The Traitors

A True Story of Blood, Betrayal and Deceit

JOSH IRELAND

JOHN MURRAY

First published in Great Britain in 2017 by John Murray (Publishers)
An Hachette UK Company

2

© Josh Ireland 2017

A CIP catalogue record for this title is available from the British Library

Hardback ISBN 978-1-47362-032-2
Trade paperback ISBN 978-1-47362-033-9
Ebook ISBN 978-1-47362-034-6

Typeset in Bembo by Palimpsest Book Production Ltd, Falkirk, Stirlingshire

Printed and bound by Clays Ltd, St Ives plc

John Murray policy is to use papers that are natural, renewable and
recyclable products and made from wood grown in sustainable forests.
The logging and manufacturing processes are expected to conform
to the environmental regulations of the country of origin.

John Murray (Publishers)
Carmelite House
50 Victoria Embankment
London EC4Y 0DZ

www.johnmurray.co.uk

To Victoria

Contents

I've gone to find a traitor. A full-grown, four-square, red-toothed, paid-up traitor.

John le Carré, *A Small Town in Germany*, 1968

Prologue

Our purpose is to crush all compromise out of existence

JOHN AMERY. HAROLD Cole. William Joyce. Eric Pleasants. Few people talk about these men any more. If I mention their names in conversation, only William Joyce – or Lord Haw-Haw, as he is better known – is recognised with any regularity; references to the others are usually greeted by blank stares. But seventy-five years ago they were among the most notorious men in Britain, renegades infamous for having thrown in their lot with Nazi Germany and betrayed their country.

These were all complex, flawed men who led existences replete with tragedy, sex, compromise, drink, scandal, exalted ambition and shabby failure. They travelled to wartime Paris as it tried to make sense of France's catastrophic defeat in 1940 and witnessed Berlin's progress from triumphant capital of the Thousand Year Reich to a bombed-out collection of ruins; they stayed in everything from lavish hotel suites to stinking cells in Stalin's gulags, and crossed paths with everyone from brave French *résistants* willing to lay down their lives in the name of freedom to remorseless Nazi killers. While fascinating in themselves, their stories continue to offer urgent lessons for our times.

The narrative starts at the beginning of the 1930s, for in their own ways these traitors were all formed by their experiences of that 'low dishonest decade', where none of them were ever able to find a comfortable home. By following their lives over the years that followed I hope to illuminate something more about how a man might come to betray his country, and how he might then go on to try to justify his actions – both to himself and to others. Occasionally these men swim in and out of each other's stories, at other times they plough their own furrow, but in telling their tales in parallel I want to show the way in which each of them embodies – though never in a neat, symbolic fashion – a different kind of perfidy. I have tried to get as close as possible to their thoughts and emotions, and in doing so I hope that to some extent I have been able to restore some of the past's immediacy, a sense of it as a chaotic bundle of contingent events rather than a stately and inevitable progression towards the present day.

The word traitor is still regularly lobbed like a Molotov cocktail into our contemporary political discourse. It is a word that demands unpacking, to show, if nothing else, that treachery is a more complex process than assumptions about Judas and his thirty pieces of silver would lead you to believe. Treason can be provoked as much by a sincerely held desire to protect one's country as by a desperate bid to save one's skin; while patriotism can turn septic, idealism can sour, and extreme politics can come to exert a narcotic and ultimately fatal allure.

Treachery is often a reaction to a very specific, often uncomfortable, historical context. This book's four subjects led untidy existences that were fat with accident and mess, but that were shaped by the epoch they inhabited. They came of age in a time of tectonic uncertainty: across Europe, country after country had fallen into the hands of nationalist demagogues, and democracy suddenly seemed fragile, unable to keep pace with a rapidly changing world. Britain, already coming to terms with severe industrial decline, its eclipse by other powers such as the USA and the Soviet Union, and a sustained economic crisis that robbed millions of their livelihoods, seemed unable to decide what kind of relationship it wanted with the rest of the Continent. It was an era full of pitfalls for the naïve and unwary, but also one that bullied its way into the biographies of even those desperate to be left to their own devices. The war that followed in 1939 became, whether they liked it or not, the central fact of these four men's existences. Their circumstances demanded a response: each answered in his own fashion, and each paid the price for the decisions he made.

★

Where I have included footnotes in the main text it is to provide supplementary information that would otherwise render a particular sentence too dense. I have not always used inverted commas to indicate when I am quoting these men's thoughts and opinions, but full references are supplied in the endnotes at the back of the book. This book draws on a number of different sources – including but not limited to memoirs, diaries and statements given to the security services – to reconstruct these men's stories. There are often discrepancies between the narratives offered by different actors in the same events; in each of these cases I have opted for the account that seems most convincing once motive, context and any other testimony have been borne in mind.

I

Hush! Do not awaken the dreamers

Late spring 1930

OSWALD MOSLEY IS surrounded by traitors. It is 28 May 1930 and in the stuffy, airless chamber of the House of Commons he has been speaking, without notes, for over an hour. All around him sit men of power and influence, 'small, dried-up men with mean faces; big pompous, pot-bellied men with smug faces'. Britain is in the grip of a ruinous depression, and they should be exerting every sinew to resolve a crisis that Mosley believes threatens to equal any in their country's long and storied history, but instead 'These old men with their old dead minds embalmed in the tombs of the past' continue to betray the promises made to the generation who came of age in the blood and squalor of the Great War. When the veterans returned they were promised a land fit for heroes, but they found themselves ignored, their sacrifices quickly forgotten. In his election address a year earlier Sir Oswald reminded voters that it is 'an offence against God and man that women should be imprisoned in the damp and disease-ridden walls of a slum house and have to bring up children to share their misery'. He might have made that observation ten years ago; nothing has changed. Nothing looks likely to.

Opposite him sits the Conservative Party, a group of reanimated fossils dressed in frock-coats. There is Neville Chamberlain, his starched wing collar and patrician umbrella marking him out for what he is, a relic of the last century. And their leader, Stanley Baldwin, a man whose complacent equanimity exemplifies the 'affinity between the love of Conservatism and the fear of ideas'.

9

He is decent, reassuring and fond of saying things like: 'one of the reasons why our people are alive and flourishing and have avoided many of the troubles that have fallen to less happy nations, is that we have never been guided by logic in anything we did.' He is not a man for these tumultuous times.

But Stanley Baldwin and the party he leads are supposed to be afraid of change. The young Labour minister may despise many of them, but he doesn't blame them. No, it is the men on his own side for whom he reserves the bulk of his ire. He has pressed and harried, but every idea he has put forward to help relieve the current situation has been ignored or dismissed.

Mosley looks back to the benches behind him. Not so long ago he believed Labour were 'the only party which had been thrown up by the mass of people to right their wrongs'. Yet they are not, he has realised, interested in radical action. Or any action at all: why call yourself a socialist if you're afraid of socialism? He has put up with a great deal in the Labour Party, but what he cannot stand for is 'the complete betrayal of the mass of the people who trusted us'. They were elected twelve months ago having pledged to solve the country's crippling unemployment problem, a problem that the great crash of the previous year – Ramsay MacDonald's 'economic blizzard' – has only exacerbated. And it is to this issue that he has turned his mind and his considerable energy, even though the prime minister MacDonald, instead of giving him any real responsibility, has made him Chancellor of the Duchy of Lancaster, a junior ministerial post within the department run by the Lord Privy Seal, that nonentity Jimmy Thomas.

Sir Oswald's powerful harsh voice – the kind it is easy to imagine carrying across a parade ground – rings out around the chamber.

> What I fear more than a sudden crisis is a long, slow, crumbling through the years until we sink to the level of a Spain, a gradual paralysis, beneath which all the vigour and energy of this country will succumb . . . If the situation is to be overcome, if the great powers of this country are to be rallied and mobilised for a great national effort, then the Government and Parliament must give the lead. I beg the Government tonight to give the vital forces

of this country the chance that they await. I beg Parliament to give that lead.

The ghoulish chancellor, Philip Snowden, who has previously claimed that Mosley's brand of socialism gave him 'feelings of nausea', glares up at him. This bitter soul – lonely and melancholy in equal measure; the son of a Yorkshire weaver who now likes to surround himself with diamonds and Rothschilds – has used his power to stamp on every idea Oswald has proposed. Snowden had once been able to summon a visceral anger at injustice, but now his energy is reserved for defending the shibboleths of economic orthodoxy, indulging his weakness for vituperation (if he has ever said anything kind or tender, there wasn't anyone around to record it) and making the most of his new position in society: his wife claims that the couple are now so intimate with the royal family that they no longer need friends in the Labour Party.

Mosley's gaze takes in Hugh Dalton, a 'third-rate don'; Herbert Morrison 'a narrow, rigid, vain little bureaucrat devoid of vision and incapable of movement beyond his office stool'. And George Lansbury. Poor George, he looks like a cross between a prophet and a dairy farmer: a heart of gold, but a head of feathers. Some are good men, like little Clem Attlee, but, good man that he is, Clem is not the kind that will get things done; you will never see a mild-mannered fellow like him change the face of the country. Sir Oswald can barely disguise the contempt he feels for the men who are supposed to be his comrades. While others such as Dalton and Stafford Cripps will devote hours to even the humblest Labour members, listening to their reminiscences as if they were the most interesting thing in the world, Mosley has no time for the 'wearisome babblings of decrepit Trade Union leaders'. 'Why,' asks Attlee, 'does Mosley always speak to us as though he were a feudal landlord abusing tenants who are in arrears with their rent?' It is a reasonable question.

Sir Oswald Ernald Mosley's hair is thick, black and shiny; his smile is a shrug. His aquiline profile is a model of aristocratic hauteur and he has perfect white teeth. He is six foot two inches tall, possesses a distinctly military bearing and, despite a limp, a panther's stride. There are very few men like him in the House of Commons. People's first reaction on meeting Mosley is to be dazzled. Their second is often to question his motives (Snowden: 'I was always suspicious of a rich man who came into the Socialist Movement and at once became more Socialist than the Socialists').

He has long been talked of as a future prime minister; and ever since he came into Parliament he has diverted his energies into moulding himself into the kind of great man – like Julius Caesar (whose biography he has considered writing) or Pitt the Elder (an imperial visionary, who believed himself to be 'the only saviour of England') – he is convinced the country desperately needs: 'Great things,' he says, 'can only be done in a great way.'

The idea that we are products of genes or our environment holds little appeal to him – instead he regards the individual as the product of a process directed by strength of will: 'The mind can be trained to do abnormal things as a muscle can be trained to lift a weight.' He was a poor speaker when he first took his seat, but has put himself through an intensive regimen in order to transform himself into one of Parliament's supreme performers. He has studied the great orators of the past; employed a voice coach; practised in front of the mirror and even honed his technique by picking a fight with *The Times* leader each morning over breakfast. Sir Oswald has taken similar care to cultivate his memory, and later in life he will boast how 'I can remember a scene, a statistic, a turning-point of action, a quotation of prose or poetry which has moved me, but not life's minor irrelevancies.'*

He has read a prodigious amount (though is curiously resistant to picking up a novel), and unlike many of his contemporaries has made a sustained attempt to familiarise himself with current

---

* It's unclear whether 'minor irrelevancies' include things such as whether or not the BUF received funding from Mussolini or Hitler (they did, to the tune of several million pounds in today's money), or if he'd seen and approved the virulent anti-Semitism that occasionally despoiled the *Blackshirt*'s leader pages (he had, the party's inhouse paper was never printed without the leader having endorsed its contents).

economic thinking. There are few, if any, other front-rank politicians who have so fruitful a relationship with intellectuals such
as John Maynard Keynes (Beatrice Webb noted his ability to 'use
other men's brains'). If truth be told, there are few, if any, who
have such an understanding of the scale and nature of the unemployment crisis facing the country.

Sir Oswald has also attended to his diet and, thanks to advice
from David Lloyd George and Winston Churchill, has acquired
the habit of taking an afternoon nap to preserve his strength.
He eschews the great quantities of alcohol consumed by other
members of the House, restricting himself (or at least so he says)
to the odd beer, and hock mixed with soda. He prefers to fortify
himself with coffee before speeches; believing this assists in the
build-up of momentum and adrenalin needed to create 'the condition of excitement which is communicated to the audience'.

There are some aspects of his personality that have escaped Sir
Oswald's passion for self-improvement. His temperament remains
defiantly aristocratic, which ensures that he remains unbound by
the same 'middle-class caution' as others, but, more often than his
friends and enemies alike find comfortable, this manifests itself as
arrogance. He has no gift for introspection, nor does he allow
himself any practice at it, and while he is all too happy to lecture
others on the importance of living like an athlete – 'statesmen
are poor fish,' he says, 'if even for the few years at the height of
their responsibilities they cannot be serious' – it is not altogether
clear how this is consistent with his unrelenting promiscuity.

One day he gives a list to his wife Cimmie of the women he
has slept with. 'But they are all my best friends!' she replies. Pained
by the hurt he knows he has caused he subsequently talks about
the exchange with his friend Bob Boothby, a young Conservative
MP, telling him how he had enumerated all his conquests.

Boothby, unbelieving, interjects: 'All?'

'Yes, all,' comes the reply. 'Except, of course for her sister and
stepmother.'

Sir Oswald is, in the words of the Liberal MP Leslie Hore-Belisha,
'the only man in the House of Commons who has made an Art

of himself'. And there was something impressively sudden about the emergence of his reputation for brilliance and wit when he first arrived in London society. Mosley had been born into an ancient family (motto: 'Our custom is above the law') that had been hitherto distinguished by a kind of extreme and reactionary provincialism. Unlike many other great families they made no attempt to fight the nineteenth century; they simply tried to ignore it.

Sir Oswald's mother Katherine 'Maud' Heathcote, a lover of animals, field sports and spiritualism, was utterly devoted to her son: to her, according to a contemporary, 'Tom was God.' Two decades on, it doesn't appear that he has quite shaken off the effects of this prepubescent deification; nor, it should be said, has he shown much interest in doing so.

He had dreamed of achieving glory in the Great War but came away with little more than a year of fairly undistinguished service and one leg that was an inch and a half shorter than the other (in May 1915, having secured his pilot's certificate, he crashed his plane and broke his ankle while showing off before his admiring mother).* However, he did emerge from the conflict with an enduring enthusiasm for military life: where harmony reigned between the classes and the country was organised (this enduring and romantic memory of a trench solidarity 'fired by struggle and suffering' was one shared by many of the other European socialists who converted to fascism). Indeed, there was a moment when it seemed that this new spirit would persist. Shortly after the peace the then prime minister David Lloyd George spoke movingly about how 'There are many things that are wrong and which ought not to be – poverty, wretchedness, and squalor. Let us cleanse this noble land. Let us cleanse it and make it a temple worthy of the sacrifice which has been made for its honour.' His high-sounding words have not yet been translated into meaningful action.

Oswald Mosley identified with the men of the trenches more completely – certainly more self-consciously – than any other inter-war British politician. He claimed their hopes, fears and

---

* An unimprovable, albeit cruel, metaphor for his subsequent career.

grievances for his own, and it was a desire to ensure that the sacrifices of his comrades were not in vain, as well as an 'almost religious conviction to prevent a recurrence of war' that led him to seek a seat in Parliament. Although he stood as a Conservative in the 1918 election, party politics had little meaning for him. He claimed that he 'knew little of Conservative sentiment and cared less' and campaigned for what he described as 'socialistic imperialism', which, if eccentric for a Tory candidate, had the virtue of being an uncanny anticipation of his later thought.

As it turned out 'business as usual' swiftly reasserted itself; almost, it seemed, before the echoes of applause for the prime minster's speech had died out. Mosley had thought the 'young men, the men of war, were in charge' now; however, of the 168 newly elected Conservative and Unionist members, fewer than forty-five were under forty and only sixty-eight had been in uniform.

His obsession is with getting things done, but he is soon disappointed by an institution that doesn't seem to share the same priorities. Sir Oswald's temperament is geared to action: he is like those sharks that must move ceaselessly if they are to continue breathing. 'I prefer,' he says, 'the errors of dynamism to the religion of lethargy.'

Even after crossing the floor to the Labour benches in 1926, joining a party that is at least in theory committed to reconstructing the very foundations of society, his disillusionment has not been assuaged: proximity to the levers of power has only served to heighten his frustration. John Beckett, a maverick Independent Labour Party MP,* was equally bewildered by the inaction and impotence he saw all around him. He is another member of the war generation who has been inspired to enter politics by a desperate passion to relieve the grinding poverty that afflicted so much of the population, but he too soon realises that his party's leaders are reluctant to make a difference, and uninterested in any attempts from their backbenchers to change this. 'There was little else to do,' he would complain in his

---

* The Independent Labour Party was a socialist party affiliated to the Labour Party from 1906 to 1932.

[handwritten annotation:] He joined Labour party and fought B'ham seat in 1924 against Neville Chamberlain. narrowly losing. In 1926 elected Lab MP for Gateshead

memoirs, 'except walk like caged lions up and down the length of the terrace.'

Mosley's warnings become increasingly urgent and he begins to assume the tone of a prophet.

> Unemployment, wages, rents, suffering, squalor and starvation; the struggle for existence in our streets, the threat of world catastrophe in another war; these are the realities of the present age. These are the problems which require every exertion of the best brains of our time for a vast constructive effort. These are the problems which should unite the nation in a white heat of crusading zeal for their solution. But these are precisely the problems which send Parliament to sleep. When not realities but words are to be discussed Parliament wakes up. Then we are back in the comfortable pre-war world of make-believe. Politics are safe again; hairs are to be split, not facts to be faced. Hush! Do not awaken the dreamers. Facts will wake them in time with a vengeance.

In an exchange of letters with Mosley at the beginning of the crisis, the prime minister, who gives the impression of being more interested in the gorse at his home in Lossiemouth than the unemployment problem, had outlined his position: 'As I see the problem (dimly) we must hang on to what we are doing but weed out the spongers all round.' It is feeble, but at least Mosley now knows where he stands.

Oswald Mosley is perhaps the man that Ramsay MacDonald wished he had been; he has been known to talk wistfully of him as 'someone who might some days do the things which he himself had once dreamt of doing'. And what would he have given to have been born with the younger minister's confidence and good breeding; not to be surrounded by men like Snowden; not to have slipped into a Faustian pact with high society designed to help him ignore his illegitimate birth; no longer to be tired, old, confused and 'hopelessly woolly'.*

★

---

* He still has one surprise up his sleeve: within months he will form a National Government, deserting his party – in the country's interests, he says – and earning himself a reputation for treachery that will last for what little remains of his life, and endure long after his corpse is cold.

There had been a time when people wondered out loud whether Jimmy Thomas, chief of the National Union of Railwaymen, might one day become prime minister. Now the question on their lips is whether he is going to drink himself into an early grave. Thomas has long since exchanged his socialist principles for a kind of music-hall proletarianism. His comic turns (usually involving the ostentatious dropping of his aitches) have been sufficient to make George V laugh so hard that he opened an abscess in his back: but though he remains intermittently good company, he's also awash in a sea of booze and corruption. There's an increasing suspicion that his waggish good humour is deployed to obscure ignorance, and he is already up to his elbows in the Stock Exchange gambles that will eventually bring his ministerial career to a brutal end.

The man who, as Lord Privy Seal, has been given ultimate responsibility by the prime minister for solving Britain's unemployment problem is patently out of his depth. Previously, on his good days he had been able to console himself with the comforting idea that 'there is less suffering in our country than in any previous period in our history', but in the aftermath of the 1929 crash he has been known to fall into a state of such panic that some, including Mosley, are concerned that he might actually descend into madness.

While Thomas has floundered, Mosley has been busy in 'a semi-dungeon high up in the Treasury' drawing up a series of radical economic proposals. Doctrinaire socialism has only ever held a 'slight appeal' for Sir Oswald; he prefers his own interpretation of it as 'the conscious control and direction of human resources for human needs'. It is as if he believes the country can be transformed by the same concentrated exertion of will that he has employed to remodel himself into a 'complete' man. He is convinced that nineteenth-century liberalism is incapable of solving twentieth-century problems: laissez-faire economics is not, he will tell anyone who listens, a match for virile state intervention. And so any scheme that might stimulate employment is given due consideration; for a while he is even taken with the idea of building an aerodrome in central London by putting a roof on top of Victoria station.

The ideas coalesce into what becomes known as the Mosley Memorandum. Thomas is unaware of its existence until Oswald Mosley tells him, with what must sound like unusual – and thus suspicious – diffidence that he has 'jotted down a number of new proposals on "our special problem"', before adding, almost offhand, 'Some of these ideas you will agree with and some you'll probably turn down; but in any case, Jim, I'd like you to see them.'

In short order Mosley sends his proposals to Keynes, who, while not agreeing on every point, responds positively, and Ramsay MacDonald. In a series of stormy confrontations Mosley's ideas are discussed by the rest of his party. Snowden, incensed by his junior colleague's temerity, dismisses him as a 'presumptuous fool and an economic ignoramus'; the home secretary John Clynes describes the memorandum as 'something approaching insanity'. 'You must make a greater effort,' Mosley snarls in a Cabinet meeting, 'or throw up the sponge.' It becomes impossible to discuss the issue without acrimony. Many of Mosley's friends and colleagues urge patience. They remind him of the glittering future that awaits him if only he will hang on: bide your time, they say, you will be prime minister before long. But with millions of his fellow countrymen condemned to near-starvation, how can he sit comfortably in Westminster, knowing his party's pledges have been betrayed? He is offered a promotion, to minister for agriculture, but his adviser John Strachey tells him to refuse: 'What the people want is action.'

Mosley attempts to force a vote on his proposals through at a party meeting. His speech defending his memorandum is eloquent, passionate and convincing, but it is not enough; his motion is defeated. Strachey watches Mosley sitting silent and alone, brooding with an indescribable bitterness, as the elderly, portly trade union officials and nervous pacifist intellectuals file out. Whatever fragile threads have hitherto bound Sir Oswald to the Labour Party are fast beginning to fray.

On 20 May 1930 Mosley, seeing no way forward, hands his resignation letter to the prime minister, who notes that his words are characterised by a 'graceless pompousness'. Snowden, going further, accuses Mosley of being 'a traitor to the cause of Labour, and one who was incapable of political loyalty'; adding that 'the English people had no time for a "pocket-Mussolini".' Mosley storms out. 'It was easy enough for them to say – young man wait, why such a hurry? – it was not so easy for people to wait in the slums of Birmingham while we drew our salaries and they drew the dole.'

So it has come to this: Mosley addressing Parliament as he defends his resignation. As he finishes, cheering breaks out, loud and prolonged, from every section of the House. There is palpable excitement in the chamber. Josiah Wedgewood, a Labour MP, would later remember how it engendered a new mood on the back benches: 'Man after man was saying to himself: "That is our leader."' Mosley has not, hitherto, been a popular man in Westminster. His air of condescension allied to 'that curious curl of the upper lip which made him always look as if he had a bad smell under his nose' have seen to that. But in the space of sixty minutes he has become 'a hero of all young members in all parties who are impatiently demanding new ideas to meet a catastrophic situation'.

The reactions in the press the next day are similarly ecstatic. The *Evening Standard* describes 'the triumph of an artist who has made his genius perfect by long hours of practice and devotion to his art. There is no politician who works harder or who takes more pains to master his problems.' Bob Boothby acclaims it as 'The greatest parliamentary tour de force this generation will hear'. Later Boothby goes to Mosley's room at the House of Commons. He is struck by 'his relief and satisfaction, his determination to go forward and "bring these grave matters to the test"'. Even amid the acclaim there is a strong sense that Sir Oswald is at risk of throwing away a glittering political career. The man in question does not share these concerns; when he goes to the Astors' house later that evening it is to celebrate. He is asked about his prospects by Frank Pakenham. Mosley stares at him 'with that odd look with which he seemed to transfix women' before intoning, 'After Peel comes Disraeli. After Baldwin and MacDonald comes . . . ?'

'Who comes next?'
'Comes someone very different,' growls Mosley.

Mosley has long hinted at a frustration with the old party system, and a belief that a new order would emerge to replace it. As early as 1922, in a letter he wrote to his constituents when he stood as an independent in Henley, he spoke of how 'The war destroyed the old party issues, and with them the old parties . . . The party system must, of course, return in the very near future, but it will be a new Party system.' He has spoken in the Commons of the need to create a 'third force' between Bolshevism and reaction.

Not everyone agrees with Mosley's analysis, even those who share his concerns about Britain's sclerotic political system. Boothby writes to Mosley, counselling him against setting up his own party. You can 'do more for us than anyone else now alive' he reminds his friend. 'Only for God's sake remember that this country is old and tradition-ridden, and no one – not even you – can break all the rules at once. And do take care of the company you keep. Real shits are so apt to trip you up when you aren't looking.'

2

I'm glad that I haven't a son

Winter 1932

THE MEN AND women for whom Oswald Mosley claims to be speaking do not, in the main, live within sight of Westminster. They inhabit what have become known as the distressed areas; regions of the United Kingdom that lie only a train ride away from London, but which sometimes must seem as if they exist in another country.

These people used to work in the heavy industries that had formed the backbone of Great Britain's pre-eminence: coal, steel, cotton, shipbuilding. Over the last thirty years they have watched, helpless, as Japan and the USA seized huge shares of the markets that had previously been dominated by the goods they'd sweated to produce. Coal and cotton, which between them had once comprised 55 per cent of the nation's physical exports, have both long been in seemingly terminal decline, unable to compete with cheap imports from places like Poland and India. Throughout the twenties, unemployment had run at about 10 per cent of the population, what the economist Arthur Pigou had dubbed 'the intractable million'. Then came the Wall Street Crash.

In the north-east, Lancashire, South Wales and Glasgow whole communities have seen their livelihoods destroyed. In shipbuilding areas the average unemployment rate is 60 per cent, a stark comparison to the nationwide figure of 22 per cent. By 1932 a third of all coalminers are out of work, and in areas where the struggling industries are concentrated the effect of the slump can be devastating: 72.6 per cent of Jarrow's insurable workforce have no job; in Ferndale in the Rhonda Valley the figure stands at 96.5 per cent. Men will walk miles each day to try to find some way of feeding their family, but there is little or no hope of finding new employment in these parts of the country, either for the forlorn multitudes who have been left idle for years, or for those boys tumbled out of school at fourteen who know there's no chance of picking up their father's trade.

'I'm glad that I haven't a son,' one unemployed Welsh miner says:

> It must be a heartbreaking business to watch your boy grow into manhood and then see him deteriorate because there is no work for him. And yet there are scores of young men in the Valley who have never worked since the age of sixteen . . . at sixteen they become insurable and the employers sack them rather than face the extra expense. So we have young men who have never had a day's work since. They have nothing to hope for except aimless drift.

The austerity measures enacted by the National Government in 1931 only make life harder. A disproportionate amount of attention seems to be given to stamping out 'abuses' of the system and trying to cap the spiralling costs of the borrowing fund. Contributions are increased and unemployment benefit cut: henceforth it can only be drawn by right for six months; after that the supplicant must apply to the labour exchange for 'transitional payments', which are so low that they serve to humiliate the receiver while giving them just enough to fend off starvation. Most severely, the household's total income is assessed under a means test. This is administered with an almost penal severity, and leads to widespread anxiety, despair and suffering. New mothers are asked whether they are breastfeeding – even this source of extra nutrition can have an effect on their allowance.

In some of the country's poorest constituencies there are women who cannot be persuaded to come out and vote because they are ashamed of their clothes. The rat-infested slums they live in are dirty, dark and damp, without the most basic amenities. Often several families share a single tap. At least a million houses are considered unfit for human habitation; 2 million houses are classified as being overcrowded. It is not uncommon for eight people to share a single room that is black with grime and mould, the plaster peeling off the ceiling. Children are crammed with their siblings on to straw mattresses stained with urine and menstrual blood, and 80 per cent of children in the poorest areas of London and mining regions of County Durham show early signs of rickets. Infant mortality can be three times the national average in depressed areas, maternal mortality double.

Years later, during the fall of France, the American correspondent William L. Shirer will be struck by how the British prisoners he sees being led away by victorious Germans are 'hollow-chested and skinny and round-shouldered'. They are, he concludes, the victims of two decades of criminal neglect.

Few politicians seem interested in combating, or even investigating, the underlying structural causes of the slump. Ministers from both parties are blinded by a mode of thinking that maintains that taxation is always a burden, that a country's economy might be saved by implementing the cost-cutting measures one might apply to a struggling small business, and that 'laissez-faire was the most perfect system of economic management devised by the genius of man.' The stubborn attachment of successive governments to an economic orthodoxy offers little or nothing to alleviate the country's woes must, to those men who survived the maelstrom of the trenches, bear a distressingly close similarity to the costly failures of the Great War's generals.

It does not help that much of the rest of the country is thriving during these years. Home ownership and light industry both grow exponentially in the thirties. People have more money in their pockets and new consumer goods such as radios and cars to spend it on. Unless you live in a distressed area, it is easy enough to put the abject poverty endured by many of your compatriots to the back of your mind. Richard Reynell Bellamy, who will become an early recruit to Oswald Mosley's fascist movement, will later write about his frustration at what he saw as the prevailing view of unemployment – that it was a 'sad inevitability about which nothing could be done'. He was almost as appalled by middle-class complacency as he was by working-class misery. One day he informs his father that he believes that the country needs a revolution. The response is dispiriting: 'My dear boy, you must not speak like that. The affairs of old England are in more capable, experienced and trustworthy hands than you imagine.'

Sir Oswald had once dismissed fascists as 'black-shirted buffoons, making a cheap imitation of ice-cream sellers', but by 1932 he has realised what a congenial environment for his beliefs and personality the ideology can be: 'I have finished with people who think,' he claims, 'henceforth I shall go to the people who feel.' He moves swiftly to unify the disparate parties of the extreme right under the banner of his British Union of Fascists (BUF), and is soon able to boast that the only fascists outside the party are 'three old ladies and a couple of office boys'.*

Fascism was, in origin, Mosley explains, 'an explosion against intolerable conditions, against remediable wrongs which the old world had failed to remedy. It was a movement to secure national renaissance by people who felt themselves threatened with decline into decadence and death and were determined to live, and live greatly.'

The ideology seems to offer the chance to exist in a heroic register, an impression that is only encouraged by Mosley's high-sounding oratory. In his speeches he talks passionately about how

> We count it a privilege to live in an age when England demands that great things shall be done, a privilege to be of the generation which learns to say what can we give instead of what can we take. For thus our generation learns there are greater things than slothful ease; greater things than safety; more terrible things than death.
>
> This shall be the epic generation which scales again the heights of time and history to see once more the immortal lights – the

---

* Those who refused tended to be the more wilfully eccentric figures on the far right's fringes. Arnold Leese, one of the world's pre-eminent authorities on camels and a virulent anti-Semite, claimed that Mosley was in the pay of the Jews. He referred to the BUF as 'kosher fascists'. Miss Linton Orman of the British Fascisti demurred from subsuming her organisation into Mosley's because she believed he was practically a communist.

lights of sacrifice and high endeavour summoning through ordeal the soul of humanity to the sublime and eternal. The alternatives of our age are heroism or oblivion. There are no lesser paths in the history of great nations. Can we, therefore, doubt which path to choose?

Let us tonight at this great meeting give the answer. Hold high the head of England; lift strong the voice of Empire. Let us to Europe and the world proclaim that the heart of this great people is undaunted and invincible. This flag still challenges the winds of destiny. This flame still burns. This glory shall not die. The soul of Empire is alive, and England again dares to be great.

It is the kind of appeal that exerts a narcotic hold over ardent young minds, of whom there are overwhelming numbers in the BUF ranks. The blood runs hotly in their veins; to them previous generations seem tired, undeserving of the deference that they had once claimed by right. The old parties cannot halt the spineless drift to disaster; instead they squat impotent in front of the problems of the day like hypnotised rabbits faced by a snake. It is a commonplace on both sides of the political spectrum that the faiths and values of the old world no longer obtain – they died, like so many millions of young men, in the blood and filth of the Great War.

The young intellectuals in the Blackshirts' ranks all seem to have read Oswald Spengler and Thomas Carlyle. They are against the decadence and materialism of the modern world 'where there are no spiritual landmarks'. Their conviction that western civilisation is in terminal decline vies with the belief that a great man is needed to salvage the situation. When one of the movement's rising stars, the coruscating Irish speaker William Joyce, asserts at a rally in Brighton that 'We know that England is crying for a leader and that leader has emerged in the person of the greatest Englishman I have ever known, Sir Oswald Mosley,' he is simply expressing a feeling shared by many thousands in the party, including Mosley himself.

The fascists have certain assumptions about the way the world is run. The press is bought; Parliament is a sham uninterested in constructive thought; the old are betraying the young; supreme power resides in the City of London; all parties are rackets;

democracy is feeble and enervated, unfit to face the challenges of the modern era: the world has changed beyond all recognition; why, they ask, is our government still the same? And then there is the spectre of communism, which the fascists see as posing a monstrous threat to everything they hold dear. They all fear the barbaric savagery of the Soviet Union, and see themselves as a bulwark against its spread beyond the USSR's borders.

For those desperate to somehow make a difference, fascism holds an intoxicating promise. At the same time, its very swagger, its violent élan, explain another element of its appeal to the young: fascism speaks eloquently to their desire to *épater les bourgeois.* Being a member is *exciting*; life before the BUF now seems grey, dull and incomprehensible. Even the movement's name is a provocation. Mosley had insisted that the word fascist should be employed, in spite of others imploring him to use a less incendiary, less foreign one. He wanted to be seen to be making a decisive break with the old world. It is intended to offend, to sort the wheat from the chaff, to show that you were willing to take risks in the name of a great cause.

The BUF provides an immersive world for its members. There is a Blackshirt Automobile Club and Blackshirt Holiday Camps, there are Blackshirt weddings, and the party even has its own brand of cigarettes (William Joyce's favourite, apparently). This world centres on their headquarters, a grey, pseudo-Gothic pile at 232 Battersea Park Road that the party christen the 'Black House', and which is run on quasi-military lines. The BUF's Defence Force sleep, eat and train there, their days regulated by the sound of a bugle. Its rooms are 'filled with students eager to learn everything about this new, exciting crusade; its club rooms rang with the laughter and song of men who felt that the advent of Fascism had made life worth living again.'

Membership of the party soars into the thousands, and it draws support from aristocrats and leading military figures. (Mary Ormsby-Gore remembered that Adolf Hitler and Mosley's new sister-in-law Unity Mitford 'used to comb through the *Tatler* every week to mark the names of those who might come over to them when he occupied England. They had great lists.') They are buoyed by the success other authoritarian parties have enjoyed across the Continent, in Italy, Portugal, Austria, Greece, Romania and, of course, Germany. An excited belief grows that they too will be in power within the year; some supporters even go so far as to start discussing the positions that the movement's leading lights will hold in the new, corporate state. The thirty-seven-year-old Mosley is more measured: I will be in power, he tells an American journalist, by the time I am forty.

3

If my mother is going to Hell, then so shall I

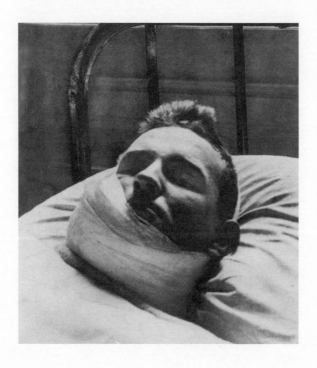

Autumn 1934

E VERY TIME THE propaganda director for the British Union of Fascists stares into the mirror he is confronted by the deep, livid scar that begins just below his right ear and loops across his cheek before joining the corner of his mouth. It dominates his face to the extent that you could be forgiven for overlooking his cleft chin, or his stern pugilist's jaw. One man who met him a decade later said that it made him think of raw pork. Another recalled how it would twitch, almost as if it had a life of its own. William Joyce knows the scar conditions the way people see him ('People would talk to me. It would come out I'd got a first at London University. They wouldn't believe me. I could see them disbelieving me') but it also conditions the way he sees himself. It is a mark that shows he's a fighter. 'Fascism,' he says, with some satisfaction, 'is not a creed for the smug mice who choose to emerge from under Bloomsbury tea-cosies to have a nibble at it.' He prides himself on being the kind of man who can effortlessly quote from Dryden and Swift, Browning and Tennyson, and yet also keep a revolver in his drawer. But more than anything it's a visceral reminder of a defeat. In 1924, as he was canvassing for a prospective Conservative MP ahead of that year's general election, he was jumped from behind by a Jewish communist.* In the midst of the struggle this assailant inserted a razor in his mouth, then drew it cruelly up to his ear.

---

* The candidate in question, Jack Lazarus, was Jewish. Perhaps this counts as irony.

Or, at least, that's the way the story he would later tell goes. You can find some people who will tell you that he did not receive the wound in open combat, but after having been hunted like a rat by a gang of Jews, held down and humiliated. Other, better, witnesses could relate a different tale: how the knife was thrown by an Irishwoman, a belated retribution for his entanglement a decade previously in the country's war of independence.

Whatever the truth, the attack left him in hospital and attracted the attention of the *Evening Standard*, who reported on 'wild scenes by hooligans'. Anxious to flesh out their story the paper sent a kindly but ill-informed photographer to the ward in which Joyce was recovering. 'Ach, these fascist blackguards are damn swine to carve you up like that,' he sympathised with the gruesomely mutilated patient. 'They should be shot.' Joyce's response was to laugh until he nearly burst his stitches, but nonetheless the picture appeared in the following edition. He looks, perhaps uniquely in his life, serene.

Subsequently he will try to make light of it, calling it his 'Lambeth Honour', or, later, *'die Schramme'* (the scratch), and recalling how 'An attempt was made to cut my throat, but the razor slashed a quarter of an inch too high. There is something to be said for having a well-fed appearance.' But no matter how many sardonic jokes he might make, it is hard to see the scar as anything other than an outward manifestation of the hate that twists and pulses inside him.

It is not clear when exactly his hatred of the Jews emerged; it is unlikely that he actually met one until he came to London as a student. Joyce is like a child who, after a lengthy period of silence, suddenly begins speaking in perfect sentences: his anti-Semitism appears to have arrived fully formed. This prejudice, which seems already to have assumed the qualities of an obsession, shares space in his thoughts with a belief in the need for a complete social revolution and a patriotism that might also be described as obsessive. His patriotism's origins are less mysterious, though it too is built on shaky foundations. In around a decade's time the world will learn that, contrary to what they'd come to believe, William Joyce was born in the USA, in Brooklyn.

What we do know is that Joyce grew up at a time when it was possible that, as the result of a pen stroke in a chateau outside Paris, a family could go to bed in Germany one night, and then find they'd woken up in Poland the next morning. The same was happening across the Continent as the borders of Europe were re-drawn by men in frock-coats and starched collars, and millions of people were left – depending on accidents of birth and geography – either bewildered, isolated and betrayed; or liberated from centuries of oppression. The Joyce family were, in their view at least, among the victims of this historical process.

Michael Joyce had moved his wife Queenie and child back to his native Ireland in 1909, when his son was three. William appears to have come away with an ability to speak German (acquired, he claimed later, from neighbours in Brooklyn), an 'unambiguous dislike' for Americans (inherited from his mother) and a firm belief that he was somehow marked out from others. William would later remember that Queenie had once told him that 'I shall never forget in my life how lonely I have felt in America. Even before you were born you were my only comfort in this atmosphere of strangeness, lack of interest and hostility.' Loneliness, strangeness, hostility: all were coursing through his veins before he had taken his first breath.

Learning came easily to him and he was obedient and helpful in the classroom, yet from an early age everything he did was coloured by fanaticism. William Joyce was always the altar boy who swung the censer too hard, who waved his staff around too vigorously. His head was a little too large for his body. Bright blue, sardonic eyes stared unnervingly out of his firmly set features. He hero-worshipped Napoleon and had a precocious interest in mesmerism and hypnotism (it could be argued that his interest in both the esoteric and controlling the minds of others never really left him). Joyce would later claim to have been a member of the 'very British' scouts – though there were no scout troops in Galway at that time. All the same, somehow it seems that he managed to obtain a khaki shirt, tie and badge, which he wore on the lapel of his coat. He liked to show off by demonstrating different scout signs and signals with his fingers.

William also came to understand, earlier, and perhaps with more force than most other boys of his age, how loyalties could clash – and how two apparently irreconcilable causes can each claim your allegiance with equal strength. He abandoned the Catholic faith in which he'd been raised because a priest told him that his Protestant mother was unlikely to be spared eternal damnation: 'If my mother is going to Hell, then so shall I,' he was heard to say in response. His teachers were by turns shocked and impressed by his defiance. 'That boy will either do something very great in the world,' one of them was prompted to observe, 'or he will finish on the end of a rope.'

However, it was another, more severe, rupture that came to define his early life: Britain's withdrawal from all but the northern tip of Ireland. The Joyces had been well off, at least compared to their neighbours, tight-knit and respectable. They were also fervent loyalists. 'I was brought up by my parents in a creed of fanatical patriotism which the English people found very hard to understand. From my earliest days, I was taught to love England and her Empire. Patriotism was the highest virtue that I knew.' William and the rest of the family were left bereft by a political decision they regarded as an act of the basest treachery: how could the British Empire surrender their home to a 'gang of gunmen'?

Joyce began to spend all his spare time in either the barracks of the Black and Tans or at the headquarters of the Royal Irish Constabulary. He claimed to have collected intelligence for them and appears to have been adopted as a kind of mascot or pet – Joyce could often be seen riding on the Black and Tans' lorries as they sped along the country's narrow roads. Though not yet sixteen, he had long acted as if impatient to be done with childish things and, at some point in this fervid time of violence, hate and betrayal, his childhood might be said to have come to an end. A building leased by Michael Joyce to the Royal Ulster Constabulary was burned to the ground. And then one day one of the officers William knew was murdered while playing tennis. William Joyce was a conspicuous presence at the funeral, offering a stiff salute as the funeral cortège passed by. On another occasion, as he was walking along a familiar path in the twilight, he saw a Sinn Feiner pursued by police, cornered and killed. Years later, amid the ruins of Berlin, these incidents would continue to haunt him; unable to cope with the images by himself, he would drunkenly tell his wife about a man haloed by a pool of his own blood, his brains seeping out on to the pavement.

It was probably too late already, but his parents decided that it was time their eldest son left Ireland.

Over the following years, William Joyce passed through the Royal Worcester Regiment (until it was discovered he had lied about his age, though this was not before his roommates realised that the young cadet would spring to attention whenever he heard the national anthem: they played it with merciless regularity), university (where he studied so fanatically that on several occasions he reduced himself to the verge of a nervous breakdown; though this didn't stop him emerging from Birkbeck with a first), a number of the nascent fascist organisations (notably the British Fascisti, run by the eccentric lesbian Rotha Linton-Orman), the Conservative Party (a relationship terminated after a scandal involving an affair with a young activist), and into, and ultimately out of, a marriage. William and his first wife Hazel came to realise that they could be far happier outside the arrangement than inside it, but not before they had produced two daughters. Hazel married one of Mosley's body-guards, while William remained, outwardly at least, unaffected by the loss of his family. His mind was consumed by the urgent demands of extreme politics, there was no space for sentiment.

The British Union of Fascists provides a home that looks as if it might endure. His exaggerated patriotism and anti-Semitism have been joined by a crude hatred of Bolshevism, and a disgust at the gross inequities that blight the lives of many millions. Fascism helps William explain away his own failures (the snubs, the rejec-tions, the world's stubborn refusal to acknowledge his genius) by referring to the wickedness of others (Jews, bankers, Bolsheviks), and offers pure, adamantine solutions to the evil and misery he sees all around him, solutions untainted by mumbling bourgeois compromise.

He soon glides up through the BUF's ranks, his fierce intelligence, forceful personality and gift for public speaking gaining him admirers across the party and a pair of nicknames: the 'Professor' is a nod to his intellectual accomplishments; the 'Mighty Atom' a reminder of his imposing physical presence. At university Joyce had trained as a featherweight, swum and fenced and now one colleague notes approvingly that 'His chest was terrific, his waist was small, his legs were terrific, his arm muscles were terrific. He had worked his body.' While his boxer's frame might be hidden beneath the dirty trenchcoat and thick woollen muffler he habitually wears over his Blackshirt uniform (his outfit is completed with a belt fastened tightly round his midriff and a heavy stick), Joyce bristles with barely contained energy, aggression and strength. But perhaps there is more than that: an ungentleness.

Although his personality is jagged and angry, there is much about him that remains guarded and obscure, covered by the soft cobweb of untruths that he has been spinning since he was young. It is hard for the people who encounter William Joyce ever to be quite sure whether what he is telling them about himself is true. He deploys his cleverness and his charisma to help him make and unmake reality. Events from his past are ruthlessly distorted: if it burnishes his legend to tell people that he passed the written exam for the Foreign Office brilliantly but was rejected because he lacked a private income, then so be it. His birthplace can lurch across the Atlantic – from New York to Galway – depending on which cradle suits him best. He can even blame his failure to complete his MA on a Jewish woman tutor who stole his research.

His new pre-eminence is confirmed in November 1933 when, as a last-minute replacement for Mosley, who has phlebitis, he addresses an audience of 5,000 people at a stadium in Liverpool. Outside are protesters wielding knuckledusters and potatoes embedded with razor blades, chanting 'Hitler and Mosley, what are they for? Thuggery, buggery, hunger and war!', but William does not show a second's hesitancy. There is no sign of anxiety, and the audience's reactions dart through him like lightning. 'Thin, pale, intense, he had not been speaking for many minutes before we were electrocuted by this man. Never before had I met a personality so terrifying in its dynamic force, so vituperative, so vitriolic. The words poured from him in a corrosive state.'

Before long Joyce is appointed director of propaganda. He speaks at countless meetings across the country and propels himself into the heart of the movement – within a year he is being talked about as a future leader. Though for the moment the BUF is undisputedly under Mosley's command, William is a natural plotter, a schemer who is so much a part of the tensions that constantly sluice through the party that it is hard to tell where his involvement in them begins or ends. There is no reason, he believes, why in due course he should not rise right to the top, where he belongs.

It is said that when he was a boy in Ireland, William Joyce's mother would whisper into his ear: 'Without you at the centre there is no empire.' Though three decades have passed since he left Ireland and he is yet to be recognised as a Napoleon or a Caesar, this narcissist goaded by a remorseless ambition is still convinced that in some way destiny has marked him out for greatness. Perhaps this is why MI5 pay him the compliment of taking out a file on him, noting the regard he enjoys inside the BUF. It ends with a summary of his strengths and weaknesses.

Good: Boundless physical and moral courage; considerable brain power; tremendous energy and application; well read politically and historically; very loyal to his friends; a sense of humour; patriotic.

Bad: Little stability due to over-developed intellect and Celtic temperament; very violent temper at times, at other times extremely quiet and calculating; a tendency towards theatricality; marked conspiratorial complex. Celtic prejudices very deeply rooted; not to be swayed by arguments where his inherent instincts are touched.

Although it has always been a home for Jew-haters, the British Union of Fascists was not, to begin with, an explicitly anti-Semitic party. But Joyce looks on approvingly as this changes once he has begun to wield more influence. They start to publish pamphlets arguing that 'These little sub-men are a nuisance to be eliminated, but their wealthy instigators and controllers, well known to us, are, in sum, a criminal monstrosity, for which not all the gold of Jewry can pay the just compensation which we will demand and obtain.' These are, he says, marvellous times.

William's hatred for the Jews consumes every atom of his body; his bones hum with a cracked loathing. He is already another Captain Ahab, and his chase after his own white whale will also drag him across seas, but if his obsession has the same propulsive force there is a crucial difference: the Irishman is chasing a phantasm of his own making, his powerful intelligence employed to construct a bizarre and irrelevant dystopia that dances atop the real world. The delirious force of his sewer prejudices is such that it can corrode his memory, erasing events that no longer fit the story he wants to tell about the world and his place in it, and replacing them with more amenable alternatives. The strange evolutions in his account of how he received the slash across his face are a case in point; there is no longer any question in his mind that a Jew wielded the razor, to him it is the only explanation that makes sense.

4

Margaret and I are making a little trip to Deutschland in the morning

Winter 1935

WILLIAM JOYCE IS not a man who has many friends: he is too awkward, too sour, too unwilling (or unable) to make the constant adjustments and compromises needed to knit a relationship together. He claims to find cocktail parties boring because he always knows what other guests are going to say before they have even opened their mouths; given that he chiefly spends his time with fellow anti-Semites, perhaps that is less than surprising. And he dislikes jazz so much (because the Nazis find it decadent) that regardless of who is present, or where he is, if it comes on the wireless he'll turn it off.

But what he will later look back on as his wilderness years are sustained by an unconventional *ménage à trois* in which, probably for the only time in his life, he finds some measure of domestic contentment. His friend from the BUF, John, or more usually Angus, Macnab, is known as Bonga, or 'the Master', a tribute to his vast erudition. He is one of those unfailingly loyal men who attach themselves to another individual, whom they believe to be a genius, and in the course of many (often lean) years reveal themselves to possess a genius of their own: inevitably something that draws heavily on both forgiveness and forbearance. Angus shares his friend's passion for esoteric knowledge – in his case Wagner, Moorish Spain and chivalry – and a disastrous spell in business has introduced him to the pain that accompanies failure, but he also incubates a seething hatred of the Jews that sits uncomfortably alongside his self-consciously professorial demeanour. Joyce and Macnab take a flat together, a congenial masculine environment that, although they do not know it yet, will soon also be home to an auburn-haired, green-eyed former dancer who will change William's life for ever.

Margaret Cairns White smiles quickly, laughs hard, and her heart is big; her home town of Carlisle cannot begin to fill it. Provincial society, to her, is dull and restrictive: she is not short of suitors, but every proposal feels like a trap. The twenty-two-year-old works as a typist at Morton Sundour Fabric Ltd in Carlisle, a textile warehouse where her father has been assistant manager since 1915. She is good at her job (her boss describes her as 'a capable girl with plenty of initiative and a low, distinctive voice' – she has lived variously in London, Carlisle and Manchester and her conversation tinted by all three accents), and knows that in this economic climate she can count herself lucky to have a job: yet she is discomfited by a growing sense that she is living in a country being run on unsatisfactory lines. Margaret is sufficiently empathetic to be moved by the suffering, poverty and stunted lives she sees all around her, and dynamic enough to want to do something about it. Her father suggested she might help him sell copies of *Fascist Weekly* outside BUF meetings, and from there she has graduated to speaking and has recently become head of the women's section of Carlisle BUF. Oswald Mosley, she says, puts into words everything she has been trying to think.

In February 1935 she organises a bus trip from Carlisle to Dumfries to hear William Joyce speak. She has seen a picture of him in *Fascist Weekly* and something about that image, and his growing reputation within the movement, makes her want to meet him in person. Because she is restless and impulsive, and has little else to detain her, Margaret is soon able to arrange a brief encounter. At subsequent meetings she learns that William Joyce has the power to mesmerise a crowd, but can be offhand, distant and dismissive in conversation.

A year later, by which time she is a full-time employee of the BUF's Manchester branch, William surprises Margaret by inviting her to see him speak at a rally at the Albert Hall, and then accompany him to a Mayfair party being hosted by the aunt of an aristocratic BUF member. Two days before she is due to travel, she catches pleurisy when the car she is travelling in gets lost in fog on the moors between Leeds and Manchester, but after spending forty-eight hours confined to her bed, she comes anyway.

Margaret will remember for the rest of her life the ecstatic crackle of excitement that coursed through her that night when she saw the fascist banners flying outside the Albert Hall. Inside, the charged atmosphere sends a thrill through her: the chants, the music, the surge of violence and energy when communists try to break up the evening by screaming abuse. Still exhilarated, she arrives at the house in Mayfair, where her coat is taken at the door by a liveried footman.

Once inside, she takes the whisky offered to her by a butler and nervously scans the crowd for someone she knows. She's relieved when William materialises by her shoulder and touches her gently on her arm. 'What are you drinking?'

'Whisky.'

'Nonsense.' He takes her glass away, and signals to the butler for champagne. The glasses arrive, and they sip from them. An anxious kind of tension seems to envelop them both.

'No doubt you've heard about my private affairs?'

Yes, she has, William's divorce is no secret within the movement. She nods distractedly and stares around the room, looking at other guests. She doesn't know when, if ever, she will be invited to an event like this again, so she intends to make the most of it.

'When my affairs are settled I hope we can see each other more often.'

Margaret smiles, and lets her eyes continue their tour of the room.

'In fact, I wondered whether you would consider marrying me.'

The background chatter suddenly fades. She stares at him in astonishment. I barely know this man, she thinks, have never even been alone with him. Perhaps the Pennine fog is still rolling through her brain, perhaps the sickness is still in her body, deranging her thoughts? She feels dislocated, and it is almost as if somebody else were speaking, when she hears herself saying, 'Well, we can try. We can always undo it if we don't like it.'

Joyce lifts his glass to hers, and as they clink he spills champagne on to her hand. Suddenly the unreality has been pierced and they both laugh. William and Margaret look at each other steadily and drain their glasses: this, then, is it.

Winter 1937

Soon after William and Margaret marry for the first time, on 13 February 1937 at Kensington Registry Office, she begins to understand what life with her husband might be like.* There is no honeymoon; instead she helps him canvass in Shoreditch, where he is standing as a parliamentary candidate. Joyce loses, but polls 2,564, almost half his Labour opponent's total – a respectable performance. Margaret watches aghast as, eschewing the normal courtesies, he stands contemptuously with his hands by his side and declares that it has been 'a thoroughly dirty fight'. Then he turns and marches from the platform to a chorus of gasps.

She rushes up behind him to tell him he has made himself look like a bad loser. He whips round and spits: 'There is no point pretending to be a good sport when both sides have been rude to each other during the campaign. When you think someone is wrong, it is dishonest to treat him as though he might be right.'

A few days later, he casually announces to his wife that in marrying him she has become an American citizen.

After a minute, she replies. 'Fancy that.'

Margaret moves into the apartment shared by William and his friend the Master. Short of cash, they spend most evenings talking, drinking, smoking and playing cards. When the rent becomes too expensive, the trio decamp to a furnished flat owned by a doctor in Fulham. Life there is full of laughter and affection. Neighbours

---

* Prickly as ever about his social standing, Joyce gave his job as 'university teacher (retired)' and said his father was 'of independent means'.

complain about them playing 'Teutonic operas' on their gramophone well into the small hours, but none of this appears to
bother them; they are, in Margaret's words, 'extraordinarily happy'.

This happiness appears to be in jeopardy when, later that year,
Joyce learns that he has been relieved of his paid position by the
cash-strapped BUF. (There is a feeling too that Mosley has become
tired of his lieutenant's restless ambition, as well as the sardonic
humour that stands in sharp relief to the personality cult he has
allowed to assemble around himself: Blackshirts salute him when
he enters the sea to bathe at the BUF's summer camps in Selsey.
While many in the movement refer to Sir Oswald in awed tones
as 'the Leader', William has his own name for him: 'the Bleeder'.)
Almost immediately the Irishman sues for wrongful dismissal, and
throws his energy into a rival organisation, the National Socialist
League (NSL), which he had created some time earlier. It seems
that Mosley's suspicion of his erstwhile propaganda chief's propen-
sity for plotting is well founded; he cannot help himself.

Joyce is joined in his new enterprise by two other renegade
fascists: Angus Macnab and the former Labour MP John Beckett.
Beckett is an irresponsible, spontaneous and passionate bon vivant;
and a speaker so inflammatory that it is said that 'He could hardly
ask for buttered toast in the morning without sending the shivers
up someone's spine.' A few years previously he had achieved
notoriety in Parliament by trying to bundle the Mace out of the
chamber in protest at another member's suspension; if he had
succeeded he had planned to stick it head first down the toilet.
His ambition is great, and his principles profound, but few consider
him to have fulfilled the promise he showed when he became
Labour's youngest MP in 1929.

In public Mosley can dismiss the NSL as a 'refuse' bin for his
movement's dissidents, cranks and extremists, but privately he
nurtures a festering sense of betrayal. A week after William is
expelled, Angus Macnab visits Mosley to complain about his
friend's treatment, and is shocked by his reception.

He thought Mosley was going to strike him or have a seizure.
Mosley went livid and thumped the desk and shouted that Joyce

was nothing but a traitor; that he would never rest until he had broken him; that he would roll him in blood and smash him. He also threatened he would smash [Macnab] and everyone else who acted as a traitor.

Traitor. The word has been used so much over the last few years (and to few public figures has the label been affixed as regularly as Mosley) that although it retains its ancient moral pungency, people have discovered that it can be employed in new and useful ways. It is a word that you can hurl like a knife at other men: it does not matter how free from treachery's taint they might believe themselves to be, if you wield more power or influence than them, the label is difficult to shrug off.

Words have always poured out of William Joyce, and in the flat with his wife and best friend they flow, unstoppably: insults, invective, endearments, lines of poetry, strings of curses and jokes. When he talks he throws back his head, shuts his eyes and begins to 'intone'. Margaret and the Master listen eagerly to what he has to say, they are impressed by his many gifts, and indulgent of his occasional flights of extravagance. There appears to be a consensus – at least in the circles in which they move – that William Joyce possesses almost preternatural talents. In the moments after Margaret and William announced their engagement, once the shocked silence had been succeeded by the familiar thrum of a successful party, John Beckett came over to shake her hand, whispering into her ear as he did so: 'I do hope you'll be happy, but it may be uncomfortable being married to a genius. And William is a genius, you know.' Margaret's response was more cautious: 'Well, he's certainly impetuous.'

One day he might announce he has conceived of a cure for cancer: as 'an anarchic disorder of the normal cell-growing function,' Joyce claims, 'it should be curable by rebalancing the cell-producing glands.' On another, he might dispatch a note to Joseph Goebbels giving advice on how to run the German economy. (The Nazi propaganda minister's response to a *Draft Scheme for a Scientifically Managed Currency as Adapted to the Needs of the Third Reich* is not recorded.)

He knew Latin so well he could actually speak it

And there is much else to admire about William Joyce. His specialist subject at Birkbeck had been Germanic philology, which included Icelandic, Old Norse and Gothic. He is fluent in German and French and has a reasonable command of Latin. He has a talent for mathematics and at some point had taught himself chemistry, medicine, physics and anatomy; once he set his own collarbone after he broke it ice-skating.

About his rages, his violence, his monomaniacal hatred of the Jews, Margaret and the Master say nothing. This is strange, for hatred remains his supreme gift. A witness of one his early speeches would later remember:

> I had been a connoisseur of speech-making for a quarter of a century, but never before, in any country, had I met a personality so terrifying in its dynamic force, so vituperative, so vitriolic . . . We listened in a kind of frozen hypnotism to this cold, stabbing voice. There was a gleam of a Marat in his eyes, and his eloquence took on a Satanic ring when he invoked the rising wrath of his colleagues against the festering scum that by cowardice and sloth had reduced the British Empire to a moribund thing, in peril of annihilation.

Joyce can start sentences reasonably, but many decay into spittle-flecked rants. His anti-Semitism continues to be so violent, bitter and obsessive that it unnerves both Beckett and A.K. Chesterton (nephew of the writer, ardent anti-Semite and another man who has passed out of the BUF and into the NSL; he will later work as a ghostwriter for Lord Beaverbrook).

How can his fellow Englishmen not see that in their cruel, calculating depravity the Jews have decided to make England the instrument of a war of revenge against Germany? That inwardly they hate the power of the British Empire? No matter how fierce or urgent his warnings, the population at large seems frustratingly unwilling to listen to him. They do not want to join his world of snarling paranoias and poisoned resentments. A couple of years ago Joyce was addressing enraptured audiences of thousands of people at a time; now he speaks only to tiny clutches – occasionally as few as a dozen. It is clear that nobody sees the NSL as a threat. They are dismissed with the offhand contempt reserved for the irredeemably eccentric: 'Bloody well go and live in Germany, then, if you like it so much!' Sometimes scuffles start. Sometimes nobody bothers to turn up. One former colleague in the BUF would later tell a story about walking past Joyce and John Beckett, who were standing on a street corner. One was standing on a portable platform and the other was heckling him. It was a popular method of attracting an audience, but they didn't seem to be having much luck.

Ever fewer prospective members make the effort to tramp up the several flights of uncarpeted stairs that lead to the National Socialist League's headquarters – a shabby one-room flat on the Vauxhall Bridge Road. Eighteen months after he had set it up as a political party, William Joyce re-registers the National Socialist League as a drinking club. It is possible that by this stage police informers outnumber the organisation's genuine believers.

William Joyce appears destined to an obscure existence on the far right's seedy borders. By the middle of 1938, with his failure patently clear, William is increasingly consumed by bitterness: yet every day he persists. He speaks on street corners, in clubs: anywhere, everywhere. But the people of England are blind and deaf to his warnings. It seems that they want war and race suicide. Joyce sees a unique glory in being English, yet the men and women he speaks to want to earn a living and pay their taxes on time and maybe go to the cinema once or twice a week; they aren't interested in glory.

His heart is with Berlin now. Patriotism alone has always seemed sufficient to William Joyce, but he knows the British Empire is dying on its feet, betrayed by liberals and Jews, and if you compare it with the miracles being wrought in Germany . . . He sees a proud nation in the throes of a revolution led by a man of super-human heroism. They are rebuilding a country and William has always possessed a mystical attraction to Germany, attributing this not just to his admiration of great figures like Wagner and Goethe, but to the German blood that he claims flowed through the veins of his ancestors. As if to emphasise the shift in his loyalties he grows a toothbrush moustache and begins to sport a trench coat notably similar to the one Hitler is often pictured wearing. Sometimes he can be found in a state of delirium, tears streaming down his face in joyful anticipation of the day when the Nazis will be masters of Europe.

William Joyce is not alone in his sympathies. He has close connections with the network of organisations designed to promote greater understanding with the Third Reich – such as the Anglo-German Fellowship, the Link, the Nordic League and the Conservative MP Captain Archibald Ramsay's Right Club – that springs up as the thirties draw on. They are permeable, compromised groups, in which apologists for Hitler, former soldiers, German spies, politicians and peers come together to swim in the same stream.

Many of Britain's leading statesmen find that it is easier than they thought to overcome the queasiness that had initially assailed them during the Nazis' first flourishes of anti-Semitic violence. Adolf Hitler's gentle reassuring words, his soft, artist's mien, convince them that he is a man they can do business with, a valuable safeguard against what Oswald Mosley describes as 'the jackal of oriental Communism'. David Lloyd George returns from the Berghof, the German leader's Bavarian mountaintop retreat, glowing at his encounter with 'the greatest living German', who, he says, 'likes to withdraw from the world for spiritual refreshment . . . he has no vices or indulgences or ambitions'. Lord Lothian describes the Führer as 'a visionary rather than a gangster', and the Londonderrys have the Nazi foreign minister, Joachim von Ribbentrop, as a weekend guest at their country house in Northern Ireland. Their enjoyment of his patronage is only slightly marred by the political considerations that prevented their 'good friend Goering' from accepting the invitation. The Duke of Buccleuch writes to the Lord Halifax, the British foreign secretary, to explain that he is taking a pair of Sèvres vases to Hitler as a fiftieth birthday present. Perhaps the royal family might like to make a similar gesture? Surely, his letter continues, only a Jew could object.

Summer 1939

The tutoring business run by Joyce and Macnab has so few students that they can no longer justify its existence. Part of this is due to William Joyce's obduracy: he refuses to teach Jews and, anyway, wishes to devote his energies to politics rather than the sordid business of working for money. To him it is a matter of principle; to Margaret it is a source of hair-pulling frustration. With a vastly reduced income, they can no longer afford South Kensington, and instead must move to a basement in Earls Court.

In the course of the first night in their new apartment Joyce is assaulted by forebodings of disaster: savage visions of failure, of death, of great cities reduced to ruins. He talks wildly, lashing out and screaming as the bewildered Margaret tries to soothe him. Finally, he gibbers and raves and, seemingly exhausted, falls asleep.

The next morning he wakes up in a cheerful, affectionate, tranquil mood, and makes no mention of the night before. For Margaret, the events of the night before must feel uncomfortably reminiscent of his behaviour a year ago, in the immediate after-math of the Munich crisis. Throughout those days when Europe seemed to be teetering on the brink of war, her husband appeared to be suffering from extreme stress; as if he were already struggling to resolve the competing loyalties inside his soul. He talked aloud about the possibility of travelling to Ireland, and then on to Germany, where he would enlist in their army. Once Neville Chamberlain returned with the promise of 'Peace in our Time' – secured by abjectly handing over a large slice of Czechoslovakia to Adolf Hitler, an act that he knows will precipitate the young nation's dismemberment – they were probably as relieved as anyone else in Europe. To celebrate, the couple decided to take a brief holiday at Ryde on the Isle of Wight. While there William received a vivid premonition that he was being prepared to play a role in momentous events: possessed by a kind of feral energy he talked rapidly and with great excitement until dawn.

For a while things seemed to calm down, and in the year after Munich he returns to the street-corner agitation that has been his occupation since leaving the BUF. Although he is still wary of making a definitive decision about leaving England, William Joyce knows that there is a lot to be said for setting plans in motion, just in case. When, in the summer of 1939, he learns that Macnab is planning a holiday to Berlin, Joyce gives him a letter of introduction to Christian Bauer, a contact of his in the German capital who is now working for the propaganda minister, Josef Goebbels.* Almost as afterthought he says:

> John, if you are willing, I want you to do something for me after you have got to know Christian. I want him to find out whether, in the event of my leaving England and going to Germany, Goebbels is able and willing to arrange for my immediate natur-alisation as a German citizen, together, of course, with Margaret, if she accompanies me.

Macnab returns on 21 August with good news: the impression he has been given, he says, is that German citizenship is all but guaranteed for the three of them. For Joyce this is highly signifi-cant. If he and Margaret do end up in Berlin, then they have an insurance policy. With German citizenship they will not have to rely on his falsely acquired passport†; and therefore they cannot, he reasons, be accused of treason.

A few days later, William Joyce's ability to reconcile conflicting allegiances is tested once again. The news that Hitler and Stalin have signed a non-aggression pact leaves him almost prostrate with shock. In his revulsion at the news he is, for maybe the first time in his life, in tune with the sentiments of the rest of the

---

* Joyce maintained constant contact with many of the Germans sent to London by the Nazis to act as conduits between them and Britain's various fascist organisations. Joyce, like the BUF, received funding from the German govern-ment. His communications with Bauer suggest that he was helping collect intelligence for the Third Reich: 'I hope that all goes well with you; to tell you the truth, I have been wondering whether my last "report" did not contain some blunder that caused you to go up in smoke . . . I am collecting some more material, though perhaps not as quickly as you would wish.' It is perhaps telling that Christian Bauer was expelled from Great Britain in November 1938.

† On the passport application form he filled in earlier that year he had lied and claimed that he had been born in the UK.

British population. For a while he broods in the gloom of their basement flat, before he decides to take to the streets. Long walks have always been his method of dealing with anguish and confusion – they were a feature of his first marriage, where he would often disappear into Battersea Park for hours at a time: leaving the house as a man incandescent with rage; returning once again as a benevolent paterfamilias.

Now he strides through the streets of a London that is already preparing for war, smoking endless cigarettes as volunteers dig trenches in parks and fill sandbags. He returns home and yet again he and Margaret find themselves talking through the night. Should they go to Berlin or Dublin, or will things blow over like the year before? Can they afford to stay? Margaret, the more decisive of the two, argues for Berlin. But Joyce, a man who enjoys complete certainty in so many other aspects of his life, remains irresolute. He gets out of bed, paces the floor, chainsmoking and reading and re-reading newspaper reports of the treaty – as if he is hoping that if he stares at the page long enough, the hateful words will disappear.

The news of the gruesome alliance the man he has come to idolise has made with the nation he believes represents the most evil force in history devastates him. It is inconceivable; everything is collapsing, falling apart. Nazi Germany and its Führer are supposed to be the saviours of civilisation, so why are they making common cause with its greatest enemy? Impossibility has been piled upon impossibility. Over the past twenty years, Joyce has invested enormous amounts of emotional energy in constructing a very particular, and highly charged, vision of the world. People, whole nations even, are expected to act in a certain way. He has his caricatured conception of Jews, and because he has virtually no contact with them, it can persist unchallenged. He thinks that the British government is run by a cynical group of cronyist capitalists: and while this may not be true in any objective sense, many of their actions, when interpreted from a highly subjective perspective like his, might appear to support his contentions. On those occasions when he is presented with evidence that might contradict his beliefs, he can generally dismiss it. But what is happening is too big to ignore: white has become black, down has become up.

He slowly, painfully, tries to rationalise the situation. A section of German opinion, he tells himself, has always wanted a pact with the Soviet Union for military reasons. And if the West has rebuffed Hitler's legitimate attempts to safeguard the Fatherland, then surely this was a reasonable step for him to take. In truth, this explanation is only sufficient to establish a fragile truce in his mind, but it is enough for now.

It is of little practical use, however, in helping him address the horrifying prospect of a war between Britain and Germany. He cannot believe that this is what the British people want. It is a war being fomented by the Jews and traitors who run the government. Surely, when the population see what they are being dragged into, they will revolt.

William Joyce is aware that this is unlikely to remain a hypothetical question for much longer. With war in Europe looking imminent, his high-profile past is likely to see him interned as a potential fifth columnist. Joyce knows that both Houses are being recalled in the next few days in order to rush through the Emergency Powers (Defence) Act, which would give the government exceptional powers in the event of war.

He is not afraid of internment in itself, but he has no wish for Margaret to witness a loss of nerve on his part, and nor does he wish to be parted from her. More significantly, sitting in a cell waiting for the conflict to end will do nothing to satisfy his desire for glory. If the war against Bolshevism is to begin − and of this he is certain − it is imperative that he is involved. To stand idle would be to make a mockery of everything he has said and done over the last two decades; it would be an act of gross cowardice. Even in the unlikely event that he is not arrested, Joyce is honest enough to realise that England seems to have increasingly little to offer him: he is an intensely proud man, and to him an existence spent on the lunatic fringe of politics is a living death. Might Germany offer new avenues of adventure and opportunity? And then there is the hatred of the Jews that pulses inside him like a heartbeat. Why not swap a nation corroded by their influence for one that has taken brave steps to crush them underfoot? He can feel Berlin's pull; it is his shining city upon a hill. With something approaching confidence he tells Margaret: 'There has to be a higher loyalty even than nationalism. Our war is with bolshevism so if that means fighting on the side of Germany, so be it.'

Yes, she agrees, it's the only logical, honest thing they can do: 'And, anyway, once there, we can let fate decide the rest.'

Yet even equipped with this new resolve they take no definite steps towards leaving for Berlin. Over the course of more sleepless nights William continues to return ceaselessly to the same questions: should they go to Germany? Would it be easier to travel to Ireland? Neither of them has any experience of foreign travel, so their putative destinations exist more as intellectual abstractions than places with a solid existence of their own. Only Margaret seems able to consider the problem from a practical perspective: 'Darling, I'm frightened. If I have to be imprisoned, at least let me be imprisoned somewhere where I can understand the language.' She watches as her husband appears gripped by a paralysis, unable to do anything but smoke and read the papers. Neither has slept properly for days, and their nerves are chewed up with anxiety.

Then, about midnight, the phone rings. They exchange startled looks. William Joyce moves hesitantly and, with evident anxiety, lifts the receiver. He says his name, listens for a few seconds, then replaces the handset.

'We must now make a final decision,' he tells her.

The following evening, after hours spent feeding documents into the fire, William and Margaret host a small party. Near its end, with his family talking excitedly in the room next door, William takes Angus by the arm.

'Margaret and I are making a little trip to Deutschland in the morning.'

'I want to come with you.'

'No. This trip is not for you. I know your loyalty but it isn't fair to you and, anyway, you're engaged to be married. I couldn't have asked you to come, and that's why I've delayed telling you until now. If I wait another day I fear it would be jail for yours truly and starvation for Margaret.'

'What if there is no war?'

Joyce shakes his head. 'I'm going to throw in my lot with Germany for good or ill. I am very sorry to leave England, which I love, but I made my choice, and Margaret is of the same mind as myself. In any event, my life in England is over.'*

When all their guests have left, William and Margaret lie down in a brief attempt to snatch some sleep. It is impossible. Doubts continue to crawl across William Joyce's mind like flies, and even his wife's soothing words are not enough to brush them away.

But the enterprise to which they have committed themselves seems to have acquired a momentum of its own. They wake up, red-eyed, almost giddy with exhaustion, and Macnab accompanies them to Victoria station, walking against the tide of people of people surging back from the Continent. 'Berlin!' exclaims the porter carrying their luggage. 'That's a rum place to be going right now.'

William's mother Queenie and brothers Frank and Robert are in attendance. As they wait for the train to depart the small group make hesitant attempts at beginning a conversation, but none of them can find the words the situation demands. It's a relief when Queenie remembers she has a gift for Margaret. She hands her a Brussels lace collar, a family heirloom; then the awkward silence resumes. It persists even after their train has pulled out of the station: as if, after the non-stop talking of the last weeks, there is nothing left to say. When William and Margaret reach Dover the man checking their passports appears to hesitate when he looks up at them, but then he evidently decides to swallow whatever words were rising up his throat and stamps their documents.

The Joyces take their place on the ship among German passengers who weep as it casts off. Perhaps more empty than truly stoical,

---

* The academic Colin Holmes suggests that in fact the reason Macnab stayed in England was so that he could act as part of a fifth column in the event of war. In this reading, it is only this particular phase of Joyce's life in Britain that is over: he intended to return as one of the country's new overlords.

William and his wife, who is gripped by seasickness and a great misery at leaving England, merely stand on the stern deck, their hands gripping the rail. Two years earlier he had imagined this moment, or something like it: 'If it ever happens to us to see the chalk cliffs receding for the last time as the water widens between us and our homeland, then the memories will come in a choking flood, and we shall know our land when it is too late. This is the land for which better than we have died.' His anticipation of the beginning of exile – and what else is it? – is oddly passive: 'If it ever happens to us.' But what is happening now is a situation of his own design; he has made it happen and will have to live with its consequences. He cannot forgive Britain for not being the country he had imagined it to be. Now he is intent on seeing if the Third Reich will be any more capable of living up to his febrile expectations.

William and Margaret keep their eyes on the horizon until they can see no more of the land that they loved and tried to serve, and which he would rather see burned than become a colony of Palestine. 'Let's go to lunch,' William says. They head down into the ship, their backs turned on Albion.

5

Bombs will speak for themselves

Late spring 1940

IN THOSE FIRST, gilded months in Berlin, the Joyces are happy, or at least close to it. They enjoy an eminence that exceeds by far the mild celebrity William had attained during his time with Mosley. The couple are feted, invited to parties and everybody seems to want to know what they think about the war. They drink, smoke and talk into the small hours with colleagues, foreign journalists and German soldiers home on leave, before groping their way back in the blackout, drunkenly colliding with lampposts and fire hydrants and laughing as they fall to the ground.

The early days of the conflict in western Europe are unworried and triumphant, and Margaret cheers the Axis advance on with a sports fan's avidity: 'We have only lost 10,000 men since the big fight started,' she records breathlessly in her diary. They watch with undisguised glee as Norway is subjugated in twenty-three days, Holland in five, Belgium in eighteen, France in thirty-nine, Yugoslavia in twelve, Greece in twenty-one; Denmark surrenders in less than twenty-four hours. A continent brought to heel in less than five months of fighting. There is food from Poland, furs from Czechoslovakia, and wine, champagne and brandy from Paris; the shops are full of silk stockings and perfume. The war's fortunes are such that, to William at least, it seems reasonable to assume that their exile need only be temporary. In August 1940 the daring are willing to lay money that the swastika will be flying over Trafalgar Square by 15 August; others, more pusillanimous, are betting on 7 September. One day Joyce turns to James Clark, one of the youngest members of the English colony in Berlin, and says, 'Well, Jim, a year from now, we will be eating as the guests of a grateful nation.'*

Outwardly, they appear to be thriving. William has much in common with the city to which they have moved. It is the imperial capital of an empire that claims it will last a thousand years, but Berlin is not a metropolis at ease with itself. Fiercely ambitious and resentful of the easily-won prestige it sees conferred on others, it has always been adept at manipulating history so that it tells a story more to its liking. The ghosts of the great betrayal of 1918, victims of the so-called 'stab in the back' and the hysterically punitive Versailles settlement, still haunt the streets, unassuaged by the Führer's realignment of Europe.

It is perhaps indicative of William's newfound contentment that he allows himself two sartorial flourishes: a bizarre confection of flags on his lapel, which somehow combines the St Andrew's Flag and the St George's Cross with a swastika in the middle; and an *Arbeitmütze*, a dark blue peaked cap favoured by workers. The latter is a defence against the biting cold of Berlin's winters, a way of hiding his thinning hair, and a statement of proletarian solidarity. As part of the naturalisation process, William adopts a mischievous, punning surname – Fröhlich – which serves the twin purposes of piquing his sense of humour (*fröhlich* is German for 'joy') and reaffirming his heritage (he affects to believe that his family are descended from Normans bearing the name Joyeux). It appears that he can imbue his choice of clothing, and even bureaucratic procedures, with dense layers of political and personal meaning. He also has started to carry a large automatic pistol around with him at all times and keeps the doors and windows of his apartment bolted: you can never be too sure.

After a couple of false starts, William is offered a post at the Rundfunkhaus (or the Skunkhouse as he calls it), joining a small coterie of English language broadcasters working there as part of

---

* Which would suggest that he had changed his mind since the year before when he'd assured Macnab that 'I have no intention of using Germany as a temporary haven or refuge, but I am making it my permanent home.'

the Nazi propaganda machine. Adolf Hitler once wrote that 'Our strategy is to destroy the enemy from within, to conquer him through himself. Mental confusion, contradictions of feeling, indecision, panic – these are our weapons.' And the motley group of washed-up actors and two-bob fascists whom the Germans have managed to scrape together to work in the English department are charged with delivering this airwave-borne blitzkrieg across the Channel. Some were admirers of Hitler before the war, but even those whose beliefs overlap, however crudely, with the sentiments they are expected to articulate, are largely motivated by the need to keep their heads above water.*

William is plainly more gifted than his associates, for whom he feels the contempt of a pike in a pond of tadpoles. It is lucky that propaganda's simplification of complex issues, its Manichean impulse, is perfectly suited to William's mindset. Lucky too that he shares the Third Reich's paranoiac worldview. Quickly he learns how the microphone exaggerates the idiosyncrasies of his voice;† he learns where he should stand in the recording studio; and he learns, most of all, how to lie. His life so far has, in many ways, been a drawn-out attempt to impose his version of the truth on the world. And if it is inconvenient that his truth's coordinates do not appear on any known map of the reality, and unfortunate that thus far so few others have been willing to take him at his own estimation, it has not shaken his conviction of his essential honesty. But honesty and truth are unwelcome intruders in the Third Reich. For Joseph Goebbels, the head of

---

* Margaret broadcasts too, though her delivery and scripts are dreary. 'Washable silk frocks are remarkably cheap, and bright and gay cyclamen stockings are readily available . . . rationing provides generous proportions: its aim is to make injustice possible. There is certainly no need for the BBC to sympathise with the Berlin woman because she can't get clothes – the great trouble is not to want to acquire too many – and too many bills.' One suspects that she was just as bored as her listeners – if there were any – must have been.

† It's a measure of how altered his voice was, both by the mechanics of broadcasting and the new persona that he had come to inhabit that even people who knew him well struggled to identify it. His own daughter remembered how 'I did not at first recognise his voice. It was too stark, too official. Then I listened again and little things that he said convinced me that, yes, it was my father.'

the Propaganda Ministry for whom William now works, the truth is not so much an absolute concept as it is a protean substance to be manipulated into whatever shape most suits his purposes.

Early on William discovered that the news scripts he was expected to follow were produced at the Propaganda Ministry by an English department that was headed by a former railway engineer who was 'conceited about his English and whose quali-fication as an authority was his authorship of a book in Nelson': he wasted little time in seeking permission to write his own. His broadcasts are soon littered with phrases that are immediately familiar to anybody who had heard him speak before the war (the gradual tightening of his grip can be traced by the increased frequency with which phrases such as 'true nationalism' and 'true socialism' began appearing in his talks), but if the sensibility and tone of the talks is unmistakably Joyce's, their content and direc-tion is determined by Goebbels.

The persona of Lord Haw-Haw existed before William had spoken so much as a syllable into a microphone.* But it is he who inhabits it more fully and confidently than any of the other broadcasters, and soon it feels inconceivable that the name could ever have been identified with anybody else. He is plainly more ambitious, more energetic, more able by far than the rest, and is the first, perhaps the only, one of them to grasp the opportunities the role offers. He sees it as a chance to leave his fingerprints on history. It is not exactly notoriety or power he seeks (though he knows both have a value) so much as *significance*.

The unprecedented potency of the Third Reich's high-powered wireless transmitters allows William Joyce to clamber into the minds

---

* He was first identified (if that's the correct word) by the *Daily Express*'s radio critic Jonah Barrington (a pseudonym, his real name was Cyril Carr Dalmain) who wrote of a broadcaster on German radio that 'He speaks English of the haw-haw, damn-it-get-out-of-my-way variety, and his strong suit is gentlemanly indignation.' The two most likely candidates were Norman Baillie-Stewart and Wolf Mittler. Another possibility is the former silent movie actor Jack Trevor, once the star of films such as *Rhenish Girls and Rhenish Wine*, *The Lady and the Chauffeur* and *Cause for Divorce*, who could often be found standing 'in the snow, with a mighty blizzard blowing, and rav[ing] to an S.S. guard outside the studio door about the urgent necessity of liquidating the Jews everywhere'.

of millions of people across Great Britain. He comes to represent Nazism incarnate: for those sitting at home he is more real, more present than any actual German could be. The impudent, incantatory rhythms of his voice stand both for the jackbooted armies massing against Britain across the Channel, and the shadowy traitors and fifth columnists waiting to bring the country down from within. By an ugly process of osmosis, his words come to absorb the fears, uncertainty and the madness of that time. Every word, every syllable that emerges from his mouth will forever remind people of the bleak months in which they stared defeat in the face.

In time he will command an audience bigger than any other English-speaking fascist has ever addressed before or since. In the summer of 1939 he was resorting to hustler's tricks to try to drum up interest in his ideas. By the end of January 1940 six out of ten Britons are gathering around the wireless to listen to him. He has 6 million regular and 18 million occasional listeners. His voice is better known than any other figure – with the honourable exceptions of the comedian Tommy Handley and Winston Churchill. Goebbels is delighted with the success of the man he describes as 'The best runner I've got in my stable.'

William revels in his notoriety. It is, after all, a sure sign that people are listening to him, that he is finally being treated with the respect he deserves. And how satisfying it must be to him to learn that Oswald Mosley is languishing in the obscurity of a cell at Brixton Prison. As 1938 rolled into 1939, and tensions across the Continent increased, the Leader had become an ever more vocal advocate of peace at all costs, and an accommodation with Nazi Germany. Hitler's ambitions were modest, he argued, and they presented little threat to Britain, limited as they were to the union of the German peoples in Europe. In a series of huge public meetings, bigger than any his movement had been able to stage for years, he continued to press his case with the same intoxicating, overwhelming, empty logic he had always used to drive his audiences into submission. 'Supposing every allegation were true,' he claimed, 'supposing it were a fact that a minority in Germany were being treated as the papers allege; is that any reason for millions in Britain to lose their lives in a war with Germany? . . . Why is it only when Jews are affected that we have any demand for war with the country concerned?' Why should Britain intervene in an alien quarrel? * Once war had been declared, Sir Oswald issued an ambiguous proclamation to the BUF – the italics are his own.

> Our members should do what the law requires of them; and, if they are members of any of the Forces or Services of the Crown, they should obey their orders and, in every particular, obey the rules of the Service. *But I ask all members who are free to carry on our work to take every opportunity within your power to awaken the people and demand peace.*

The great majority of British fascists were, at heart, uncomplicated patriots who rushed to serve their nation, but Sir Oswald's own protestations of loyalty were given little credence. His arrest and internment were applauded by a British public who were alternately thrilled and terrified by the idea that a fifth column might be active within its borders. While it was acknowledged that Mosley had been condemned as much for what he *might* do as for any treason he had actually committed – and some of his followers were arrested as they stepped off the boats from Dunkirk†– the general sentiment was that 'it should have been done a long time ago.' There is relief at the thought of him under guard, as of a crisis averted, or a dragon conjured and then dispatched before it has a chance to breathe any fire.

With Mosley safely behind bars, his former deputy cheerfully

---

* After the war, in his memoirs, Mosley continued to return, disingenuously, to the topic: 'It is true,' he conceded of the Third Reich, 'that people were in prison and concentration camps in Germany before the war, as some of us were in prison and concentration camps in England without charge or trial, and I am prepared to believe they were badly treated, though I had no proof of it.' But it was only after the onset of war that mass murder became the rule: 'If war had been avoided, the lives of 6,000,000 Jews would have been saved.' This was, apparently, a result of the opportunity for secrecy that conflict afforded, and also the maleficent effects of wartime conditions, which apparently afflicted the German Führer more strongly than most: 'Most people go rather mad in war, and Hitler in this respect went very mad.'

† Though, needless to say, very few of those MPs and peers who had, overtly or otherwise, supported the movement suffered the same fate.

assumes the mantle of being Britain's bête noire. The opening pages of *Twilight Over England*, a bizarre screed William writes at the behest of the propaganda department, are marked by a kind of cackling, black-hearted glee at his newfound status.

> The preface is usually that part of a book which can most safely be omitted. It usually represents that efflorescent manifestation of egotism which an author, after working hard, cannot spare either himself or his readers. More often than not the readers spare themselves. When, however, the writer is daily a perpetrator of High Treason, his introductory remarks may command from the English public that kind of awful veneration with which £5000 confessions are perused in the Sunday newspapers, quite frequently after the narrator has taken his last leap in the dark.

Now that William has grabbed the attention of a whole nation, he does not intend to let the opportunity go to waste. His voice seeps like smoke into living rooms up and down the country, providing a soundtrack to the first years of the war. It is an alien, unsettling, but exciting contrast to the suffocatingly deferential tone of most of the BBC's output.* 'When someone tunes in to Lord Haw-Haw,' the BBC reports anxiously, 'the whole room gets up and gathers round the wireless.'

The names of downed ships and lost battles roll from his tongue with vicious relish. He gives advice on how to dress the more fearful types of wounds that will, he says, become commonplace when the Luftwaffe starts bombing Britain in earnest. He talks – again with the same tone of earnest concern – of the straitjackets that will be needed once thousands start going mad.

He does not mind that, for the first time in his life, the hatred he feels for the vast proportion of humanity is being reflected back at him on something approaching a scale commensurate with his own vituperation. His threats continue, week after week.

---

* William Joyce's very confidence that he knew best, his occasional suggestions that he cared profoundly for his listeners' well-being, might be taken for an ingenious subversion of the BBC's blithe paternalism.

If the people of England silently allow these rulers to commit them to annihilation, then silence must be taken to signify consent. It is a pity! It is a thousand pities! It is a tragedy the Führer went out of his way to avoid. But if those who rule England and those who live in it care less for their country than the Führer has cared, force, which they regard as the sole arbitrator, must arbitrate . . . And that is the end of England, not within a few years but within a few days to come.

It is unnecessary to say that a terrible retribution will come to the people who tolerate as their Prime Minister the cowardly murderer who issues these instructions. Sufficient warnings have already been given. Bombs will speak for themselves . . . The people of England will curse themselves for having preferred ruin from Churchill to peace from Hitler.

Londoners will now know the taste of monkey or alligator, and the Zoo will continue to be one of the few institutions to keep to the old slogan 'Business as Usual'. Starvation now threatens England. Who is to blame for this? No one but the small circle of rich people which is indifferent as to whether the people starve or not. These people have already got their children to safety. When things get bad enough they will make a getaway as well. The British will, in the meantime, starve. Is this the wish of the British people?

It is said that one lady is so depressed by William Joyce's broadcasts that, after having finished the night's washing-up, she put her head in a gas oven. Even the phlegmatic Commander Leonard Burt, who at the end of the war will convey Joyce back to Great Britain, attributes his mother's death from a stroke to the septic mixture of anxiety and terror induced in her by the Irishman's broadcasts. One listener blurts out how: 'I think that, secretly, we are rather terrified by the appalling things he says. The cool way he tells of the decadence of democracy and so on. I hate it; it frightens me. Am I alone in this? Nobody has confessed as much to me.'

There is a kind of measured lunacy to William's sentences. More often than not they unspool in orderly cadences, his voice giving a specious impression of sanity that blinds you to the fact that the speaker has long since cut his moorings and drifted away towards a cracked, paranoiac's vision of the world.

He leaves long pauses between his words, as if inviting you to fill them with your own fears. And, before long, people do. The cheerful, stoic indefatigability of the 'Blitz Spirit' has a counterpart in the form of a succession of panics about fifth columnists (which range from easily resolved misunderstandings about flashlights through to the internment of German Jews who had fled Hitler). Astrology, spiritualism and séances all become far more popular than they ever were before the war. Even pigeons cannot be trusted: the authorities use birds of prey to intercept pigeon-borne German messages released by German agents in Britain. And it is in this climate that rumours ascribing almost preternatural powers to Lord Haw-Haw begin to circulate.

But still people listen. And if his radio voice terrifies many, its very power makes it seductive to others. There are even some who are impressed by the sex appeal of what they consider to be his virile, commanding tone. Though he speaks as if he were better clothed and fed than his audience – and knows it too – many working-class listeners say they like Lord Haw-Haw's understanding of their social conditions. He comes across as the kind of man who knows the price of a loaf of bread, and what it is like to struggle – which, given his penurious existence before the war is literally true, but acquires a paradoxical aspect given the persona he inhabits is widely regarded as an epitome of aristo-cratic degeneracy and corruption. There is something bracing about his Punch and Judy sallies against the fat old men in suits who seem to be making such a bad job of running the war. Nobody commissioned by the BBC has ever referred to Winston Churchill as 'the degenerate of Downing Street' before.*

★

---

* Much the same might be said of the output of Workers' Challenge (a Nazi radio station designed to give the impression that it was run by disaffected proletarians broadcasting from somewhere within the United Kingdom), whose liberal use of words like 'bleeding', 'bugger', 'old cock', were some of the first profanities to be broadcast in Britain. It is said that the programme also marks the debut of the word 'fuck' on British airwaves. In keeping with the more proletarian audience to which it was supposed to appeal, Joyce's scripts extended their fire to figures such as the doughty Ernest Bevin, dismissed as 'Mr Bleeding Bevin' or 'Hoary Ernie'. However Workers' Challenge was fatally hobbled by Joyce's tin ear – reading the bilge the actors were expected to deliver you might

69

His broadcasts are a vehicle for the seething resentment that he has incubated for decades: against the government who betrayed the loyal Joyce family by ceding independence to Ireland; against the diplomat who had written on his Foreign Office application 'A little oily, don't you think'; against the BUF, who treated him like an officer who had risen from the ranks; against the Conservative Party, for whom he was good enough to 'work like a black', but did they ever offer him a seat?; against the ordinary people of Great Britain, who day after day had complacently ignored his frantic warnings; against everyone who ever held him back in any way, 'determined that people like me should never come into our own. They were the murderers of the heroes of the true blood.'

But William has never stopped loving England. His rage at the country in which he had once reposed so many unrealistic hopes is the rage of a wounded suitor. Sometimes it feels as if the abuse he hurls over the airwaves is designed, as much as anything else, to convince one person in particular that Britain truly is an enemy: William Joyce. While on one level he knows that some people might regard him as a traitor, he cannot accept that he has in any way actually committed treachery. So the very fierceness of his attacks is a device that allows him to persuade himself that Britain, through its blind obedience to plutocratic frauds like Churchill, its supine surrender to Jewish influence, and its continuing refusal to acknowledge that Adolf Hitler is at the helm of the greatest revolution since the Renaissance, has in fact betrayed him. He cannot allow Germany, and by extension himself, to be anything other than a victim.

> Must we remind them of the fact that it was Britain who declared war on Germany, who started to wage it on women and children by preparing the hunger blockade? Must we recall to their memories the air raid in Freiburg when children were killed in an attack on an undefended town in broad daylight, with no military target even in the vicinity?

---

reasonably conclude that while the Irishman might have met a working-class person before, he had certainly never listened to him actually talk.

He is lonely for London, although he will not – and perhaps cannot – admit the fact to anyone. Whenever Margaret tries to talk to him about how isolated and homesick she feels, he swiftly changes the subject, or simply aborts the conversation. It is as if he considers that to confide to her that he misses their life in England would also in some way be a confession that their decision to come to Berlin was defective.

William is permanently draped in memories of Albion: he always wears an overcoat purchased on Regent Street, and his pockets are invariably filled with English cigarettes. The land he left behind is present to him at all times in hallucinatory, taunting detail. There must be a reason why the couple has kept trinkets such as an old newspaper cutting about Joyce's sacking by Mosley, and tickets from Kensington Public Library (for books that are now years overdue). In the midst of their self-imposed exile, they ache for home. One evening he turns to one of his few friends in Berlin, and tells him that he hungers for Britain every hour that he lives.

Night after night, as he makes his broadcast, he haunts the country he had abandoned in 1939, continuing to inhabit it by way of a jagged proxy. He is like a man who has walked out on a lover he believes has hurt him, but who is compelled to return again and again to stare at her window, or to write long wild letters in which every sentence is formed of equal parts of love and hate.

From time to time the Joyces are given stinging reminders that in the eyes of many people traitors – whatever their allegiance – carry a contagion. Traitors are exiles from the normal arrangements of society and should be shunned, consigned to the margins; as if contact with them might lead to pollution.

William knows what it is like to walk into a favourite haunt like the Press Club and be 'shunned like the plague'. Occasionally he receives letters from German correspondents informing him, with some regret, that they have nothing but contempt for the traitor Lord Haw-Haw. And even some of his superiors seem only to be able to contemplate the renegades in their employ with their fingers clamped tightly over their nose. Questioned after the war, Professor Herman Haferkorn of the English department said that 'they were not the type of person from whom one chose one's friends', though they were useful at the time.

At some point during the war Eduard Dietze, a senior figure at the Rundfunkhaus, will present his star employee with a caricature of him that appeared in an issue of *Punch*; beneath the drawing he scrawls: 'From Mephistopheles to Faust. With Best Wishes – Dietze.' It is an acknowledgement of the bargain Joyce has made. But it appears that even Berlin's Mephistopheles is revolted by his Faust's decision to leave Britain, a revelation whose force is borne, inevitably, by Margaret: 'W found out that it was true that Dietze said he was a traitor,' she records in her diary, 'why blame me?'

Spring 1941

Margaret fears the city's dark streets. From the earliest days of the war a draconian blackout has been strictly enforced in Berlin. Every night, lights in shop windows, advertisements, railway stations, buses and trams must be extinguished, and all windows shuttered and curtained. In their place, a ghostly filigree of phosphorescent paint covers kerbstones, street corners and crossings. Luminous arrows point towards bomb shelters; steps are painted with a glowing zigzag.

Although sometimes the blackness is momentarily pierced by shards of light from the S-Bahn and subways, or the firefly glow of cigarette ends, none of this is enough to prevent many, including Margaret, from feeling as if they have been cast adrift. The darkness gives rise to strange and unsettling experiences. Buses roam through the night like sea monsters; dislocated conversations drift through the air. One evening Margaret sees a woman being dragged struggling and shouting into a car. She rushes home to tell her husband; together they manage to quell her fears by agreeing that it is likely that she has simply witnessed the Gestapo at work. Strange days indeed when this represents a reassuring explanation. It does not appear to bother the couple that they are part of a regime capable of snatching civilians off the streets.

A few evenings later William is walking home along the broad Kaiserdamm when suddenly he stops with a sharp intake of breath. For a few seconds the buildings on either side of the street, which had looked so solid and intensely black against the moon's eerie light, dissolve into jagged ruins. He will not be afflicted by this particular vision again – which shares a macabre similarity with the apocalyptic dreams that had descended upon him in England – but reality seems intent on supplying a more tangible form of horror.

Night after night the air raids come. Darkness falls, the city's 20,000 sirens blare and, in the ghostly light cast by phosphorescent paint, you are forced to contemplate, all over again, how and when you might die. It is, for many, an intolerable burden: the thought that you might be crushed in a building's smoking ruins; reduced to a bloody smear by shrapnel, identifiable only by a wedding ring; or found bizarrely unmarked, victim of an unseen but lethal percussive detonation. Even on those rare nights when bombs don't fall, the city's denizens are afflicted by attacks of anxiety, and recurring nightmares that rip the tattered fabric of their sleep apart. Like all Berliners the Joyces have learned that very few shelters offer protection from a direct hit – many are simply old railway buildings, or brewers' cellars – that in the dubious safety of the shelters smoking is utterly *verboten* (oxygen reserves below ground are consumed with a horrifying speed), and that when shrapnel descends from the sky it makes a sound like hail on a tin roof.

The first air-raid casualties in Berlin came on the night of 28 August 1940. Ten people were killed and twenty-eight wounded. As soon as his shift at the Rundfunkhaus ended, William made his way over to view the damage. In the street behind the apartment he shared with Margaret, a house had been cut clean out of the block by a direct hit. Glass, rubble, bedding and splintered furniture were strewn across the ground. Disoriented survivors littered the pavements, unable to absorb what had just happened to them. Joyce stood for a while watching, moved by the human consequences of a bombing attack. As he walked home, he could talk of nothing else.*

So he knows how bombs can devastate a city, and the lives of the people living there. He knows too that each night, when the Luftwaffe's huge armadas fly over London, the massed ranks of planes heave countless tonnes of incendiaries and high explosives on to homes inhabited by friends such as John Beckett and Angus Macnab, his parents, his brothers and sisters, his own daughters. Yet he has greeted the consequences of these attacks with a kind of reptilian delight: 'Now just retribution has befallen Britain. If there are civilian casualties and destruction of homes in London, then these are such as cannot be avoided in any really large-scale attack on the main objectives of military and economic import-ance in the East of London.'

At no point during the Second World War does William Joyce ever fire a gun in anger, or drop a bomb, nor does he issue any orders to do so. But his work has an intimate connection with the Heinkels and Junkers that rumble across the Channel each night to deal out death and destruction to the men and women of the country he left so precipitately in 1939. Every time he steps up to the microphone he is contributing to a war effort whose stated aim is the subjection of the United Kingdom – no matter how much British blood is spilled. The same is true (if in varying degrees) of John Amery, Harold Cole and Eric Pleasants: this knowledge has an awkward, prickly presence, and for the rest of the war it will sit stubbornly on the renegades' shoulders like ragged crows on a fence, no matter how many frantic self-deceptions they employ to try to shake it off.

Before long William Joyce will feel for himself what it is like to lose someone in the assault on London for which he has been such an ardent cheerleader.† Michael Joyce, William's father, dies

---

* Hitler, by contrast, never displayed any emotion when driven past the smoking ruins of his capital city.

† By its end the Blitz will have killed almost 45,000 Britons, and seriously wounded a further 50,000.

in an air raid in February 1941, his heart giving out when a bomb falls close to the family's flat. Queenie Joyce finds that she does not have enough money to cover the funeral expenses of her husband. It is only some time later – through a foreign press report – that their son will learn of this. William is a sophist who can argue that white is black, or that down is up, or indeed that the defeat of England would also be its victory, but on this subject he is silent – perhaps because there is nothing he can say.

Schnapps, white wine, champagne, sekt, brandy, whisky, Burgundy, Mosel, sherry, hock, red wine, cognac, opium, Steinhäger, kummel, beer, gin, Riesling. It is a drinker's war, and William and Margaret Joyce (who faithfully records much of their carousing in her diary) are two of its greatest topers, their days irrigated by a stream of booze. They drink because they can: *Was in one of my drinking moods – kept pace with W. & was sober when he was tight.* They drink because it is fun: *terribly drunk. W made me flirt with a Bavarian!* And they drink to keep their courage intact: *Several bombs about 150 yds from us. We drank all through the raid. I was scared.* But, most of all, they drink because they must. What before 1939 had been an uncomplicated pleasure is now a consuming desire.*

In the first year of the conflict, whenever William and Margaret felt like strangers in a foreign city, they knew that they could turn to each other for comfort. They were lovers and comrades then, both engaged in the same great struggle. But now they use drink to dampen the pain of exile, and to help them forget that the foundations of their marriage are eroding with every passing day.

William, his devotion to National Socialism undimmed, works punishing hours at the Rundfunk, where his colleagues cannot help but notice how often he reeks of drink. He persists with his labours, even though he has little or no respect for most of the Germans he encounters, and is frequently asked to perform tasks

---

* The back endpaper of Margaret's diary for 1944 reads: 'NUNC EST BIBENDUM' – *now is the time for drinking.*

that he finds degrading. He has not managed – he will never manage – to achieve the kind of ecstatic communion with a renascent race of Teuton heroes he had envisaged finding in Berlin.

By contrast, Margaret is lonely and bored ('The heating in the hall blew up at about 2am,' she notes, listlessly, in her diary. 'That was the only excitement') and starved of affection. For her, life in Berlin feels like a holiday that was exhilarating and exotic to start with, but has now gone on for far too long. She finds her work at the Rundfunk dreary, and with her husband so often absent she struggles to fill her time. Coming to the city has driven them apart and their marriage has been hollowed out until it resembles little more than an empty schedule.

She has lost her husband, the kind tender man who gently observed that her laugh (which he wrote as 'Yp-baa') was like the noise made by a sheep calling its young; who called her affectionately, among other things, Peggy, Peg Mae, Meg, Meb, Freja, Mother-Sheep, die Olle, Ol and Little Ape Face. It does not matter to me if you are here or not, he tells Margaret. He screams at her when he feels his breakfast has been served late, nearly knocks her unconscious when she forgets his cigars.

Margaret's diary entries reflect her isolation and emptiness, with the occasional moments of effusion – 'Free day (oh yeah)' – balanced by more frequent complaints about a parade of ailments ('I have caught cold & life is a Bad Thing as smoking hurts my throat') and her husband's behaviour ('Rat Will being a real Rat Will again'). But more eloquent than any words are the vast blank spaces she leaves on each page.

6

In the name of my King and Country
I thank you

Spring 1941

IT HAD STARTED with spontaneous efforts by local patriots after the fall of France. Someone had to help the hungry and bewildered men in khaki battledress who were hiding in barns, sheds and basements across the Pas-de-Calais, and even on the streets of Paris. Weeks earlier they had drunk, fought and swaggered, now they were happy to submit meekly to whatever assistance they were offered. After Dunkirk, one family in ten in the Lille area kept a Tommy hidden, and a further five families knew of their presence but kept their lips sealed. Some escapers settled down temporarily in northern French families, a handful, reluctant to leave, even married and stayed there for the duration of the war. But the majority walked or cycled from village to village until they reached the unoccupied zone in the south of the country.

They quickly learned how to avoid capture: stay away from third-class train carriages, the passengers are too talkative; police dogs are your great enemy, and if you are attacked by one give it a good kick under the jaw; posing as a football team provides unexpectedly good cover. It helped that the Germans, as stunned as anybody else by the scale and speed of their success, were too busy trying to organise the finer details of the vastly expanded new Reich to devote much attention to the British Army's waifs and strays.

It wasn't easy to keep the Tommies sober, or stop them fooling about. One horrified *résistant* witnessed her charges performing a wildly exaggerated goosestep behind the backs of German officers waiting on a railway platform. Another English soldier was found in a village bar playing darts with a German; luckily each was as drunk as the other.

By 1941 the escape operations had begun to operate on a more professional footing. The British established MI9, a dedicated escape organisation, and increasing numbers of *résistants* were drawn into the networks that helped ferry the ragged remnants of the BEF, as well as downed air crew, across the demarcation line that separated Vichy France from the occupied zone, and then spirit them away to Britain (most often across the Pyrenees). These escape lines – of which the one established in Marseille by Ian Garrow (a 'great devil of a Scotsman with a genial and somewhat round face and a *sacré calme*') was perhaps the most significant – performed a heroic and highly valuable function: they helped safeguard the government's substantial investment in the men charged with prosecuting the war in the skies – it cost £10,000 to train a bomber pilot and £15,000 to train a man to fly a fighter. Just as importantly, at a time when Britain felt as if its back was truly against the wall, 'The miracle of [the evaders'] reappearance at Air Force bases and stations had a marvellous effect . . . on the morale of all who flew against Germany.'

Helping the evaders is a gruelling, nerve-fraying business, but, most of all, it is dangerous: by the end of the war 500 civilians in France, Holland and Belgium will have been executed by the Nazis for their work on the escape lines. The Continent abounds with German agents, and the Gestapo is adept at insinuating traitors into the heart of even the most close-knit resistance organisation; still, though, men and women come forward.

One of the more notable figures operating in the north of France is a mysterious Englishman known to the men and women he works with as 'le Capitaine Anglais' or 'Monsieur Paul'. He goes by other names too: he has papers in the names of Paul Delobel and Joseph Deram; both identities that – with the help of a pair of glasses, or a different way of combing his hair – he can slip into at a moment's notice. But his real name is Harold Cole. He was born in Hackney in 1906, the son of an itinerant and unskilled labourer; by the time he was ten his family had moved five times. Harold watched his father struggle to hold down a succession of menial jobs – bottlewasher, cooper, stoker, docker – before he died in the service of his country in 1916. Cole's mother married a carter named Robert Moore a year later. In short order five half-siblings followed, as did a lurch into an even more unsteady, impecunious existence. Though Cole was bright enough to earn a scholarship to Stormont House School in Hackney Downs, he had to leave in 1923 when his stepfather told him that it was time to start earning his keep.

It is not long before he commits his first crime: stealing a bicycle in Southend. On this occasion he is discharged under the First Offenders Act and returned to his home by the police. 'Almost immediately I left home again stealing a car, went up to Kings Lynn to look for work and was picked up by the police on my return to London.' A pattern of petty crime and deceit begins. He flits in and out of his family's life, increasingly luke-warm about either working hard or admitting to his humble origins. It is clear to Sonny Boy – as he is known to his family – that you can work your fingers to the bone and struggle every day and even shed blood for your country, but that it doesn't matter and nobody will thank you because the system is rigged against people like him. He knows that Britain remains a deeply class-ridden nation; that you are judged on the way you dress and the way you speak, and the school you went to.

One of his cousins would later remember of Harold that: 'You never knew when he was in the nick or away somewhere else . . . To us he was a toff – he didn't speak like us. He was a six-footer, slim-built, and always well dressed, the type of person that can walk into clubs, attractive to gullible women.' In the service of disguising his background he begins to sport an aristocrat's mous-tache, oils his conversation with phrases like 'old boy' and 'old man' and makes sure he is always dressed in a dapper suit; though anybody who looks closely will notice that his cuffs are thread-bare, and the elbows shiny from wear. He is the kind of man who always likes to make sure he has cash in his pocket, a glass of champagne in his hand, and a pretty woman on his arm. He views the world with a bleak and chilly cynicism, and solidarity is not a word that means anything to him. Everybody knows that you are on your own in this life, and he is out for what he can get.

In 1925, perhaps because he has exhausted the goodwill of everyone around him (he once swindled his half-brother out of the money he earned as a milkman), he joins the Queen's Royal West Surreys. Initially he seems to thrive in his new environment, and is promoted to corporal – perhaps this will be the making of him? In 1928 he is sent to Hong Kong as a chauffeur, where his good intentions falter. 'A new C.O. was appointed to change the routine and as a result I stole a car and went for a holiday around China.' Eventually he is caught, given six months' imprisonment and discharged from service.

Finding no work on his return to London, Harold falls into old habits. He becomes a persistent but somehow rather hapless criminal. Whether he is stealing cars, breaking into houses, embezzling funds, obtaining money under false pretences or passing bad cheques, he rarely seems able to escape justice for long and his rap sheet – for crimes committed everywhere from Stoke Newington to Oldham – swiftly expands. Exhilarating, larcenous months of freedom are invariably followed by tedious, incommodious years behind bars. Harold remains obdurately unwilling either to go straight, or to learn how to be a better criminal (though he is cunning enough to secure his release from behind bars in 1935 by persuading the warden he has TB – that his lungs were evidently well enough to play both trumpet and trombone in the prison band seemed to have escaped notice).

He has shared little or nothing about his pre-war career, and nor has he told anyone that he had carried his light-fingered habits over into a trouble-filled spell in the British Expeditionary Force. (When his unit's mess funds were discovered, along with two whores, in an apartment he kept in Lille, he had been confined to jail. Two short-lived escapes later, Cole was encouraged to fend for himself as the rest of his regiment fled back towards the English Channel. 'I don't care a bugger what you do,' he was told by the sergeant who flung his cell door open, 'we're off.')

Instead, he has let it be known that during peacetime he was an inspector at Scotland Yard (where he had had the special responsibility of guarding Wallis Simpson) and that on the declaration of war he had joined the intelligence services, where he holds the rank of captain. He is not always consistent about his rank – sometimes in an unintentional access of modesty he demotes himself to a mere lieutenant, but nobody picks him up on this inconsistency.

Harold Cole moves busily around the villages and towns of northern France. Sometimes he uses the black Peugeot 302 sedan he has been provided with to deliver black-market supplies and ferry escapees; but just as often he relies on his long, very thin legs, striding nonchalantly from house to house as he makes new contacts and connections. He speaks such bad French that he might as well speak none, and is so shortsighted that he must screw up his eyes to see into the distance, yet somehow he has always managed to stay out of trouble. This is despite the fact that everything about his person seems designed to make him conspicuous. He laughs with a loud guffaw and a list of his physical features reads like the text from a wanted poster: angular frame; hair plastered down; reddish rims on eyelids; very narrow, bent shoulders; false teeth, some crowned with white gold; shifty glance; long, bony hands, rather hairy; prominent Adam's apple; one earlobe cut off; sticks out tongue when writing or concentrating; scar on his chin. Most of all though, with his russet hair and those small dark eyes that shift quickly between sharp hunger and an anxious watchfulness, he resembles nothing so much as a fox.

The people in the network he has built – such as the strikingly beautiful and clever hairdresser Jeannine Voglimacci, who arranges food, clothes and shelter for the evaders; or the one-legged François Duprez, whose job in the local mairie means he can create false identity cards for them – feel a fierce loyalty towards him. When he speaks he gives confidence to others, and makes them believe in him. 'If Paul ever quits we won't go on with all this dangerous work,' claims one of the *résistants* inspired by his example. This is combined with a kind of vulnerability: he can draw your sympathy, make you want to help him.

They are enchanted by his panache and disregard for danger – he is regarded as '*un type très chic*'. Every mission is attended by tension and excitement, but nothing seems to faze him. It is as if the parade of deceptions that had characterised his peacetime life was simply a rehearsal for this new existence. He loves the secret meetings and sudden journeys, the adrenalin induced by the constant fear of discovery. He drives cars without a licence, and sits fearlessly among Germans in cinemas, drinks with them in bars, and dines beside them in restaurants (always in the company of a girlfriend). For those situations when he would prefer to avoid speaking directly to the grey-clad troops he has created a document in German certifying he is deaf and dumb.* Sometimes, though, he cannot resist thumbing his nose at France's occupiers (to whom he refers, in a gallant echo of local tradition, as 'les Boches').

When his car – with François Duprez and six British evaders inside – breaks down on the way to Lille train station, Cole, wearing boots and a black leather coat, leaps out and runs into the Renault dealership on the boulevard, which also happens to house the German motor pool. He persuades the Germans to tow their car the several miles to the station, then dismisses them with a staggering haughtiness. A few months later he is the victim once more of mechanical failure; he hails a Wehrmacht lorry and politely approaches the driver: 'I say, *mon cher*, could you be kind enough to have a look at this engine for me?' His displays of chutzpah are a welcome morale boost to people straining under the yoke of a humiliating occupation.

And while everybody knows that he is regularly responsible for great acts of heroism in the name of freedom, he is becomingly modest. He seems the very model of an English gentleman; whenever a local patriot performs a kindness for him he responds with elaborate courtesy: 'In the name of my King and Country I thank you.'

At the same time there is a minority who, mistrustful of his

---

* An important component of his suite of false documents is a membership card for a local pigeon racing association.

ersatz gallantry, feel that he is too quick to make himself at home in other people's houses, draping his elongated frame across favourite chairs and helping himself to special bottles of whisky. Some think him boastful and conceited; and perhaps there is a defensiveness about the way he is always exaggerating the difficulties he faces. Occasionally this shades into what sound like lies. Had he really escaped from the clutches of the German police by kicking one of his pursuers in the groin and then quickly disguising himself in a set of *bleu de travail*? Did anyone actually believe that he was in touch with a British lieutenant from the intelligence services who was working undercover at the German headquarters in Lille? Was it true that before anybody else could meet him this agent had been shot by the Germans while shouting 'Long live King George VI'?

Cole's success means that few pay much attention to these criticisms. Who else in the network can match his ability to draw new members into the organisation, or to secure the funding they need so desperately? Henri Duprez, the owner of a string of textile factories, was taken aback by the abrupt request for financial support Cole made within minutes of their first meeting. Something about the question – its indelicacy, perhaps – disquieted him. For a moment it appeared that the old Harold Cole, the grafter and small-time swindler, had flashed to the surface. But Duprez's doubts were soon swept away by the enthusiasm Cole displayed. He had talked knowledgeably and passionately about his work and he left Duprez, who was somewhat overwhelmed to be in the presence of an English agent, feeling as if he had met someone special.

The eighteen-year-old Roland Lepers had also been completely 'dazzled' by Cole from their earliest encounter, and he now follows him everywhere he goes, part aide-de-camp, part starstruck fan. Lepers and Cole make an odd pair – so much so that they unsettle many of the pilots whom they ferry to safety. There is Cole in his baggy plus-fours, 'so obviously English it wasn't true'; even all his close shaves never seem sufficient to deter Cole from 'chattering away in this frightful French with Germans around'. At his heels is Lepers, who, when he is not cheerfully whistling British popular songs, spends his time showing off his English to the men in their charge.

It is Lepers who, having just escorted a group of evaders south with the intention of travelling with them to England, makes the connection with the escape line operated by Ian Garrow in Marseille. When Garrow persuades him that he would be more useful in France, Lepers suggests he might like to meet Cole: 'I know an Englishman who is working for the resistance. I think it would be good for you to get to know him.'

'Bring him along,' says Garrow, handing him 10,000 francs to cover his expenses.

Garrow reports enthusiastically about his new agent to a Major Donald Darling in Lisbon, who has been charged by British intelligence with trying to rebuild the communication lines and networks that have been demolished by the Germans' implacable sweep through Europe. This is the first time that MI9 have become aware of Cole's existence and, without quite knowing why, the cockney's story unsettles Darling. It is inconceivable to him that this man – who speaks such atrocious French, and who dresses as if he were attending a golf tournament – has managed to evade capture, let alone that he has played such a central role in the escape of so many British soldiers and airmen.

He sends a coded telegram to London. Surely they know more about this mysterious figure; Darling cannot be the first person to have been perplexed by his success. The reply, when it comes, offers little help. Yes, they are aware of his work and what is more they feel as if he has 'a sporting chance of getting away with it for a while'. Unsatisfied, Darling makes a series of requests: Cole's background should be investigated. What kind of man is he? Even at this early stage in the war, when most intelligence officers work by a combination of trial and error, Darling has learned enough to know that when somebody seems too good to be true, they usually are. But another thing his experience had taught him is that while his controllers can often come across as obtuse, some-times a very good reason lies behind what might otherwise have looked like negligence. Somewhere in MI6 a decision has been taken to allow Cole to continue his good work unhindered, even if it means keeping Darling and Garrow in the dark.

Meanwhile, Garrow looks on approvingly as the British money he sends to Cole ensures that the cockney's network starts to function with ever greater efficiency and speed. More men and women are joining – *passeurs*, couriers, forgers and suppliers of clothes and food – and the network expands to cover thousands of square miles. Cole begins to collect information about troop movements and the damage caused by RAF bombing raids, and asks his agents to discover the exact locations of flak batteries as well as fuel and ammunition depots.

Maurice Dechaumont, a railway employee, is charged with stealing maps of airfields and copies of German transport orders; in Dunkirk, the ropemaker Raphaël Ayello is requested to keep an eye on any German preparations for a cross-Channel invasion, and also to provide information on the defences surrounding the town; while Henri Duprez is given the responsibility of collecting German occupation documents like ID cards and travel permits – he is assured that even theatre stubs and matchboxes will be useful.

As ties with Garrow's escape line grow, Cole spends more time in Marseille. Whereas others in the network are uncomfortable among the pimps, pushers, gangsters, spivs and spies who swarm in and out of the brasseries, cafés and *dancings* of the Vieux Port, Cole thrives there. Black-market goods, false paperwork and information are all commodities to be bought and sold: if you have the right money and the right contacts, and are willing to take a risk, then there is little you cannot lay your hands on. Cole always seems to know where to find the restaurants that still serve a dinner that almost matches pre-war standards, and he always has the money to pay for the privilege. That Cole plainly has a taste for good living is not in itself considered to be a problem. Nor, for the moment, is the fact that he has access to large amounts of cash, coming both from London's deep pockets and the rather shallower ones of the French patriots who have supported the network's activities so generously. He is a hero who deserves the trust of the people he works with – and surely even heroes are allowed to let their hair down once in a while.

It is also recognised that Marseille is a good place to pick up new members for the network. One recent recruit is a bored and frustrated young girl called Suzanne Warenghem, who had been working as a secretary in Le Havre when war broke out. Suzanne is still an innocent – even the mention of the word 'brothel' can make her blush – but she is brave, resourceful and desperate to help the struggle against the Germans: the first time she saw a British plane shot down she was so angry that she developed a red rash that spread across her entire body.

Having escorted two British officers to Marseille with a view to escaping with them, she had been persuaded by Ian Garrow to stay and work with his escape network. 'If you go to England and join de Gaulle you'll just be another person in the army,' he had told her. 'All very nice, of course – but if you stay with us in France you can do work that's fifty times more valuable.'

Suzanne is sent back to the north of France by Garrow, which means that more and more often she finds herself in Cole's company. She knows he has other women, and yet it is difficult not to be swept away by his élan. Nobody would call him good-looking, but she notices that there is something about him that turns heads – and gradually she too finds that her head has been turned. Over dinners that stretch late into the night, Suzanne returns constantly to her favourite theme: that France at heart is defiant and unbeaten, and that its people want freedom. Cole agrees with everything she says: 'My dear, you are absolutely right,' he says. 'It is just wonderful what you are doing.'

Harold gives the impression that he too is an ardent patriot. He stands to attention when he hears the British national anthem played, spits meaningfully (though discreetly) in the direction of passing German soldiers, and regularly expresses his certainty at the inevitability of an Allied victory in the war.

When they are both next back in Paris, Harold introduces Suzanne to the tall, slim, grey-haired Eugène Durand, proprietor of a brasserie called the Chope du Pont Neuf, on whose plush red banquettes English soldiers can often be found eating, their ears ringing with Durand's warning: 'Eat, drink and keep quiet.' 'She's one of us now. She'll probably be bringing you quite a lot of guests,' Harold tells the Frenchman. Durand smiles at her.

After Durand has left them, Cole turns to Suzanne. 'First-rate chap, that,' he says, pointing to the Chope's owner. 'Known him for years. When I was a small boy my mother, who was widowed, used to bring me to Paris and we stayed at a little hotel just across the street. I was an only child, you know – and I was very fond of my mother. Anyway, that was when I first got to know M. Durand – and that was when I started to learn French, of course.' It is another of Harold's inexplicable and risky lies, but Suzanne has no reason to question a word he says. In September 1941 she accepts his proposal of marriage.

As time passes Suzanne makes the acquaintance of a number of the other members of the network. In Paris, among others, there is Vladimir de Fliguë, owner of a small factory making electrical parts, and the eminent Professor Fernand Holweck of the Radium Institute. Further north, in Abbeville, she meets the tall and handsome priest, Abbé Carpentier. Carpentier, with whom Cole is good friends, finds food and clothes for the evaders, but most importantly he helps them obtain French ID cards, without which travelling across the country would be impossible.

Suzanne is soon incorporated into the escape line's operations. She becomes familiar with the journey across the demarcation line – forty-eight hours or more of shattering travel. It is some-times grindingly dull, often hideously uncomfortable, and always pregnant with danger. Days begin and end in sleazy, lice-infested rooms and when they move it is on cold and dirty trains that are so slow that she sometimes thinks they must have square wheels. Eventually they reach Marseille, where Cole relieves her of her charges: 'Now you needn't worry any more, my dear, you can leave it all to me, I'll do the actual handing over; it's better that way.' Afterwards she throws herself down on her hotel bed and sleeps for twelve hours; but even this is not enough to shake the adrenalin from her veins, or the exhaustion from her bones.

7

I've got the Germans in my pocket

Late autumn 1941

LIES COME SMOOTHLY when they enjoy some proximity to
the truth. And yet lately the distance between Harold Cole's
lies and the truth has been growing quickly. Once so busy and
brave in the escape line's service, in the space of a few short
months the man who had been a hero has given himself up to
dissipation. He appears to have lost any interest in discretion,
content for friends and enemies alike to look on aghast as he
drinks, whores and spends vertiginous amounts of money that
plainly does not belong to him. Many men like Harold Cole have
thrived in the disarray the Second World War has left in its wake;
for them it is less a catastrophe than it is an opportunity. In 1939
his dingy swindler's tools were tired and stained from over-use,
but since then he has used them to forge a reputation for heroism;
and a reputation for heroism can get you a long way in the bars
and *dancings* of Marseille's Vieux Port. But just because you have
started talking like a public-school-educated intelligence officer
doesn't mean you'll stop thinking like a small-time swindler from
Hackney.

In many ways the demands of life as an evasion organiser and
agent (the false identities; the sense of always being hunted; those
giddy, dizzying moments when a German soldier stares sceptically
at your forged papers, a question bubbling on to his lips as sweat
prickles the back of your neck and your breath turns sour with
fear) are similar to those of his previous existence as a confidence
trickster and crook: how can he be expected to slough off his

old skin completely? There is a yawning chasm between the man he wishes he could be and the man he *is*, and sometimes it must seem to him as if he were in danger of disappearing into it. The edifice of untruths he has built remains worryingly insubstantial; it would not take much for it all to be blown away. Harold Cole has enjoyed the freedom his fraudulent existence as 'Monsieur Paul' has given him to reinvent himself, but he has also come to understand that the fabrications that seem to liberate him can just as easily come to press on him with the same suffocating force. How to keep track of all the false stories he has told? How to impose some kind of consistency on the deceptions he has spread the length and breadth of the country? Some days he must feel as if he were wearing borrowed boots on a slippery floor.

If he had a confidant, someone to whom he could unburden his heart, he might explain to them that sometimes an excessive craving for women descends upon him; it grabs him and won't let go, and leaves him feeling like a sexual maniac. It is hard, then, to resist the urge to start spending the money that sits in his apartment like a promise, and so easy to get more from the honest, open members of his network. Gradually the complexion of his commitment to the network has changed: the long hard nights spent ushering evaders across the demarcation line have given way to evenings sitting at expensive nightclub tables; the funds he had once used to feed and clothe the tired, cold and hungry men now sit fatly in his wallet, ready for another night on the town. The escape line is still functioning, men are still being ferried to safety; it is just that it is increasingly difficult to discern what contribution Harold Cole is making to its operations.

Recently it has mostly been Roland Lepers, and a new contact, a Scot called John Smith, who undertake the risky and physically punishing legs of the journey south. Only when the exhausted, dirty evaders and their escorts arrive in Marseille does Cole take suave control. Lepers begins to feel used, and, as his resentment grows, he starts to entertain other concerns about Cole's behaviour, concerns that he learns are shared more widely in the north of France. Others have noticed that Cole is spending far more on wine and women than he could possibly be earning from his work. Even in Lille – a sedate city by comparison with Marseille – he can regularly be seen drinking champagne and shooting his mouth off in his own language: increasingly the tall, garrulous Englishman with deep pockets is the subject of feverish gossip. Those members of the network who witness his wild behaviour know that it will not be long before Cole draws the Gestapo's attention – that is if he hasn't already. And if he is caught it will mean the sure destruction of the escape organisation that they have all worked so painfully and bravely to establish, and with it, in all likelihood, their lives.

On top of this, Henri Duprez has heard a steady stream of stories from men and women who have given money to Harold Cole in return for a pledge that British intelligence would repay them. There has been no reimbursement. From Marseille they learn that he has coached Jewish refugees he met on the water-front to pose as Polish pilots – offering them safe passage to England in exchange for a hefty consideration. Visitors to his home in the north are surprised to see how much food, how many clothes and provisions he has stored there; it is as if he were running a curious kind of wholesale business. François Duprez discovers that whenever Cole has been asked to account for the thousands of francs that have passed through his hands, he has simply asserted that it was left on deposit with Duprez himself. He has not, it goes without saying, seen so much as a sou. More alarmingly, some escapers – who should have been passed on to Pierre Carpentier in Abbeville – have disappeared without trace.

It is now, belatedly, that the other members of the network begin to realise how little they really know about the Englishman. He has always been an enigmatic figure who has come and gone according to a timetable of his own devising, but as time has passed he has become more secretive. What had once looked like sensible precautions to protect the group's safety – such as keeping different parts of the operation ignorant of the actions of others – now seem as if they were only there to safeguard his own.

That he has been dishonest; that his behaviour is reckless to a degree that terrifies his colleagues; that on some level he has betrayed the trust invested in him and has come to represent a danger to their safety: all this is beyond doubt. What they do not know is whether they have worse to fear. The members of the network begin to try to restrict what Harold Cole does and does not know about their activities. French helpers delivering airmen to the safe houses used by him are instructed not to give their names or any other information: 'You knock three times on the door, and you hand over the Englishmen that you are guiding, and you say, "Here's a package for Madeleine-Marie,"' they are told. 'Don't go in, don't try to make contact. Because you never know what may happen.'

Before long Henri Duprez receives an urgent summons from Maurice van Camelbecke, one of his most steadfast and active companions. Camelbecke had first become suspicious of Cole when on a visit to the apartment above Voglimacci's shop he discovered him in the company of a man who Cole claimed was a Polish airman, but who spoke poor English and had no papers. On this occasion Camelbecke was able to satisfy himself by taking the serial number stitched into the flier's underwear, which Duprez then radioed back to London to establish his credentials. But their fears had been reawakened when they learned that the Pole had been arrested that same evening; more worrying still, Cole had gone missing.

As they discuss the situation Camelbecke tells Duprez about another incident involving Cole. The Englishman had arrived at Camelbecke's home driving a distinctive black Citroën sedan – a car alarmingly similar to one he'd seen driven by the German secret police stationed in Roubaix. Like all Frenchmen he enjoyed seeing the Boche humiliated, but stealing one of their cars and driving it around in broad daylight felt like an incitement too far.

'Don't worry, Maurice,' Cole had told him, when Camelbecke suggested he should be more cautious in the future. 'I've got the Germans in my pocket.'

What had seemed to Camelbecke like a simple, if imprudent, act of theft when he had first considered it – he checked the licence plate and confirmed that it had indeed been owned by the Germans – now begins, in the light of what they have since discovered, to take on a more sinister cast.

'This is impossible,' says Duprez, who has become incandescent with rage. 'We've got to eliminate Cole. Otherwise we're heading for a disaster.'

When Duprez calms down he contacts London again. Much as he would like to act unilaterally he knows that the organisation is too reliant on English support for him to do so. He puts the problem before them, as well as presenting his solution. A few days later he receives a response: 'London does not agree.' Somebody at MI6 is protecting 'Paul', although they do not care to explain why. Undeterred, Duprez presses his superiors to arrange a meeting in Lille with two men he is told are British agents. Patiently he lays out the evidence he has collected so far; patiently they listen. 'Cole is a traitor,' he concludes. 'He's got to be killed.'

'If you touch one hair on the head of Paul Cole,' one of the agents tells him, 'you yourself will pay the consequences.'

They leave, assuring him that if there *is* a problem, it is one that the British will deal with themselves. It is clear that somebody is protecting the cockney, but why? And *who*?

In Marseille, Garrow has for a long time turned a blind eye to Cole's swindles and deceptions. Months ago, when the cockney had first appeared, he had consulted Pat O'Leary, a fellow member of his network, about their new associate. O'Leary, a Belgian whose real name is Albert Guérisse, had warned him that Cole had a 'funny smell', but Garrow paid no heed. Harold Cole was a British NCO, a good Englishman.

Now he reluctantly comes to the same conclusion as Duprez: Cole must be killed. He does not share his French colleague's suspicions of treachery, but it has become clear that the Englishman's tawdry stream of deceit represents a serious threat to the line's security. Like Duprez he is aware of the risks involved, so he takes Dr Georges Rodocanachi, one of his organisation's most stalwart members, into his confidence. Almost without blinking the physician presents him with a plan that will ensure they avoid any unwanted attention. If they can inject Cole with a large dose of insulin they will be able to induce a coma, and the unconscious victim could then be slipped discreetly into the sea. With their plan set they await Cole's next visit to Marseille. O'Leary is dispatched across the demarcation line to fetch men such as François Duprez and Roland Lepers who can act as witnesses in the 'trial' to which they plan to subject the man they know as Paul before they dispose of him. Lepers is charged with arranging a convoy to Marseille and ensuring that Cole travels with it.

While they wait, Garrow and Rodocanachi start looking for somewhere they can dispose of the body.

'Hello, Paul. Glad to see you back in Marseille.'

Harold Cole is sitting in a small back bedroom situated deep inside Georges Rodocanachi's labyrinthine apartment. It is a cold November day, the bedroom's curtains are drawn and the air is thick with cigarette smoke. In front of him are Pat O'Leary, Mario Praxinos and Bruce Dowding. Cole had expected that Ian Garrow would be here too; and so, in truth, had Garrow. But Garrow, who was unlucky enough to have got himself arrested a few days ago, is sitting in a prison cell at the Fort Saint-Nicholas. Cole has not been informed of this, nor does he know that in the bathroom next door François Duprez is listening intently to everything that is being said.

Cole takes a drag on his cigarette and sips his whisky as O'Leary lies fluidly and explains that in an unforeseen turn of events Garrow has had to travel to Perpignan to meet with the Basque guides the network uses to ferry evaders across the Pyrenees.

Still friendly, still welcoming, still giving Harold no reason to think that today is different from any of the many other visits he has made to this apartment, O'Leary makes solicitous enquiries about his journey. 'Tell us, is everything all right? How many passengers did you bring down?'

Familiar questions. Familiar answers. But then O'Leary edges the conversation to money.

'We've got plenty of money in the north,' Cole tells them complacently. 'As you know, we've got our banker there, François Duprez. Of course, it's better to have money in security with people like that.'

Cole is good at this, spooling out the lies he has told over and over again. He knows how the conversation will proceed and looks forward to finding himself in more congenial company once he has got this little interview out of the way.

It is at this point that everything changes. Cole leaps up, all his bravado atomised by the sudden appearance of Duprez, whose patience has been pushed beyond its breaking point by the untruths he has been forced to listen to. '*Salaud!*' screams the man who has just appeared, as if conjured, from next door. 'You lying bastard! Not only did you never give me a penny, but you owe me a lot of money!'

Harold momentarily throws a panicked look around the room but it is clear that the game is up. The man who has defied Germans the length and breadth of the country, who has regaled rapt audiences with tales of his derring-do, collapses to his knees and begs for mercy.

'I've done something terrible – I admit it – terrible – it was a moment of weakness – I'm sorry – sorry . . .'

There is a moment of silence before O'Leary speaks again: 'We cannot trust you any longer.'

Cole crawls forward on his knees, arms spread in supplication.

'Oh, I know it's terrible – terrible – but I've done some good things too – I did bring men down from the north – you know that.'

Silence again. Then, disgusted by the performance, O'Leary steps forward and punches Cole in the face. The blow is hard enough to fracture O'Leary's knuckles, but the rage he shares with the other men lingers. 'I knew you were a bastard from the very beginning. Now you are in front of a tribunal, and here are your two judges.' O'Leary points to Dowding and Praxinos. Your fate is in their hands, he tells Cole.

Next the Australian, Dowding, speaks up. 'Pat, let me kill him. Let me kill him.' There is no question in any of their minds that Cole is guilty; no question either that their organisation's safety would be imperilled if he were allowed to live. But none of the men in the room was privy to Garrow and Rodocanachi's carefully devised plan to murder Cole discreetly and then dispose of the body, and they are leery of murdering a British agent without securing some kind of authority from London first. So although Cole has returned to his knees and is beseeching them to spare his life, it is prudence rather than mercy that informs O'Leary's response: 'No. I cannot permit that.' It would be best – and they all agree on this – to lock him in the bathroom recently occupied by Duprez and try to establish what their next move should be.

Just as they are settling down to discuss what they will do with Cole they hear a noise next door. Dowding rushes through but is only in time to see the Englishman's back disappearing through the window. As he looks ruefully at the handily placed airshaft that Harold has used to assist his escape a thought rises irresistibly: we should have shot him when we had the chance.

Winter 1941

Cornelius Verloop of the Abwehr is entitled to pour himself a large drink. His agents have long been on the trail of the heedless Harold Cole – or Captain Colson as they have become accustomed to calling him – and now he is in their clutches. That morning Verloop had at last given the order to swoop on a man who for months had been a key figure in running one of France's most successful evasion lines. Two full cars of German troops had descended on the house of Madeleine Deram – one of Cole's many mistresses, with whom he has been sheltering while he tries to decide what to do in the aftermath of the confrontation in Marseille – and dragged him shoeless into a waiting car. 'You see your "Captain Cole" now, eh?' one of the officers had sneered at her.

Verloop chooses not to take an active role in the Englishman's interrogation. Instead, he conceals himself behind a curtain as his operatives present Cole with a series of choices, which all sound like threats. There is only one way to avoid torture or a bullet between your eyes, they tell the cockney: you must help us. Cole agrees; then begins to talk. And it is now that Verloop is, momentarily, wrongfooted. Surely the Englishman knows that the Abwehr agents' menacing words are empty, that all he need do is claim ignorance each time a question is put to him, and then sit the rest of the war out in a prison cell. But as details about every element of his activities, along with those of the network, spill from Cole's mouth, Verloop realises that this man is a far more significant player than he had previously thought. Cole gives enough information to fill thirty typewritten pages. He has an astonishing level of recall, able to give the names of men and women he has met only once, mapping out for Verloop – who, though overjoyed at the intelligence windfall, is rendered some-what queasy by this man's complete abandonment of all self-respect – the network's structure and operating practices.

Perhaps Harold Cole still retains some shreds of chivalry, perhaps he is keen to put some kind of insurance policy in place in case he manages to escape, but he withholds the names of Suzanne Warenghem and Jeannine Voglimacci, as well as information about the escape network in Marseille: everyone else he throws to the wind. And he does not limit himself to giving names: in each case he takes care to furnish his interrogators with as much in-criminatory evidence as possible. He tells them about the arms hidden in Carpentier's home; tells them addresses, names. It is as if he is determined that once arrested his erstwhile friends will be so thoroughly damned that there is no chance they will re-appear and tell others of his treachery.

William Joyce is consumed by the idea of Britain as a nation. In his eyes it is a living entity, and the thought of its history, of its noble qualities, of its vast empire, makes him giddy. He is sensible too of the matrix of responsibilities and obligations that binds the government to its people, and vice versa. But he draws a sharp division between this priceless civilisation and those leading it, who are criminal and corrupt, and dangerously in hock to Jewish international interests. It is, he believes, his duty as a patriot to oppose these traitors. Harold Cole only sees the state, a set of institutions that, given they have spent the better part of the past two decades trying to stifle his attempts to get on, he can feel no affection for. But the speed with which he shrugs off whatever residual loyalty he might feel towards the country in which he was born is striking. Maybe the process is made easier by the fact that he has long ago lost, or perhaps never possessed, any sense of fellow-feeling. Much of his pre-war life was spent trying to part his countrymen from their property; he cannot be expected to discover a sense of public-spiritedness now. And his professed disdain for the Boche (perhaps the patriotism that had so impressed Suzanne was simply a Briton's instinctive xenophobia) is easily overmastered by two puissant facts: the Germans have him in custody, and thus hold his fate in their hands; and, just as pertinently, they currently exert a similar control over the vast majority of continental Europe. He has witnessed the collapse of several countries and the BEF's feeble part in their defence. He has seen France swarming with stunned Britons barely coping with the consequences of an abject defeat. It is perfectly reasonable to conclude that the future lies with the Third Reich, and equally reasonable, for a man like Cole at least, to decide to throw in his lot with it. At least, that is, until such time as he can wriggle free and return to a less circumscribed existence.

And yet self-interest alone is not sufficient to explain why treachery spills so readily from Harold Cole's mouth. There is an implacable vindictiveness about the way he helps to condemn these men and women; it is as if he wants to punish them for his own exposure as a fraud and a coward, and blames them for the fact that he can no longer pretend to be the courtly, lion-hearted officer that he wishes to be taken for. He has been hurt deeply by his humiliation in Marseille, and now fate has handed him an unexpected opportunity to take revenge.

François Duprez is the first victim. On 6 December – just hours after Cole's arrest and interrogation – the Abwehr descend on his home. François is out, so they try to reassure his wife: 'It's nothing. We're just looking.' But within minutes the house has been ransacked. The Germans leave, clutching samples of his hand-writing, and head towards the town hall, where they tear Duprez's office apart. It is at this point that Duprez approaches the Germans. Though others have urged him to disappear until the interest in him has blown over, Duprez is anxious that this might lead to reprisals against his family. The horrified Roland Lepers watches as his friend is led away in handcuffs.

Reprising his old role, Cole arrives at the homes of his unsuspecting colleagues, accompanied by men he claims to be Polish airmen. Once the network member has had enough time to incriminate himself, the Germans make their entry. Désiré Didry, Pierre Carpentier, Alfred Lanselle, Drotas Dubois, Maurice Dechaumont, August Dean, Mary-Louise Gallet, Fernand Treveille – even Bruce Dowding, who had come north to warn others about Cole's duplicity – are all dragged away into waiting black cars. They are brave, resourceful, gallant people. They are good people. Few have any kind of experience in this sort of cloak-and-dagger work and precisely because they are honourable patriots they have chosen to trust this Englishman who they have seen work so assiduously for their cause; those whom harboured reservations about Cole's conduct or character have suppressed them. But now they realise – although it is far too late – that he has betrayed them. They shoot murderous glances at the lanky ginger figure who watches impassively, or shout recriminations, but what good will that do?

Five days later, Harold Cole is escorted by two German agents to Paris. His first stop is Vladimir de Fliguë. He tells the Russian that the two silent men he has brought with him are English pilots, one of whom will be joining the escape network. 'I want you to explain to him everything he needs to know about the organisation,' Cole says, 'because he's going to take over from me for a while. I have to go on a trip to Brussels.' De Fliguë obliges, as he always does when Cole makes a request. They part, agreeing to meet later that day; Cole is insistent that Holweck – the professor at the Radium Institute – joins them for this second encounter, and, again, de Fliguë sees no reason to demur.

They reassemble at two thirty in a fellow *résistant*'s fourth-floor apartment, where Cole tells de Fliguë that the two escaped fliers need papers. When they head downstairs to de Fliguë's workshop – they can talk properly there, he says – the two supposed pilots suddenly announce that they are all under arrest.

Cole makes a feeble show of resistance, but the burly Holweck wrestles himself free and gets as far as a nearby garage. He is cornered and receives a brutal beating before being bundled into the car, his white shirt streaked with blood. As they are driven away, de Fliguë takes one look back, perhaps wondering if he will ever see again the street that has been his home for years. Cole, the man who had recruited them, is standing with the two German agents. His body language is relaxed, he seems at home with these men. De Fliguë realises that he has been betrayed.

Cole has barely seen Suzanne since his return to Paris; now he contacts her, and arranges to see her at the Chope. He has no intention of entering into a permanent association with the Germans, so more lies are essential. He tells her a hair-raising tale of how he, de Fliguë and Holweck were captured, and of their miraculous escape. The two other men are safe now, Cole assures Suzanne, waiting to be whisked south, away from the Gestapo's clutches. How can Suzanne know that Holweck is dead already (perhaps by his own hand, perhaps weakened by torture), or that de Fliguë has disappeared into what the Nazis have begun to refer to as the Night and Fog. They are joined at their table by another agent, the journalist Édouard Bernauer, who has contacts with the Deuxième Bureau* and access to large amounts of money. Bernauer arrives to find Cole has descended into a state of distress. For a while he is even unable to prevent his limbs from trembling. He recovers sufficiently to demand cash and false documents to facilitate the escape of de Fliguë and Holweck, a request that Bernauer refuses: not until I've seen them in the flesh, he tells Cole.

Cole contents himself with the promise of some clothes from Suzanne and arranges to meet her in the restaurant the next day. She offers to take the clothes directly to their hiding place. Harold pauses . . . no, he says. Almost without warning he has

---

* The name by which the Vichy's military intelligence agency was known. Many of its members had little sympathy for the Nazis, and often frustrated their efforts, or actively worked against them.

become evasive. Hurt, thinking perhaps that Harold doesn't trust her, Suzanne pushes again, but he is adamant. With some reluctance Suzanne agrees. Breezily, as if he has not noticed Suzanne's uncertainty, or has simply chosen to ignore it, he takes his leave: 'Well, I must be on my way now. Got a lot to do. But I'll be back here tomorrow evening and pick up the clothes.'

Suzanne arranges for the clothes to be brought to the restaurant the following afternoon and arrives there promptly as arranged. She nurses a beer as she waits for Cole; listening to the steady beat of her heart, watching shadows edge across the floor. Then dusk falls and with a raucous bang and clatter he bursts through the glass door of the brasserie. He is breathless and dishevelled and is plainly in a desperate rush.

'Quick, Suzanne, get out of here. The Gestapo are after us. Get to the corner of the street and wait for me there.'

Suzanne sprints into the night, her footsteps echoing in the dark and empty street. Just as Harold joins her there is a snarl of brakes and a black Citroën saloon skids to a halt before the restaurant. She realises that it is the kind of car favoured by the German secret police, but before she has time to try to absorb the significance of that information Harold drags her away; they turn once, then twice, then dash through the entrance to the Pont Neuf Métro station and clamber on to a train.

Momentarily they enjoy the relief that surges through them, but this soon gives way to the realisation that Harold has become a hunted man; that they are adrift in a city teeming with agents, informers and spies; and that unless they find somewhere to hide, and fast, matters will not turn out well for either of them. Every encounter in their journey through Paris is now freighted with danger. A policeman stops them as they change trains, and for a heart-stopping moment it seems certain that Harold's lack of papers and atrocious French will give them away. Somehow Suzanne talks them out of it, but they know that they cannot rely on the next officer they meet to be quite so pliable. The problem they face is that Harold's new status means that nobody will take them in.

Suzanne knows that by taking Harold to her Tante Jeanne's apartment she will be exposing her elderly relative to danger: sheltering a fugitive from Nazi justice is a serious crime, and the Gestapo would not think twice about sending someone far older than her to a concentration camp. But, she tells herself, Harold has risked his life over and over again in a noble cause and her aunt is a redoubtable woman . . . They take the train to Bécon-les-Bruyères and resolve to let Jeanne make her own choice.

Her aunt welcomes Cole without blinking an eye. But almost as soon as they cross her threshold he falls sick with a raging fever; he is red-hot, delirious and too weak to leave the bed. He sweats so much that the women find themselves changing his soaking sheets every few hours.

To begin with he cannot eat; he is desperately thirsty, but as his fever mounts he becomes so feeble that he cannot even lift his head to drink water. His babbling becomes more frantic, and there is nothing that the meagre means at their disposal – cold compresses, aspirin and water – can do to relieve his state. Under the circumstances it is plainly too dangerous to risk calling a doctor, and as panic begins to course through their veins Suzanne and her aunt start to discuss how they will be able to dispose of his body with sufficient discretion. The stairs to Jeanne's apartment are narrow and winding; if rigor mortis sets in they will never get him outside. How far away would they need to deposit his corpse?

Terrified, they watch Harold fall into a deep sleep. When he wakes, the fever has gone, as suddenly and as mysteriously as it appeared. 'Sorry to have given you both such a lot of trouble, ladies,' he tells them nonchalantly. 'Must have been a touch of malaria. Got it during my service with the Indian Army.'

Whatever he may have said, it is hard to see Cole's collapse as anything other than a reaction to the extreme physical and moral strain under which he has lived for the previous months. The floods of tears he shed in Dr Rodocanachi's apartment might simply have been prompted by terror, but they might also be taken as an indication of the elevated emotional pitch at which he existed already. That this shattering confrontation was followed in short order by his capture by the Abwehr, the betrayals of his close friends and allies, and the desperate escape with Suzanne can only have wound him still tighter (witness his trembling limbs at the Chope du Pont Neuf). He does not have access to the self-deception that allows Joyce to persuade himself that his decisions are motivated by a higher form of patriotism. There is more than that, too: Joyce's treachery is abstract, debatable – it is unclear what, if anything, it will lead to. But Harold Cole knows, intimately, the men and women he has betrayed to save his own tawdry skin, and he can be under no illusions as to his actions' consequences. In a prison cell three years later he will confess to a former lover that he has a 'shabby make up', that he is 'a pshycologically [sic] complicated, unbalanced criminal'; he has lived with this uncomfortable knowledge for much of his life, now he realises that he has been left with a black stain on his soul.

Inside Loos Prison Abbé Carpentier sings 'It's a Long Way to Tipperary' while he is tortured, and grimly continues to argue that he alone was responsible for the escape network in his area. He also manages to smuggle out a pencil-written indictment of the man he had once been proud to call a friend.

I, a priest, would not hesitate to coldly burn him. If you leave him breathing, he can only make every situation worse and he will remain a danger for you . . . This man does not deserve the slightest pity; he is a monster of cowardice and weakness.

8

We are not ordinary people. You can't do anything to us

Autumn 1942

JOHN AMERY HAS a thin face, dark hair and restless eyes, and is given to sudden bursts of vehemence that make him at once attractive and pathetic. His persona is a chaotic, contradictory amalgam of Reinhard Heydrich, Sid Vicious and Sebastian Flyte, he carries both a gun and a teddy bear around with him wherever he goes, and he exists in a blitz of sex, lies, drink and confusion; but somewhere beneath all this burns a fierce idealism. Although he is a fanatical patriot, he wants to tear the country's foundations to pieces and build a new nation out of the dust ('I am myself,' he says, 'a revolutionary, both by nature and through force of circumstance'). He has enjoyed almost complete freedom throughout his life, has given in to every impulse almost as soon as it surges into his brain, drinking and screwing and paying no mind to the destruction he has left in his wake, and yet John has never been able to will himself into the better, happier life a part of him so plainly desires. He is furious and awkward and boundlessly insecure; at the same time is buoyed by grandiose delusions about his own significance. He is a riddle that few have ever been able to solve.

He was born some thirty years earlier on 14 March 1912, in Chelsea, the first son of Leo Amery and Florence Greenwood. His father, who had previously written for *The Times*, had entered Parliament the year before, the first step in a long and distinguished career. Florence, the daughter of a Canadian barrister, doted on her child and displayed towards him a totally uncritical devotion.

This was rewarded with at best complacent affection from her son, who reserved his veneration for his distinguished but somewhat distant father, a confidant of Stanley Baldwin and subsequently a Cabinet minister in Churchill's wartime government.

By the age of two John Amery had been considered unteachable. Jack, as he was known to his family, was a promiscuous and unrelenting bully of every child he came into contact with, but was also liable to manifest bizarre and perplexing behaviour – such as arriving at school wearing an enormous necklace of highly coloured wooden beads stretching almost to his knees. At the first sign of trouble he could be relied on to run away. Amery started masturbating at five, as well as acquiring the habit of making obscene drawings of women with breasts. His *pièce de résistance* was to scatter pictures of penises around his nursery for his nurse to find. It was as if he were determined to demonstrate the truth of the belief, held by many at the time, that children were naturally evil.

At his preparatory school, West Downs, he immediately caused anxiety. 'Ideas of right and wrong,' said his headmaster, Mr Tindall, 'seemed to mean nothing to him.' John Amery's behaviour was always shot through with a profound strangeness: his sentences sometimes degenerating into nonsense verse, his thoughts subversive and out of kilter with those of everyone around him. He dressed like a tramp, rarely washing and horrifying his parents by sporting a broken-down hat with a large piece bitten out of it.

Amery followed in his father's footsteps to Harrow, though he wasted little time before making an audacious flit to the Continent. After escaping through the skylight of the family home, equipped with his father's wallet and service revolver, he briefly held a French customs officer hostage at gunpoint. In the hastily scribbled note he left behind he explained that his aim was to make for Lausanne, where he would work as a mechanic (he had recently become consumed by a passion with cars, an enthusiasm that would never leave him). 'In the position of a garage hand,' he said on his reluctant return to school, he 'would be his own master, would not be driven, and need not do more than he liked'.

The next few years of the 1930s would be punctuated by similar outrages. On a trip to Norway Amery sold the overcoat of a guest at his hotel and used the proceeds to buy the telephonist a gift; another time he tried to stab a tutor who had attempted to force him to take a walk. When caught he either laughed or flew into a violent rage. Amery elevated refusing to show remorse to a point of principle: 'Only saps wait,' was the law he lived his life by.

Amery, who had always given the impression of being older than his years, would regularly escape Harrow to go to London clubs, including Mrs Kate Meyrick's infamous '43' on Gerrard Street, and lost his virginity at fourteen. In desperation his parents sent him to a school for English boys in Switzerland. On his return he was found to have contracted syphilis, which he claimed to have caught prostituting himself to men.

Although Amery asserted that his formal education effectively ceased at the age of fifteen, he was nevertheless bright enough to secure a place at Oxford – which he promptly abandoned in favour of entering the more glamorous film world, with which he had become obsessed. His mentor was Reginald Fogwell (telegraph address: 'Attaboy, Piccy, London'), a director with a talent for raising cash to make expensive disasters. Aged eighteen and armed with what he had learned from Fogwell (which was not much; by all accounts he was ignorant of even the most basic cinematic techniques), and an ambition to become the youngest living film director, Amery set up a film company with his schoolfriend David Mure and a couple of other contemporaries. They were joined in the enterprise by 'Count' Johnston Noad, an adventurer who had gained some notoriety in the twenties racing speedboats but subsequently turned to scams and crime. Noad claimed to be the cousin of the King of Montenegro, married a woman sufficiently notorious in the underworld to have earned the nickname the 'Black Orchid' and, on being convicted of fraud after the war, shared a cell in Wakefield Prison with the atomic spy Klaus Fuchs. Nonetheless, Leo Amery laboured under the cruel misapprehension that his son's new friend would be a beneficent influence.

History does not record whether Noad knew much, if anything, about film-making. But he was an expert at parting people from their money and his young friend learned quickly at his side. The self-proclaimed count knew that as the son of a prominent politician, John had the kind of social prestige that could open doors that might otherwise have been locked against a confidence trickster like himself. He encouraged his protégé's gift for extravagance, and showed him how smart clothes and flash cars could be used to burnish your credentials. Thus far, when John had lied or cheated, it had been prompted by a sort of feral amorality; now Noad taught him how to swindle. He taught him other things too: why fight with your fists when you could carry a gun? Why settle a bill when you can get someone else to pay it for you? Why bother making a film if the money is in your pocket already? John believed that other people were sheep – while he was a lone wolf. His ambition was to reach great heights by dishonest means in a life designed to ensure that he had no obligation to anyone or anything.

Amery's undoubted charm was enough to persuade family, friends and a string of deep-pocketed but gullible investors to fund *Jungle Skies*, a high-budget Great War flying film described as 'strong drama embracing wild animal photography', to be made in Africa. Much of the money that he and Noad gulled went on Rolls-Royces, smart clothes, jewellery and maintaining extravagant business premises staffed by beautiful secretaries whom Amery invariably attempted to sleep with. The film was never finished. Viewed generously, the affair was an incompetent shambles attributable to his naivety, but looked at from another angle it was uncomfortably close to fraud. It ran parallel with an attempt to set up a company to smuggle silk stockings into Britain by aeroplane. That operation was perhaps more honestly crooked, but it too foundered.

The *Jungle Skies* fiasco was probably his biggest disaster, but its combination of incompetence and almost delusional grandiosity, glued together with low deceit, was typical of his business ventures over the next few years. Attempts to resurrect his film career were interleaved with persistent drunkenness, sexual perversion, dalliances with petty crime (generally in tandem with the count) and the odd desultory attempt to live something approaching a conventional existence. Amery's life was one of furtive deals made in the corners of Mayfair nightclubs, diamonds that were only diamonds if you didn't look too closely, companies that folded almost as soon as they formed, dusty lock-ups filled with French liquor and perfume, bad cheques, bad faith and lies. He had become the kind of fur-coated playboy who drove around the West End in a Rolls-Royce with gold fittings but still cadged a pound from waitresses to buy a round of drinks. He lied so much and so often that even those who considered themselves his friends called him the 'Rat'. Before he was twenty he had committed seventy-four motoring offences, thinking nothing of stopping his car and leaving it in the middle of the road if he fancied a drink.

It seemed as if he might be about to settle down when in 1933 he fell in love with an older woman, Una Eveline Wing. Unfortunately, as far as his family was concerned, she claimed to be an actress. Worse still, as far as everyone but John was concerned, she was a prostitute.

Despite his parents' attempts to stop the marriage, they ran away to Athens (though not before John had gone to the press to try to drum up sympathy for his 'plight': both his father and his fiancée first learned of the engagement after reading the press release he issued to announce it), where he married her in a Greek Orthodox church. Soon after, Amery was arrested trying to buy diamonds with a bad cheque. It fell to his father to satisfy the claims of the offended parties, as it would on many other occasions in the future.*

For all the effort he had invested in entering into the marriage, Amery proved an appalling husband. Una had an early taste of her husband's gift for dishonesty when she discovered that, contrary to what he had told her, he was neither twenty-eight, nor an orphan. And she learned more about his cupidity after their return

---

* Leo's diaries are eloquent on the serious strain John's misdemeanours exerted on the Amery family's finances. 'If only Jack behaves,' reads one startlingly patient entry, 'I might be able to work my way back towards reasonable solvency.'

from Greece when he informed her that he had only married her to enhance his position in the eyes of his many creditors, to whom he had given the impression that his wife was a rich woman. Obviously nobody was stupid enough to be taken in by this for long, especially when he started trying to persuade people that Una was in fact his mistress, and that he was kept by her and by women who made their fortune from immoral behaviour and blackmail. John once brutally attacked Una in a Paris cocktail bar for 'revealing' to a fellow drinker that she was his wife. From the very beginning of their marriage Amery continued to visit prostitutes, whom he paid to beat him and tie him up. He even inveigled Una into having sex with him while other women watched. John also resumed his career as a male prostitute. Whether he regarded this as a further avenue for securing delinquent pleasure, a necessary expedient to solve their dire shortage of cash, or a convenient combination of the two, is unclear.

This period gave further evidence of John's mental instability. He was convinced he was in constant danger of violent assault. He remained fixated by his teddy bear, and developed an obsession with his overcoat. He was in the habit of buying an extra seat at the cinema or theatre for it and would refuse to stay in a hotel or restaurant if staff insisted on putting his overcoat in the cloakroom.

John did not recognise what passed for conventional morality in the thirties: he was grubby, dishonest, flashy and cruel, and laughed at the values held by his contemporaries (the final straw at Harrow was not, as might be expected, his 'shop stealing, moral breakdown and unsatisfactory work', but his refusal to submit to the prescribed punishment for 'deliberately slacking at cricket' – he had walked a bye rather than run it). On one occasion he pulled a revolver on another driver after their cars had collided. When the other man complained and threatened to call the police, Amery replied, 'We are not ordinary people. You can't do anything to us.'

In 1936 his father finally allowed him to be declared bankrupt, owing the sum of £6,000 (approaching £300,000 today). Amery vanishes almost completely from the records until the beginning of the Second World War. Occasionally a fleeting encounter – usually in a seedy European resort town – is recorded in Leo's diary; just as rarely his name appears in his father's letters, recounted in a bare style shorn of information, as if omitting detail can inure him to the bewildering pain his elder son continues to cause him. In another kind of story, if perhaps he had been a different kind of prodigal son, John would have emerged from his exile in triumph, having finally found a way of making something of his restless energy and grandiose ambitions. He could have joined the long line of bad boys and troublemakers, such as Hernan Cortés or Robert Clive, who found adventures far from home that allowed them to become great men in the countries of their birth. It was not to be.

But what did happen was just as significant in terms of his own fate: he fell under the spell of a charismatic French fascist leader called Jacques Doriot. 'Grand Jacques', the self-made son of a blacksmith and seamstress, is many of the things that Amery is not. He is big and strong, his shoulders are powerful. He exudes health and confidence, and loves fighting and women. Amery's new friend is a former communist who at one time looked set to assume leadership of the party in France, but was instead defeated in a power struggle. His response was to launch his own Partie Populaire Française (PFF), which rapidly veered towards the extreme right. Doriot's fascist beliefs, a contemporary claims, are just the same as those he held as a communist, but 'turned inside out'.

Amery finds Doriot and everything he represents irresistible. John discovers that his flesh has changed, that a set of beliefs has slid beneath his ribs and into his soul. It is all too tempting to conceive of John Amery's fascism as being of a piece with the moral squalor that had defined his existence up until this point. But he saw it as good and true. It was not pure – he could never have claimed to possess a coherent set of doctrinally sound beliefs – but it was undoubtedly sincere. His existence was so disordered, shameful and absurd that without this belief in something better, something that gave meaning to his life, his brief spell on the planet may well have been briefer still: long before his encounter with Albert Pierrepoint he would have choked in a pool of his own vomit, or met his end staring wildly in a back alley as a knife sliced through his throat.

Fascism allowed John Amery to convince himself that perhaps the causes of his unhappiness and insecurity might be located outside himself – in the actions of the wicked Jews, the exploitative capitalists and the sclerotic governments. It expanded his world – providing a home for his inchoate sense of rage and resentment, his narcissist's desire to be acclaimed – at the same time as it shrank it by prescribing the narrow and rigid doctrines of anti-Semitism and authoritarianism.

Continental fascism was shiny, bright, hard and modern. It was a philosophy incarnated in sleek new bombers, in elegantly cut uniforms, in the thrilling yet brutal sight of thousands of men and women marching as one, in the cleansing fire of burning books. And it worked, or at least it appeared to. John was a privileged witness to fascism's seemingly unbroken series of triumphs in the late thirties. According to an interview he gave to a Berlin reporter in November 1942, he had accompanied the Italians to Abyssinia, watched the panzers roll into Vienna during the Anschluss and witnessed the Wehrmacht's entry into Prague.

John had also been a participant – though to what degree is disputed – in the Spanish Civil War. Amery asserted that he had fought for Franco, and had been rewarded with a promotion to lieutenant legionary and a decoration from the Nationalists' Generalissimo. There are documents that would seem to confirm this, and also that he had obtained Spanish citizenship during this period; but most observers have cast doubt on the veracity of both the paperwork and the activities that they purport to represent. He was undoubtedly intoxicated by the rebels' conception of themselves – 'the last lovers of hierarchy and order, unselfish devotion and all that is chivalrous and clean' – and correspondingly disgusted by the Republicans' depredations: until the end of his life he would remain haunted by the evidence he saw in Barcelona's gruesome torture chambers of the atrocities committed by the Reds. What effects the brutalities perpetrated by the Nationalists had on John Amery is not recorded.

John's passport records, however, do show him flitting around

Europe throughout the late thirties, which supports his contention that he was smuggling arms for the Nationalists. He was reputed to be a reckless gunrunner and, whether this was an extension of his work for Franco, or simply an overflow of his newfound passion for fascist movements, he became involved with the French proto-fascist Cagoulard. The Cagoulard (Comité Secret d'Action Révolutionnaire) was the brainchild of Eugène Deloncle, a decorated artillery officer and a shady, unstable character with close connections to right-wing executives at L'Oréal. He and his anti-communist militia were plotting a coup d'état of their own in France, and were trying to get hold of all the weapons they could.

John Amery also fell in love in Spain. Jeanine Barde was another former prostitute. That she was brassy and coarse, that she talked too loudly and wore too much make-up, did not seem to bother John (nor did the fact that she was half-gypsy; his prejudices were fierce, but not always ideologically coherent). She was vivacious, outspoken and witty, and shared his passionate new interest in extreme right-wing politics: he called her his 'beloved friend and revolutionary Jeanine Amery-Barde', or sometimes just 'Chicky'. Before long he was telling anybody who would listen that he and this 'thrilling and beautiful' woman were man and wife.

9

Simply as an Englishman

IN SEPTEMBER 1939 the outbreak of hostilities finds John in San Sebastian, Spain, where he may well have been smuggling guns for Franco's regime. He heads to Portugal and then France, where he lives with Barde and a group of Cagoulards. John is a busy correspondent during this period, writing letters to his abandoned wife which combine affection, scorn and self-pity, sometimes within the same paragraph.* Writing from the Hotel Do Parque Estoril he complains that 'at the moment my little capital is exhausted, the sands are running out . . . I still hope to get round the corner to prosperity again.' Una has heard it all before. Much of the letter that follows must feel awfully familiar, too:

> I know perfectly well I ought to be there to assist you and arrange everything, however that is impossible and I do beg you baby bear not to sit down and spend your time thinking how bad it is of me not being there because that is f— all good to anybody . . . I leave it to you knowing that my little girl is going to be really clever and make me so proud. When I am in the money again I

---

* Later, during the war, Una will be found working part-time at a motor engineer's in Pyrford, having swapped Chelsea for Cobham. The MI5 report notes primly that she resides in a house that is 'believed to be the property of Miss Erica Marx, with whom Mrs Amery is associating'. There is an almost audible note of distaste as the memo's author goes on to describe how Miss Marx and Mrs Amery spend the weekends at the White Horse Hotel.

will buy you some more ice [diamonds, presumably] to make up for what you have know [*sic*] to sell . . . Father would I am sure at least guarantee to continue paying you the £8 a week for another 2 years . . . God bless you, good luck I will do anything I can to help, you know how much I really love you,

Keep your chin up baby bear
Your
John

For the first year or two of the war, he lives in the unoccupied zone administered by Marshal Pétain's Vichy government, where he keeps a relatively low profile: his main activity seems to be complicating the lives of the consular officials in Nice, where he is loathed (something that must be at least partly due to his predilection for swindling money from his compatriots, or denouncing them to either the Vichy police or the German authorities; occasionally he subjects the unlucky victim to both fates at once). Despite the £20 weekly allowance he continues to receive from his father he remains fatally short of cash.

In July 1941 he raises himself from his torpor sufficiently to cheer on Hitler's invasion of Russia, though is despondent when he discovers that few others in Vichy share his admiration. He is perturbed by Operation Barbarossa's realignment of the world's loyalties. Britain is now fighting on the same side as the nation that he believes poses an existential threat to civilisation, whose tortures and transportations bear comparison with the monuments of human skulls that Tamerlane erected in the countries he conquered. In his view, 'the people responsible in London were acting in a manner that no longer coincided with British Imperial interests.'

Russia! Our ally! What sort of an ally was Russia? We went to war to defend Poland, didn't we? And what did Russia do, when she marched into Poland? Well then, why wasn't Russia our enemy, as much as Germany?

He is maddened by how illogical the situation is. Does nobody else but he remember the attempts in Britain to raise a volunteer force to help the brave Finns in their unequal struggle against the Soviet Union? Had everybody in Britain forgotten the attempts by French communists to scuttle the war effort, and how their leader, Thorez, had hightailed it to Moscow as soon as his call-up papers dropped through his door?

He thinks about how many lies circulate about what is going on at home: can you believe that there are still people who imagine that it's a prosperous nation, or that it's a free country? Well, all that is a lot of bloody rubbish. There are people living there in a state of undernutrition, of filth and misery that would never be tolerated anywhere in Europe – and in the capital of the richest empire in the world, too. It would be laughable if it were not tragic. He is enraged by the way in which the ruling classes treat the working man, whom they have never ceased to exploit and for whom they don't give a damn. He thinks too of the appalling decadence that has descended upon the country: of the politicians, homosexuals, bankers and bourgeois, of the priests and prostitutes and anarchists, about the quarrels in which they are all mired, quarrels that will be unintelligible to history, and of the barbarians who, when they have 'smashed us will leave a name a thousand times greater than ours'.

It is not clear why Amery, who has not returned across the Channel for almost a decade, and who has kept up only a desultory correspondence with friends and family in England, feels qualified to speak so knowledgeably about living standards in Great Britain. But then the fact that his life is not itself on nodding terms with anything other than disorder and vice, and perhaps a muddled sense of how the world might better be ordered for his own convenience, has never given him much pause for thought.

His attitude to Britain, which in many ways is not dissimilar to that of William Joyce, is rather like that of a spoiled child forced to share a favourite toy, and his decision to commit treachery is frictionless, largely because he does not consider himself guilty of the crime. It is all so terribly, tragically, simple. The country has been betrayed, sold out to Moscow and New York (America's victory, John believes, will be the empire's defeat), and the only remaining bulwarks against communism are the armies of the Third Reich. He thinks of the British corpses that lie abandoned on foreign beaches, thinks too of the senile Victorians in Parliament, and of the Jews in London, striding around the city in their hammer and sickle ensigns, blowing cigarette smoke in its people's faces. When a state has abandoned any semblance of moral authority, and shown itself so incapable of governing in its citizens' interests, what loyalty can it continue to command? It can never be treason, in wartime or at any other time, he argues, to ardently love one's country and to take up arms against it because all the things that are sacred to it are being systematically violated. He does not wish, unlike William Joyce, to see Britain reduced to ruins so that it might be taught a lesson before being welcomed into the Nazi fold. No, what he wants above all is to preserve his country and its empire, and the only way of ensuring this is to reach an understanding with Adolf Hitler. He knows that the responsibility for this solemn task sits heavily on his frail shoulders, but how much better life will be when one can have a drink among Englishmen in an English pub, without the presence of the American soldier, the insolent Jew, the professional communist agitator!

His frustration grows as he begins to find Vichy France an increasingly uncongenial place to live. It is a pygmy regime run by the decrepit former war hero Marshal Philippe Pétain and his prime minister, a fat greasy-haired intriguer called Pierre Laval. In theory its emphasis on the values of 'work', 'family' and 'father-land' will help regenerate France through a 'national revolution' – it is considered a matter for celebration that the country is no longer 'rotted by politics'. But Pétain is purblind to Hitler's true motives and to the hideous pathos of the uniformed youth move-ments, military music and empty anthems to his greatness that he foists on his dominion. However often patriotism and nationalism are evoked, there is nothing that can hide the fact that France has suffered a catastrophic defeat at the hands of its bitterest enemy: self-preservation becomes the rump government's dominant impulse; collaboration its method.

Amery's commitment to radical revolution is anathema to the deeply conservative Vichy regime, which he describes as 'an ultra-reactionary government, of priests, the worst type of French industrialists and militarists'. They are not much more keen on him: in October 1941 he is thrown into jail at Vals les Bains (this, at least, was not personal: he was with fourteen other British subjects, their detention was a reprisal for the arrest of a group of French nationals in Syria), where he finds himself in close proximity to George Mandel and Paul Reynaud, the Third Republic's recently deposed Minister of the Interior and Prime Minister respectively. He promptly begins to inform on both. Once released from internment John embarks on a series of unsuccessful efforts to secure a way out of France, which include an attempt to persuade the authorities that he has tuberculosis and should be sent to Switzerland. The visa to leave France as well as an ambulance to take him to Switzerland are organised, but at the last moment, when John discovers that he cannot take either Jeanine or his pet Pomeranian, Sammy – to whom he is desperately attached; the two creatures share the same feral amorality and indifferent attitude to hygiene – he pulls out of the journey.

This incompetent farce, which exposes his fragile terror of being alone, and will ultimately seal his fate, is another instance of how foggy and deluded his mind has become. He can tell as many people as he wants that he suffers from consumption (and it is not just his concerned parents and embassy staff – he also has a habit of picking up cigarette ends in the street and osten-tatiously lighting up; if anyone tries to stop him he tells them it doesn't matter since he is about to die) but he does not have it, and will never have it, and a medical examination in 1945 will confirm this. In Amery's complex and contradictory fantasy world he is adorned with phantom medals and riddled with hallucin-atory diseases. There is something else too: while he was interned in Vals les Bains, Amery would drink an entire bottle of gin, or *fine*, every night, taking it to bed with him. Nobody consumes that amount of alcohol without wishing to numb, or obliterate, something in their life. Perhaps it is significant that of this time he would later write: 'I was cut off from evryone [sic]. Including England.'

A couple of months later, on 3 March, Amery writes a letter

to a French paper, the *Petit Dauphinois*, condemning an RAF bombing raid of the Renault industrial complex at Boulogne-Billancourt in which 400 French civilians were killed and 600 severely injured.* Amery's contribution amounts to little more than a few lines amid a hail of blood-curdling outrage in the collaborationist press, but it is at this point that the British intelligence services prick up their ears. Hitherto he had been a minor nuisance among many other greater ones; now he'd become . . . well, it is not clear what exactly, but certainly someone deserving of closer surveillance. Amery follows this up by writing letters to the Italians offering his services but they go unanswered. A similar attempt to contact the Finnish army receives a 'charming reply which was as negative as nicely as one can say it'. No matter, by this time he has finally caught the attention of the German Foreign Office.

In the autumn of 1942, at the invitation of the Third Reich, Amery arrives in Berlin accompanied by Jeanine Barde. Over the next few months they will strike new acquaintances as an unlikely couple. John, sporting a neat moustache, appears frail but clever, and typically English. Beside his wife he is a faint pencil sketch of a man. The vivacious Jeanine Barde, with her painted face and ample figure is, by contrast, a whirl of heavy strokes and colour.

To begin with John and Jeanine stay in the apartment of a Foreign Office official called Werner Plack, who has already played a role in the Germans' attempt to woo the young Englishman. At the suggestion of Hitler's interpreter, Dr Paul Schmidt, Werner Plack is induced to keep a closer eye on John Amery. Before the war Plack spent a number of years living in Los Angeles, where he combined working as an extra in Hollywood with sidelines in German wine sales and espionage (he boasted that he had reported back to Dr Goebbels about the goings-on in Tinseltown). He emerged from his time in the United States having acquired a perfect command of English, which he speaks with a pronounced

---

* There's a note in his file that suggests he may have been paid 10,000 francs for this.

American accent, a 'sports tan', and a reputation for drinking too much. While his taste for dissipation precludes him from occupying a senior post, he is still considered an asset and, by the time Plack meets Amery, Ribbentrop's department has for some time been using him as a chaperone for renegades or potential renegades of the social class he was likely to have mixed with in Hollywood. Charming, convivial and always well dressed, he is considered the ideal man to convince British expats of the merits of cooperation with the Third Reich; it was Plack who had persuaded P. G. Wodehouse to make his infamous series of broadcasts to the US.*

Werner Plack is friendly with a number of the other Britons eking out marginal, compromised existences in Paris and Berlin, but it is Amery for whom he develops a particular fondness. Before long the two playboys are so close that they start sharing an office at the Foreign Ministry, and a nickname: the 'gold-dust twins'.

Over the next couple of weeks John Amery meets twice with Dr Fritz Hesse, head of the England Committee, to discuss how his collaboration with the Third Reich might proceed. At their first encounter, Amery, fired by excitement, holds court. The problem, as he sees it, is that the foreign service of the Reichsrundfunk has been carved up between William Joyce and his friends and Baillie-Stewart (who, for his part, regards the Irishman as 'a thug of the first order') and his. More than that, both the tone and content of the material produced so far is completely misguided, to the point of being self-defeating. It is, he argues, 'absurd for me as an Englishman to talk about us all getting together if, five minutes later, from the same station, another

---

* The MI5 report into his actions makes it clear that it is unlikely Plack had to exert too much pressure. Wodehouse, it says, 'gives the impression that he lives in the same world as his own characters, a cosmopolitan apolitical place into which conceptions such as the state and the nation do not intrude . . . while he would probably not willingly help "the enemy" he has no very clear idea what "the enemy" is and has difficulty in recognising as such the individual Germans with whom he finds it so easy to get on.' 'I thought that people, hearing the talks, would admire me for having kept cheerful under difficult conditions.'

Englishman was to yell out abuse of my countrymen'. John says that all he wants is to be allowed to speak 'uncensored and uninterfered with' to the British people. He also asks, rather pompously, for 'precise guarantees' about 'British Imperial territory'.

Hesse, a suave operator who considers himself to be a 'sort of living dictionary' of all matters British, is cautiously enthusiastic, pointing out that John was 'asking a very great deal without giving any assurance of success'. For the moment he also opts to keep the Führer's interest in the project hidden from his interlocutor. What, he wonders, choosing his words carefully, does Amery want in return for his broadcast? Amery announces that he is not looking to make any money, but would be much obliged if they could cover his expenses. And if they can arrange diplomatic status, a bodyguard and the use of one or more cars, then all the better.

His proposition is, like *Jungle Skies*, another false prospectus, but he has always been good at selling these. A pulse of excitement passes through Berlin at the idea of the son of a member of Churchill's Cabinet conducting propaganda on their behalf; he is treated with the kind of deference normally accorded to movie stars. After a fortnight Hesse summons Amery to the Foreign Office and gives him the green light to prepare ten broadcasts, which he is assured will be uncensored; the announcer will make it clear that the German government does not endorse whatever views John chooses to articulate. He is also informed that the Führer wishes him to consider himself a welcome guest of the Reich, free to travel unhindered throughout the country. John is, the German leader believes, 'by far the best propagandist to England that we have'.

It is not clear how familiar Hesse is with his new charge's extravagance, but any illusions about Amery do not last for long. All his adult life, John has combined a prodigious gift for spending vast quantities of money with an uncontrollable terror of being without it: another of the pathological problems that he has dragged across the Channel. Now, for the first time, he is completely freed from financial concerns of any kind. It is soon evident that the young Englishman's understanding of living expenses can be expanded to absorb expensive dinners, trips to nightclubs, disturbing amounts of alcohol, and jewels for the disreputable-looking woman who accompanies him everywhere.

With his lordly entitled manner, John Amery antagonises any other Englishman he meets, but his appearance in Berlin kindles a special hatred inside William Joyce. Nobody would claim that the English section of the Reichsrundfunk is distinguished by a collegiate atmosphere: for years it has been a pit of jealousy; other people's jobs are coveted, plots seethe. Denunciations are common and it is not uncommon for people to disappear suddenly. Joyce generally views the department's sewer politics from a position of Olympian disdain, his interactions with the others limited to snarling at them when they fail to greet him with a 'Heil Hitler'. But Amery's appearance presents a threat to the comfortable pre-eminence he has enjoyed since 1939. Sitting in his suburban apartment, Joyce watches the sudden elevation of 'that quarter yid' to celebrity status with equal quantities of disgust and disdain. Frustrated and jealous, he warns Eduard Dietze that Amery is an irresponsible and silly playboy, but his counsel falls on deaf ears.

Amery's speech is to be broadcast by the New British Broadcasting operation, who give his performance an unprecedented amount of publicity ('Many Englishmen who share my views would now be in Berlin if there was no channel between England and the Continent,' he tells a German paper. The interview goes on to say how 'The inglorious collapse of the Third Republic made a profound impression on young Amery who stresses however that he was anti-communist and anti-semitic ever since he left Harrow'), something that is duly picked up by the British press and which ensures an impressive number of listeners tune in to hear him on 19 November 1942.

> Listeners will wonder what an Englishman is doing on German radio tonight. You can imagine that before taking this step I hoped someone better qualified than me would come forward. I dared to believe that some ray of common sense, some appreciation of our priceless civilisation would guide the counsels

of Mr Churchill's government. Unfortunately, this has not been the case! For two years living in a neutral country I have been able to see through the haze of propaganda to reach something which my conscience tells me is the truth. That is why I come forward tonight without any political label, without any bias, but just simply as an Englishman, to say to you: a crime is being committed against our civilisation . . . You are being lied to, your patriotism, your love for our England is being exploited by people who for the most part hardly have any right to be English. Between you and peace lies only the Jew and his puppets.

His voice is well-bred but dull, and he retains the peculiar habit of sounding 'th' as 'f', but more than anything the problem is that his script is a tedious assembly of anti-Semitism by numbers and a series of weightless criticisms of the British government. There is nothing that has not emerged before – with considerably more wit and vigour – from Joyce's mouth; and nobody in England seems to be persuaded by his calls for a rapprochement with the Third Reich. It is perhaps unfortunate that he delivers these words against an unsympathetic backdrop: the Battle of the Atlantic is still raging; British spirits have been lifted by the Battle of El Alamein, their first major victory of the war; and a wild admiration for the Russian soldier's fighting spirit is abroad, stoked by the government, and embodied in Stalin's surreal mutation into 'Uncle Joe'.

Five hundred miles away, in the house in Eaton Square that stopped being his home almost a decade before, his family gather around the wireless to face 'the miserable ordeal of listening in to John's broadcast'. They try to persuade themselves that it is not Jack speaking – they tell each other that it is too hard and staccato to be him, too much the voice of a polished radio professional. They speculate that he has been replaced at the microphone after a last-minute change of heart, or a sudden illness.

But over the next couple of weeks they slowly accept that John is guilty of treachery. Although they are touched by the concern and understanding shown by their friends (when Leo offers to step down from his post, Winston Churchill reminds him that it is hardly fair to blame a father for the aberrations of his grown-up son), increasingly their sorrow runs in parallel with a rueful kind of bitterness and rage. John's younger brother Julian, who is busy forging an impressive career in the British Army, vows that if he meets Jack at any point in the conflict he will kill him with his bare hands.* At the end of the year Leo reflects in his diary on the effect John's treachery has had on both him and his wife. He writes of the hurt already caused and the need to somehow cauterise themselves so that they might be spared further pain. For the moment, though, he cannot even bring himself to mention his son's name.

---

* His brother's actions may not have been a complete surprise to Julian. He had been in Belgrade when he heard news of the French Armistice. 'There's going to be a disaster,' he told his friend, Sandy Glen. 'I know exactly what will happen, Jack will go over to the other side.'

10

It was our one hope. It still is, if you could only realise it

Winter 1942

FOR A WHILE John Amery remains wreathed in the same sense of excitement and glitz that accompanied his broadcasts; his reputation has not yet been affected by the muted reaction in Britain to his overtures. He is still seen as one of Goebbels's favourite children. He can do as he pleases, draw all the money he wants and live in the best hotels. Everywhere he goes a cohort of guards follows closely: whether through assassination or an inconvenient change of heart, it would not do to lose a high-profile guest like John. If it ever strikes him that he is trapped in a gilded cage, then he does not let it spoil his fun. But, reluctantly at first, his new masters begin to accept that, once you strip away the frisson that comes from knowing he is the son of one of Churchill's closest allies, then Amery, with his weak uncertain voice, is an uninspiring radio performer. There are also whispers that he has struggled to cope with the demands of recording. He is so crippled by a form of stage fright that every recording session requires several takes, and engineers report their concerns about his constant drinking; it is said he always arrives at the studio equipped with a bottle of whisky, from which he sips constantly. One of the Rundfunk employees responsible for the broadcasts will later remember him as a man 'full of inferiority complexes and a dreadful type, who was always accompanied by a French woman who was even worse . . . He was much too nervous to broadcast directly.'

Another concern is the antipathy that exists between him and

Joyce, which shows no signs of abating. Eventually only seven of the ten talks he has prepared are broadcast. The feeling persists that he remains a catch in propaganda terms, yet nobody seems sure quite how he might usefully be employed. In the absence of any definite plans, Amery and Barde are allowed to leave Berlin.

Paris: a city made for a man like John Amery. He speaks French fluently, and though he will never lose his English accent, many who meet him come away impressed by his command of Parisian slang, which he likes to distribute liberally throughout his conversation.* The couple arrive in a city that has changed far less than anyone can have expected. Hitler believes that the French ardour for music, books, food and fashion has contributed to their decadence; their tastes can safely be indulged. There are differences, some quite substantial, but nothing likely to trouble Amery and his partner unduly. They swiftly check into the lavish surrounds of the Hotel Bristol – a favourite of John's from before the war – and start to look around for fun.

If you know the right people and the right addresses and have enough money the occupation makes little material difference. You can still get caviar at Petrossian's; Paul Valéry is allowed to continue his poetry lectures; and the doors of the great fashion houses remain open (as do, cynics claim, Coco Chanel's legs; she has spent much of the war in the Ritz in the arms of an aristocratic German officer). It soon becomes easy to tell who is having a 'good' war. If somebody has no interest in discussing heating or food, then they are likely either to be extremely rich, or very well connected. For the majority of Parisians, getting enough to eat and keeping warm have become endlessly absorbing topics of conversation.

Other changes are harder to spot, and far more sinister. It starts with what might be seen as minor details; matters, perhaps, of

---

* Along with Italian and German, or at least so his mother claims. His governess when he and Julian were young was the orphaned daughter of a deep-sea trawler fisherman from Finistère in Brittany. Pippette spoke no English, so the boys had no choice but to learn her language. John would often speak French to his baffled contemporaries, a process he seemed to enjoy more than they did.

taste. Streets named after Jews are re-christened, and one day Parisians wake up to see that the Sarah Bernhardt Theatre has become the Théâtre de la Cité. A relief celebrating the Great War nurse Edith Cavell, who was executed as a spy by the Germans in 1915, is desecrated.

Without any audible complaints, French publishing houses consent to a process of self-censorship: books by German-speaking émigrés such as Stefan Zweig or Albert Einstein, French writers such as Louis Aragon and André Malraux, the majority of English authors, and, of course, Jews, are purged from their lists. Displaying the taste for expensive real estate possessed by most totalitarian secret police forces, the Gestapo occupy three imposing mansions on the Avenue Foch and establish a network of branches and substations throughout the rest of the city. They waste little time in recruiting legions of informers from every level of French society, who will work alongside the armed guards and fleets of black cars sweeping through Paris's streets. The new Parisian taste for *délation* – denunciation – generates a flood of tens of thousands of anonymous letters that threatens to overwhelm the German administrators and their native cohorts.

There are reminders, too many, that anti-Semitism existed in France long before the Nazis came: the French are perfectly capable of conducting their own pogroms. As early as August 1940 militants from one of the country's numerous far-right sects smashed the windows of all the Jewish-owned shops on the Champs-Élysées. Thugs find they have a licence to beat Jews up in the street, and there is nobody to stop openly anti-Semitic newspapers from celebrating the violence, or from trying to incite further outrages. Later that year *Au Pilori* runs a competition: three pairs of silk stockings for whoever comes up with the best proposal for what should be done with the Jews. Competition for the prize is fierce, as are the suggestions as to how men and women who have long lived and worked alongside the entrants should be treated: 'I can see myself wearing shoes and a matching handbag made from the skin of a Lévy,' one submission reads.

In requisitioned houses once inhabited by Englishmen or Jews the new occupiers hold extravagant dinners attended by sympathetic members of the Parisian *beau monde*. The guests, unconcerned that they are all party to a kind of theft, eat off the former owners' silver and expensive linen, and are served by white-gloved soldiers. Next, Jews are banned from using public telephones. Slowly but surely their rights as citizens are stripped away. Some find themselves subject to extortion and blackmail from fellow countrymen who are operating in a semi-official capacity. They discover there is no longer anyone to whom they can appeal. Some French Jews had hoped they might be spared the depredations heaped on their co-religionists elsewhere on the Continent but they now begin to realise how remorseless is the Nazi desire to wipe them from the face of the earth.

On 27 March 1942 the first transport leaves Paris for Auschwitz, carrying 12,884 Jewish men, women and children: the tailors, furriers, bakers, mechanics, artists, cobblers, teachers, journalists and carpenters whose families have been sheltered in this city for centuries. Two months later, on 29 May, Adolf Hitler acts on the advice of Joseph Goebbels and decrees that all Jews in occupied France must wear a yellow Star of David on the left side of their coats; veterans may not wear their medals alongside it. An internment camp is established north of the city in Drancy. Occasionally Jews are shot attempting to escape, their deaths recorded laconically in the German ledgers; these lists will eventually record that 75,721 French Jews were sent east. Despite its appearance of meticulous accuracy, this figure is undoubtedly a very modest representation of the true number of the victims. For one thing, it does not take into account the hundreds of Jews who will commit suicide: poison, chloroform and defenestration are considered preferable to whatever the Nazis have planned for them.

The sight of their friends and neighbours being led away becomes increasingly familiar to Parisians. People discover that it is impossible not to stare at the overloaded cattle trucks: you can see the white faces of young children pressing through the narrow openings, behind them the sad and amazed expressions of their parents. Some of the spectators are bemused, some indifferent, some are haunted and shamed; but there is a disconcerting contingent who look triumphant.

It is inconceivable that John Amery would not have witnessed these deportations; inconceivable too that given his close contacts with the Nazis and the leading French collaborators – his mentor Jacques Doriot's PFF are zealous accomplices as the French police round up Jews – he would not have been aware what fate waited for them after they had crossed the French border. This, then, is the regime, these the people, with whom he believes Britain must ally itself.

John's close friendship with Doriot gains him a place among France's quisling elite, whose careers offer him a foreshadowing of what he might expect in the event of a British defeat. There is Marcel Déat, who has made the same journey from left to right as Doriot, though they have little else in common. In contrast to the brawling, beefy autodidact Doriot, Déat is a fussy and austere pedant. He has none of Doriot's charisma, but is still able to attract enough followers to set up his own party – the Rassemblement National Populaire (RNP).

John also re-encounters Eugène Deloncle, the founder of the Cagoulard, who had been briefly imprisoned at the beginning of the war (unsurprisingly, his loyalties were a matter of concern), but has been released in time to set up a new revolutionary organ-isation, the Mouvement Social Révolutionnaire, which is a fervent supporter of the Pétainist regime. Deloncle's brief career exempli-fies, with a particular kind of brutality, the dilemmas faced by French collaborators. All are invested in ensuring that, in the words of Doriot, 'France must pass from the camp of the conquered into the camp of the conquerors,' but there is no consensus as to how this might be achieved. The Germans are the masters of Europe now, and the country's spiritual renaissance under Hitler offers an inspiration for those Frenchmen who are convinced their nation needs the same. But the Third Reich hoards power jealously and the Führer himself is wary of other national socialist parties, conscious of the potential challenge their revolutionary ideologies imply. The gaudy trappings of power are dangled before the collab-orators' wide eyes, but they cannot see that they are no more than scraps designed to provoke discontent and disarray among them.

In truth they are little more than jobbing *petits* autocrats; collaborationists who swap insults and interrupt each other's meetings. Later in the war Déat and Laval are shot point-blank by a young Frenchman as they review troops. They both survive, each convinced he is the victim of a hit arranged by one of his fascist rivals. The collaborators all have their own newspapers, platforms and almost identical political perspectives: the Gaullists are traitors; communism must be resisted; democracy is bankrupt. It is a shaming parody of pre-war democracy that serves nobody's interests other than the Nazis, who can point to the existence of what appears to be an energetic political culture, safe in the knowledge that no movement or figure will emerge who might present a serious challenge to their rule. And if any of the collaborationists are unwise enough to try to embroider themselves into the Third Reich's own factional disputes, then little mercy will be shown: Deloncle's involvement with the Abwehr, the German military intelligence, is ultimately enough to ensure his assassination by the Gestapo, while Deloncle's son is beaten into a coma, and his wife and daughter taken to Fresnes to be locked up alongside *résistants*.

One enterprise in which Doriot, Déat and Deloncle, who by now each command a substantial level of political support (by 1942 the PFF can boast a membership of 100,000 in Paris alone), do work together is the establishment of the Légion des Volontaires Français in July 1941. Once proposed, the idea quickly secures permission from the Germans to proceed; though this of a rather grudging kind – Hitler is unenthusiastic about the idea of arming Frenchmen, so decrees that its numbers should be limited to 15,000. There is a blaze of euphoric publicity in the collaborationist press: radio broadcasts, posters, cinema newsreels. The politician and journalist Pierre Costantini (who had personally declared war on Great Britain after it had sunk the French fleet in July 1940) salutes them as 'the crusaders of a new order against Anglo-Jewish-Bolshevik disorder', and it receives support from prominent industrialists and clerics as well as some of France's haughtiest families.

The new organisation secures 13,400 volunteers by October

1941 (of whom only 5,800 pass medical tests – bad teeth rules many out). Among them are wild-eyed fanatics ('Our leader, Chancellor Hitler, can give whatever orders he likes. We will carry them out with our eyes closed') as well as men who feel they have a moral duty to fight Bolshevism ('You just had to go. There was no choice'), but, for the most part, those who sign up are a mixture of the curious, the impecunious and the bored; there are also large numbers of prisoners of war, who consider the legion preferable to forced labour in Germany. Doriot heads off with them to the Eastern Front. Déat has no intention of following him: 'No question of my going,' he confides to his diary. And he is wise to do so; before the spring of 1942 is over, the unit will lose half its men to bullets, shells and the terrible Russian winter.

John Amery, who is still trying to find a way of translating his inchoate desire for action into something tangible, has observed all of this with keen interest. Amery wants desperately to be involved and Doriot's boldness is an inspiration: who better to teach you how to hunt than the wolf himself? In December 1942 Doriot returns from Russia. When they meet later on in Paris he tells John that after Stalingrad and El Alamein the Third Reich is on its knees. Britain must make peace with Germany or Europe will be overrun by communists. John has long talked about raising a force of British volunteers to fight the Bolsheviks; Grand Jacques's apocalyptic warnings serve to rekindle his grandiose sense of mission. Towards the end of the little life that is left to him John will recall this encounter with his mentor: 'I believed him,' he said, 'I still believe him – you'll see . . . It was our one hope. It still is, if you could only realise it.'

Spring 1943

Though the idea of establishing the Legion of St George is never far from his mind, on his return to Berlin John writes a book, *England Faces Europe* – a reassembly of the incoherent and un-savoury prejudices he had aired in his broadcasts, liberally interspersed with material imported uncritically from the *Protocols of the Learned Elders of Zion*'s bogus pages. His use of the ugly phrase

'Judaeo-plutocracy' gives a good measure of its tone, as do the 'quotations' from the Talmud he introduces, such as 'non-Jews are but the spunk of animals'. He and Jeanine, who has faithfully typed much of the text for him, are so convinced of its importance that they begin to put together a plan that will see 5,000 books dropped over London, each copy addressed to one of the city's most eminent figures. But in the course of the bender John initiates to celebrate the completion of his manuscript, Jeanine dies.

Lurid rumours instantly proliferate. One of the other foreign nationals who worked at the Rundfunkhaus is accosted by a gleeful William Joyce, who turns to her, his broad, toothless grin splitting his scarred face. 'Have you heard the latest news? That little French girl Jack Amery brought with him has killed herself. She was found dead in bed. Last night she handed Amery a pill, asking him to dissolve it in a glass of water, which she then drank, and she died.'

There is a suggestion that after a political discussion decayed into a quarrel Jeanine told Amery that she would rather die than live with him a moment longer. In this telling, Amery put some powder in her drink and said, 'Good luck to you.' By the next morning she was dead. Another variation attributes her death to a tragic accident: Amery had intended to give her a headache tablet, but instead handed over one of the poison capsules he carries with him at all times to ensure a quick and painless escape in the event of capture.

The German Foreign Office immediately launches its own investigation, drawing on witness statements and an autopsy; this is accompanied by a concerted attempt to keep the story out of the papers. Its conclusion is that after complaining of a headache Jeanine took from her handbag a powder contained in a small box labelled 'Asciatine' (a form of analgesic). John, swimmy with booze, provided her with a glass of water into which Jeanine, who had also been drinking heavily, poured the powder. Just before she tasted the contents of the glass, Jeanine announced she was about to poison herself; John paid little attention to this. On the way home, Jeanine fell asleep at the tram stop. John, apparently under the impression that she was simply drunk, hailed a taxi and they drove back to their 'sumptuous' suite at the Hotel Kaiserhof. After they arrived at the hotel Jeanine regained consciousness and was able to walk without any help up to their room. But she then collapsed again and began to vomit. This lasted for a while before she collected herself, regained her calm and started to breathe deeply. As before, Amery attributed this to intoxication. He undressed her, put her to bed, then took a sleeping tablet of his own and lay beside her. The following morning he awoke to find that the person he loved more than any other in his life had choked to death on her own vomit.

There are no words that can do justice to the depth of John's grief: an acquaintance noted with horror that he had become like a man whose world had collapsed; that he was no longer capable of anything and had turned totally to drink. The sorrow will persist within him until the day he meets his own untimely end, and yet his misery manifests itself in a manner that to anyone else would seem incomprehensible. Within days he is seen in the company of yet another prostitute 'fiancée', Michelle Thomas, whom he met on the train on his way to deliver Jeanine's ashes to her parents in Bergerac, and who bears a striking resemblance to the woman who has just died beside him. It looks on the surface like a callous exchange: as if one body warming his bed is as good as any another (even Plack feels this, insisting that his friend spend two months mourning Jeanine before he takes up with her replacement). But it is clear that John does not feel that life can be faced alone. It is too fierce and sharp, too full of ragged holes that one is liable to disappear into unless someone else is there to light the way. As with Jeanine, he does not mind that Michelle's table manners are bad ('*elle fait un peu "demi-mondaine"*' sniffs one Frenchman), that her lipstick is invariably a bright shade of red and that she bedecks herself with imitation jewellery; he loves her.

Years later, Michelle, married to a Swiss insurance salesman, will maintain a fond correspondence with Julian, John's brother. '*C'était un amour si merveilleux et si lumineuse, qui restera dans mon Coeur pour l'Eternité,*' she writes. '*Notre Johnny est notre plus magnifique exemple et c'est lui qui nous donne le courage et la force!*' It is as if the gentle Michelle cannot see the drink and the whores, or the bitterness that twists his narrow little features out of shape. Or perhaps she just is able to ignore all this. And why not? Most people these days, it seems, only see of the world what they can bear to observe. How else are they to get by?

Almost a fortnight later, still distraught, John Amery lurches into a misguided enterprise that he believes will be hailed as an epochal new page in the history of mankind.

II

Don't wait until the truth stabs your eyes out

April 1943

HERE IS HOW it may have started. Perhaps Amery and Plack
met in the bar of the Bristol Hotel in Paris. The evening
before – 20 April 1943 – they had been at a party hosted by the
Villette and Montparnasse branches of the Nazi Party Abroad to
celebrate the Führer's birthday. There had been plenty of important
figures to meet, and a stream of booze that belied the privations
being experienced by millions across the Continent. Bleary-eyed
from the previous night's excesses, they look around the familiar
room, its grandeur intact, the waiters as smart as ever, its cellars
still full of champagne. They have plotted here, they have talked
and they have also had a lot of fun: the staff either too cowed or
too polite to get in the way of their worst behaviour. And, best
of all, the German Foreign Office always picks up the bill.
Sometimes they cannot believe the things they can get Ribbentrop's
lot to pay for: their expense claims include one for four bottles
of Pernod, a twelve-bottle case of champagne, three pieces of soap
and four neckties. It is not clear how any of this is going to help
the war effort, but neither man is complaining.

Yet even this and the strength of his hangover aren't enough
to subdue the queasy sense that has been mounting in Amery
over the last couple of months that they've been sidelined, that
their talents are not fully appreciated. Look at the attention that
fool Joyce receives, and here we are, kicking our heels. John wants
to contribute, to make a difference, if only they would let him.

The idea of raising a British unit from the POW camps to fight in Russia had been his, but now the Germans will not allow him near it. He is not interested in taking credit for it. Well, not that interested. But they're going about it the wrong way – what honest patriot is going to come forward if it's a Hun asking them to sign up? What they need is a Brit, someone well known whom the lads can trust. He thinks about the great adventurers such as Drake, Clive, Cook and Raffles, who helped to create the British Empire. That they might have committed acts of piratry and banditism in the course of their conquests ultimately means little, given that they were all inspired by an ardent patriotism. Surely this is a similar situation? Last night he remembers hardly being able to contain his excitement about his idea. He knocks back his first brandy of the day and signals to the waiter for another. His throat burns a little, his mind clears. A plan forms.

The internment camp at St Denis, in the northern suburbs of Paris (an easy drive from the Bristol Hotel) is home to around a thousand British men. They are mostly civilians who had not been able, or willing, to escape across the Channel after the fall of France. Although food is scarce, the camp operates under a relatively relaxed regime and its inmates are given time and space to pursue their own interests.

On the day Amery and Plack descend – without any authorisation – on St Denis, Mohr Keet, a bacteriological student from South Africa who had been captured at sea and interned there since July 1940, is working in the camp's laboratory when a guard tells him he is wanted in the visitors' hut. He is joined by Raymond Perrodow, who had been working as a gardener in France around the time of the invasion, and twenty other inmates. They quickly begin discussing why they have been summoned.

After a few minutes a man in a dark suit enters, followed by two others in plain clothes. Perrodow notes that he carries a black hat in his hand, and is struck by his sallow complexion and high cheekbones. Brilliantined hair sits above delicate, enervated features: there is so little flesh on his face that it is easy to believe that nothing lies between his pallid skin and the skull and bones beneath. The men are soon joined by a dozen men in civilian clothes, who are plainly from the Gestapo, together with the camp commandant, Modius, and several German officers in uniforms. The man sits down at a table in front of the internees and ostentatiously produces a revolver, which he lays on the table's surface, before covering it with his hat. This piece of theatre out of the way, he begins to speak. To the surprise of his audience, the small, slight man who has just swept in waving a pistol round like a Chicago gangster is British. He introduces himself as John Amery, son of Leo Amery the Cabinet minister, and tells them he is recruiting for a military unit called the Legion of St George.

All the men gathered in this room are used to a certain amount of compromise with their captors. The camp's senior man, Fletcher, nicknamed the 'errand boy of the Germans', is held in universal contempt, and it is thought that there are at least three stool pigeons at work within the camp's barbed-wire perimeter. More ambiguous is the position occupied by the Red Cross administrator, Hadkinson, a man who does a great deal for the rest of the internees, but even more for himself. He is always in and out of the camp, spending days at a time, including most weekends, away from it (it is thought he goes to an apartment he owns in Paris), and has free use of a Red Cross motor car. There is much that does not add up about Hadkinson, who speaks fluent German but imperfect English, and it is not hard to believe that he is a collaborator. But what Amery is offering to them, what he represents, is something different. The mood in the shabby hut swiftly sours. It is not just that they object to the idea of what is clearly treason; the fact of just being present is likely to open them up to opprobrium from their fellow internees. How are the rest of the blokes to know that the men inside this room had never asked to be here?

Oblivious to the deteriorating atmosphere, John continues his pitch. He tells them they will be paid 500 francs a month. Three months of training will be followed by a month's holiday with free lodgings: there's also the tempting inducement of the right to unlimited numbers of letters and parcels to and from home.

'You have no chance of getting out of this camp,' he says, 'but if you join up you will be free men.' Free men like the thousands of others who are joining the legion from the POW camps. Leaflets are distributed, and he talks at length about the Soviet menace. John tries to explain to them that Britain's only hope is an alliance with the Third Reich. Do they not realise Churchill is in thrall to a bunch of murderous parasites, that he's willing to throw the empire away for a cause that isn't worth fighting for? Do they want to see the country they love brought low by Jews and communists?

Suddenly, a disturbance in the corner of the hut interrupts Amery's flow. He turns and sees a tall bearded man elbowing his way past the guards stationed at the door. Amery peers at his face, anxiously trying to place this intruder. He seems familiar. John turns to the Germans who have accompanied him, but none of them offers any help. The man demands if he remembers who he is. He does. It is Brinkman, Wilfred Brinkman, the man he swindled out of thousands of dollars back in Nice. And Ogilvie? Brinkman asks, does Amery remember him too? Yes . . . yes he knew Ogilvie, he says. He had denounced him to the Vichy authorities and picked up a tidy sum in exchange, but this probably is not the best time or place to broadcast that. John glances again at his German escort, and again they ignore him. The interrogation continues, with Amery plainly out of countenance.

What is he doing here?

Amery tells Brinkman that he was explaining the advantages of joining the Legion of St George.

What authority is he acting under?

A committee existing in England, the names of which he cannot divulge, which is fighting for the freedom of England.

What is the Legion of St George?

A body of about 1,500 men recruited from the camps plus three or four heavy bombers whose crews had flown over from England.

Where will they fight?

The Russian Front.

What will happen if they face British troops?

They will be moved to a different sector.

What about if any of the men are taken prisoner?

No reply.

What will happen to them after the war?

No reply.

Do these men realise that they will be traitors to their own country?

John maintains his sullen silence for a few moments more before briskly announcing that he has nothing further to say. The meeting is over. As the men exit noisily, Amery, struggling to make himself heard, shouts that he will be more than happy to supply further information, or to respond to any letters they might wish to send. Brinkman makes to walk to the door with the rest of the internees but John stops him and asks him to stay behind.

> Amery said to me that I seemed to misunderstand his position. I said I was fully aware of his past, particularly his activities in Nice. He continued that his work had been solely on behalf of the common good. To which I replied that I doubted it. He then begged me not to mention in the camp anything which would appear derogatory to him. I replied that was precisely what I intended to do. He repeated his request and offered me his hand to shake. I replied that I was not in the habit of shaking hands with traitors. He said nothing in reply and walked away.

John emerges into a prison yard that is in the throes of something close to a riot. The last four years have been hard for the men assembled here: they have been hungry, bored and subject to an almost daily diet of humiliations. This quisling's appearance in their midst is an indignity too far. He is greeted with a chorus of catcalls and boos. The internees crowd around him, some screaming abuse, others gesturing wildly, and for a moment the camp guards seem close to losing control of their charges. Amery's escort surrounds him, ushering him as quickly as possible to the camp's exit, fending off a hail of stones as they do so. The commandant, already seething at the disruption this visit has brought to the camp's usually serene existence, informs Amery that this will be the first and last meeting of its kind. Any attempts at recruitment in the future will have to be preceded by the distribution of propaganda – to prepare the men psychologically – and should take the form of private meetings with volunteers. Disheartened, Amery agrees. The day has been an ignominious failure. It probably finishes where it had started, in the bar of the Bristol Hotel.

Over the next two days copies of his book *John Amery Speaks* are distributed to each of the barrack huts, and the camp is plastered with a range of posters. They broadcast a mendacious confection of disingenuous patriotism and false promises. One shows a picture of a British soldier with blood streaming from his eyes, and above him the words 'Don't wait until the truth stabs your eyes out'; the second shows a Russian soldier shooting a child; the third depicts British soldiers wearing German uniform with a Union Jack on their arms; and in the fourth, German, British and American flags appear together, united in the battle against Russia. Pamphlets addressed to 'Fellow Countrymen' announce the formation of the Legion of St George and claim that 1,800 POWs are already in Berlin training to fight the Russians.

> I have approached the German Government to form a British Legion against Bolshevism known as the British Legion of St. George. I appeal to all Britons to answer this call to arms in defence of our homes and children, and of all civilization against Asiatic and Jewish bestiality. Within the limits of military possibilities, the Legion of St. George will fight at the junction of the German and Finnish troops.
>
> British representation in Berlin formally guaranteed to all ranks a permanent and well-paid job in the British administration and all priority in any other employment once peace is signed, or the possibility to form the elite of the British Army. Hundreds of soldiers have volunteered to join the legion and many R.A.F. aeroplanes are coming over to us . . .
>
> . . . The world is watching us. Europe expects every civilized man will do his duty. National England desires that you will show yourselves worthy of Nelson's immediate signal.
>
> We are going to write a new page in the history of the British

Empire. Englishmen never, never will be slaves of the plutocratic tyranny. Pay no attention to opposition.

The new approach yields barely more impressive results: when Amery and Plack return to the camp forty-eight hours later, only four men express an interest in joining the unit. Of these, one is soon recruited by the Abwehr, another finds his way to Sofia, where he resumes a research project that had been interrupted by the war, and a third disappears entirely. This leaves a lonely and immature eighteen-year-old merchant seaman as the sole prospective member of the British Legion of St George.

Kenneth Berry is a fresh-faced kitchen boy from Cornwall who, in a fit of pique, ran away to sea before he'd turned fifteen. 'I did not get along very well at home. I had been prosecuted in the local Juvenile Court, once for stealing a golf ball from an un- attended house and the other time for stealing a fountain pen flash lamp from a car, and was fined on both occasions. As I could not get along with my father, I went to sea.'

He joined the SS *Cimbeline* on 27 May 1940. Four months later, on 2 September 1940, it was sunk by a German raider, which took all the *Cimbeline*'s crew on board prisoner before landing in France. Since then he has spent much of his time in various forms of detention, eventually finding his way to the camp at St Denis, where John Amery walks into the young Cornishman's life. The next few months of Kenneth Berry's existence might have been precisely calculated to unsettle and disorientate him. He is unworldly, immature and in an unfamiliar and potentially hostile environment. He had left his family in fractious circumstances when he was little more than a child, and then been in and out of detention for four years. At an age when his fellows were still at school, Berry led a 'precarious existence as a messenger for a group of black marketeers'. He had been ostracised by both his closest friends and an entire tranche of his fellow internees ('when I returned to Camp I had a dogs life from the Jews because they belived I gave one of there number away'); and finally he has been pulled into the orbit of a man who appears at once sophisticated, dissolute and powerful.

Life in the camp was austere and dull but secure. Now he experiences wild-seeming bouts of freedom followed by perplexing stretches of imprisonment more cruel than anything he had been subjected to before. One moment he must feel as if he were at the centre of this charismatic new friend's world, the next he is left to languish in a lonely flat. And can he call John a friend? Or . . . what, exactly? Is this some kind of game? Is he telling the truth – but then why would he lie? Why spend all that time on persuasion – seduction even – only to ignore him? Kenneth is a victim of the same games and careless cruelties that John Amery has previously visited on his first wife, on investors, on his family – anybody, really, whose path has crossed his. When he was a schoolboy, John – Jack, as he was then – subjected a weak-minded fellow pupil to a programme of torment so bewildering that he allowed himself to be manipulated by Jack into shooting at a teacher with an air gun. During the suspension from school that followed, the poor addled boy burned down his family's home.

Berry's statements to the security services, which were committed to paper soon after the war, betray the confusion he continued to feel, even after the dust had settled and he was back in Cornwall.

> Then he [John Amery] put some big Poster in the Camp, which said that a said Legion had been formed and the strength of this Legion was a little over 1,800 men P.O.W.s and those R.A.F. Planes that had come from England to fight, Bolshevics which I can truly say I did not understand what it meant until a few months ago, he said it was our duty to come and fight for England and Europe. So I spoke to the Camp Captain Captain Gillis a German who said it was good and that most of my friend had vol. but he could not tell me their names, so I thought if he said was good it must be so, I told him I would Join Too. So he sent me to live with some French People near Mr Amerys Hotel with another Vol. who Dissapered 10 days afer. and I was arrested the next day and put in a house with Political Prisoners, and they put a gard in my

room with a tommy gun. 8 days after I was taken to Berlin with an English Proffeser Lorgoe there I met Amery and the Minister of the German Foreign Office, and he asked me if I was going to fight Bolshevism and I asked him 'What does Bolshevism mean?'

When Berry agrees to sign up he is taken to a comfortable boarding house by Plack, where he waits in vain for Amery to visit him again. Berry spends his days at the zoo, sometimes staying overnight to snare rabbits. Occasionally he is arrested for drunken behaviour. When he needs money he works for the Abwehr, who pay him to go into prison camps and listen in on the inmates' conversations.

Amery becomes a liminal figure during this period, only occasionally swimming into view: it is as if he has drifted to the margins of his own story. He continues to make desultory attempts at recruitment, but meets with little success. Some of the men he approaches have been surviving for three years on a daily ration of two slices of black bread, four or five small potatoes, a mug of soup (which looks more like coloured water) and a couple of mugs of ersatz coffee. They live in poorly lit, poorly built huts which were cold, unsanitary and cramped to begin with and have deteriorated as the war progressed. The endless, grinding tedium of their existence is conducted in such claustrophobic close contact with other men that privacy becomes a forgotten dream and even close friendships fray. They have lost almost all control over their lives. Inside the camp they are vulnerable to diseases like TB and typhus and outside it life continues remorselessly without them: relatives killed in air raids, homes destroyed, babies that aren't yours being brought up under your roof.

And yet the POWs are almost completely unreceptive to promises of a house in Berlin, 10,000 marks and a mistress; and their officers tend to be actively obstructive. John Amery's patience with the process soon begins to fray. He had grand plans for the Legion of St George, an organisation he believed had the potential to change the course of the war. He had envisaged himself one day marching at its head through the Arc de Triomphe, his leadership a triumphant rebuke to all those people who had dismissed him, including the goading voices inside him that drive his savage inferiority complexes. Why is he not enjoying the same success as his friend Jacques Doriot? Occasionally his frustration spills out into uncontrollable bursts of rage. When the senior British officer at at Marlag Milag Nord, a merchant seamen's camp near Bremen – Captain Findlay Notman, 'a Scotsman and a sea captain to the last barnacle' – refuses Amery the use of the camp's facilities, John spins round and snarls, 'You know, I could have you shot for this.'

Notman's response is quiet, but forceful. 'Really? Let me tell you – you will be hanged before I am shot.'

12

The average decent-minded Englishman

Spring 1944

'BE STRONG, BOY. You've got to be strong,' his father used to tell him. Because if you aren't strong in body and mind, 'you will be stamped on, dragged around and ground down until your life isn't your own.'

At the age of thirty-two Eric Pleasants is undoubtedly strong in body: he is, in his own words, 'a fine specimen of manhood', who has stubbornly refused to allow five years of war to interfere with his obsessive interest in every form of physical culture. The son of a Norfolk gamekeeper, in the years before 1939 he had been variously a wrestler (200 bouts, only one defeat, good enough to make the squad for the 1936 Olympics in Berlin), a weightlifter, a circus and cabaret performer, a qualified physical culture instructor and, at least until the morning he woke up seeing double, a professional boxer. When he wrestled he competed as 'The Panther' or 'Bobby Gardner', and liked to pose for photographs wearing leopard-print trunks and Roman sandals whose thongs crept as high as his knee: sometimes he'd balance a plank on his shoulders and hoist two or three smiling friends high above him. Another trick was to lift a piano: two men sat on it while one played. Though Eric stands no higher than five foot four inches, and at first glance you might be forgiven for thinking he is slightly built, his clothing camouflages taut, cable-like muscles. An officer who passed through the ranks of the British Free Corps would later talk about Eric's 'enormously powerful physique': he must project an air of power and strength, for the officer remembers him as being six foot tall.

He is strong in mind, too. Eric has always prided himself on reaching his own conclusions about the world (when the 'religious caper failed to make sense to me . . . I cut it out'). He is brisk and decisive and has little time for what he sees as the unthinking deference to authority displayed by his contemporaries. Determined to preserve his independence, he has spent most of the war trying to have as little to do with the conflict as he possibly can. It is, Eric has decided, none of his business: he cannot see any justification for slaughtering those with whom he has no personal argument. What authority, what moral right, he asks, does any government have to order him to do so? His position is an ethical one, but it is also informed by an unrelenting individualism: he believes that the war has been forced on him, and as such he is on nobody's 'side' except his own. He is neither for nor against the Germans or the British, and despite a brief flirtation with fascism a decade ago ('I was looking,' he says, 'for something in which to express myself') he does not hate the Jews or have any strong views about the Soviet Union; he has never fought, and will never fight, for anybody except himself. Eric Pleasants recognises the existence of a community beyond the state, but does not see why he should feel any sentimental attachment to this polity at the expense of any others, or accept that it commands any allegiance from him. An accident of birth placed him in Great Britain, but that, for him, is where the connection between him and the other inhabitants of the island begins and ends.

Perhaps this is one of the reasons why he has never been able to settle in a regular trade. The years he spent in a travelling circus were his happiest; he loved the whiff of circus sawdust, talc and animal piss, the smell of the greasepaint, the roar of the crowd, the sham and the artifice of it all. But most of all he loved the chance to inhabit a world of his own making, where he was constantly on the move, free. It is his misfortune (though needless to say, not his misfortune alone) to have emerged into an era that has little interest in leaving him to his own devices.

Eric Pleasants knows about the horrors that lie in wait on the twentieth-century battlefield; his devout, patriotic father came back wounded from the Great War, and Eric is haunted by images from that conflict: the memory of twisted limbs and unseeing eyes on a visit to a war veterans' hospital; the way the small metal wound badge pinned to his father's jacket used to glint in the sun as he limped painfully about his gamekeeper's rounds; a neighbour's recollection of bilious clouds of poison gas.

In a manner that is perhaps unusual for his generation, his life has been devoted to his body: he does not drink or smoke or do anything that might harm it; he cares for it, exercises it, anoints it with oil; and it is admired and celebrated by others in turn. Why should he submit to see his limbs ripped asunder by a shell, to feel shrapnel flay his torso, or bullets thud into his shoulders?

At the outbreak of war, Eric Pleasants was working as a physical training instructor at a Butlin's holiday camp – he thought this would be the best way to further his ambition of becoming an osteopath. As the initial shock gave way to hysteria, he was horrified by the reactions of the men around him. He remembered hearing some of them parting with a cheery, 'See you in Berlin, Eric,' and knowing he could not share in their complacency. After giving long and hard thought to the matter, he decided he would not fight. His wrestler friends talked and argued with him: the charge of cowardice, never explicitly mentioned, lingered above their conversations. As if to ensure that nobody would go so far as to actually articulate this accusation – being called yellow leaves a stain that is difficult to eradicate, and whether consciously or not it seems that Eric had already begun to rehearse a story that would justify his decision, to himself and others – he offered to fight any of them, to death if need be. 'I have my own code,' he says, 'I have lived by it – I shall most certainly die by it.' He also has a gift for sewing high principle and low self-interest together so seamlessly that even he cannot see where the stitches are.

Instead of joining the army, Eric Pleasants travelled to Jersey as part of a contingent of approximately 100 Peace Pledge Union (PPU) volunteers – including his wife – who had been charged with helping on local farms. It might simply be a coincidence, given the direction Eric Pleasants's life would subsequently take, but there was substantial overlap in policy between the PPU and the BUF – most notably in terms of its obdurate refusal to countenance any kind of conflict with Nazi Germany. The BUF itself was campaigning hard on a similar platform: 'Mind Britain's business' and 'Britons fight for Britain only' were two of its most popular slogans at the time. If it stopped short of outright advocacy of the Third Reich, then the PPU undoubtedly displayed an unusual sympathy for it and its objectives. The organisation was a stubborn supporter of appeasement, even going so far as to argue that Germany should be permitted to 'absorb' France, Poland, the Low Countries and the Balkans. One contemporary remembers that 'occasionally when reading *Peace News* [the PPU journal], I (and others) half think we have got hold of the *Blackshirt* by mistake.' (There is evidence that fascists infiltrated the movement with the intention of subverting it, and some members of the PPU did join the BUF.)

The idyll, such as it was, lasted only until the Germans took possession of the Channel Islands on 30 June 1940. In the weeks before the occupation, Jersey's authorities had gone out of their way to reassure its population, even while German planes flew daily overhead on bombing missions to England, that the island would never fall into Nazi hands. 'Don't be like rats leaving the sinking ship,' the posters warned. The governor left, claiming that the pressure of his duties meant he had to return to England. He confidently assured the islanders that they should not worry. But the few boats that came to the island were filled instantly by anyone rich enough to bribe a passage to Britain. Those left behind reassured each other by telling themselves that their government would not abandon them, that even if the worst were to happen, the navy would come and evacuate every last man, woman and child. Then, one day in June, a German plane dropped a bomb on Jersey as a warning. It was followed by an ultimatum: 'Surrender or we will bomb the island.'

Soon, Jersey was plastered with white sheets. Eric Pleasants watched the population adapt to its new circumstances. How quickly bobbies on the beat learned to salute German officers! How swiftly anyone with sense started taking German lessons! How little time the girls wasted before dropping their knickers for any oaf in a Wehrmacht uniform! Eric may have felt entitled to be bitter: his wife left him to take up work as housekeeper (and, Pleasants believed, likely lover) for a German officer. Since the only legal employment on the island involved working for Germans – something he had no intention of getting involved with – Eric soon fell into the company of a gang of thieves called the Jersey Jackals, where he became close friends with John Leister, a blond, softly-spoken seventeen-year-old baker. Though there was a decade's difference in their ages, they were both independent and reckless men who did not take kindly to being told what to do.*

Eric had never broken the law before the war – though as a boy he'd idolised the raffish local poachers around whom he grew up – yet he took to his new profession, which more often than not involved looting abandoned houses, with aplomb. Like many thousands during the conflict, his actions were animated not just by hunger but also by a feverish spirit engendered by the strange times in which they were living.

Carefree soon became careless, and he and his companions caught the eye of the local constabulary. Eric and John, or 'Blondie', as he was known, decided to make a run for it and for a while they slept in fields and barns, stealing food whenever they got desperate. The appeal of this vagabond existence soon paled, even for an avowed country boy like Eric, so, along with a young compatriot called Keith Barnes, they contacted an alcoholic fisherman Eric knew and swapped ten bottles of illicitly obtained cognac for an old lifeboat. More cognac and a couple of boxes of cigarettes secured them a motor and thirty gallons of stolen petrol. The two men spent days working on the boat, trying to make it seaworthy. Days before they were ready to depart, a German patrol came across their stash of petrol and they were hauled in front of the island's commandant where Eric and John were sentenced to two years' hard labour in France; Barnes was exonerated of any blame.

★

---

* Another acquaintance during this period was the notorious double agent Eddie Chapman, whom he met during a brief spell behind bars before the Germans came. Eric had been caught disturbing the peace; they both agreed that 'the average Jersey man has no guts'. Eric helped secure Chapman's release, a favour Eddie repaid by writing Eric's first memoir for him a decade or so later.

Dijon prison was a tough place, 'the arsehole of the universe'. The cells smelled like manure, the food was disgusting, and they were surrounded by hardened criminals. One sported a tattoo on his neck that read: 'Executioner, please cut here.' Keen to keep their stay in the prison as short as they possibly could, Eric and John sold their wine ration to other prisoners to help fund an escape bid and were soon in a position to be able to offer enough money to persuade an accomplice to send them a circular bar-cutter and an address where they could go for help on arrival in Paris, hidden in a huge lump of farm butter and a pot of jam respectively. After breaking free from gaol they briefly stayed in the French capital (with a family of unregistered Jews) before they decided it was time to try to make for Marseille. The journey was less successful than they had hoped, largely because they ended up in St Malo instead. Here they hid for several months with some Polish labourers with whom they stayed until their money ran out.

Their freedom did not last much longer than their money, and they were caught and sent back to Jersey, and then on to Camp Ilag VIIIZ, Kreuzberg, an English internment camp in Upper Silesia, which had previously been an asylum for the insane.

Eric Pleasants is revolted from the very first moment by the depressing combination of barbed wire, skeletal guard towers and relentless patrols. He is not much keener on the men he finds there, many of whom, though they hold British passports, have never visited the country, nor speak the language. And anyway, he says, the vast majority are either unlikeable or uninteresting, and sometimes both.

A perverse sense of vanity drives Eric and John to pose as merchant seamen, victims of enemy action; the discovery that merchant seamen receive better rations than ordinary internees helps sustain this pretence. The pair also try to keep themselves entertained by organising sports and boxing matches, but they soon fall prey to the stultifying boredom that is such a fundamental feature of camp life. Monotony becomes the central fact of their existence. They fight, quarrel, forget why they had fought and fight again, read, study, lose their heads over trivial incidents, dream and tell the same stories again and again and again until, thin and worn, they become senseless and hollow.

Eric can feel himself becoming more petty by the hour, drawn into the noxious rivalries that simmer between rival groups of prisoners. He is choked by the thousands of tiny infringements on his freedom: his heart, his lungs, his guts are gripped by a constant tension. Transgression offers relief. He and John use a bow to send messages attached to arrows to the Polish girls working in a laundry on the other side of the wall, and transfer the effort they had previously invested in arranging sporting events into making trouble. It helps that they pay little mind to what the other prisoners think of them.

Eventually the two men cause enough fuss and disruption that a deputation of prisoners demands they be transferred elsewhere, which is how they end up at Marlag Milag Nord, or the 'City of the Lost' as it is known to its denizens. Among the 4,000 inmates Eric recognises old friends from Norfolk and from his wrestling days, and they do their best to fill him in on the complex web of rules that governs the camp. There are two types of men incarcerated here. The passengers – civilians unlucky enough to have been captured at sea by the Germans – each have their own bed with clean white sheets. Eric hears how they have more than their fair share of Red Cross parcels and other luxuries, and he also hears about other kinds of procurement. Male prostitution, his friends tell him, is rife. The seamen are the scum, forced together in squalid, cramped barrack rooms where they must sleep in rows of three-tiered bunks.

But here at least the inmates – a cosmopolitan mixture of Australians, Canadians, Irish, Americans and Chinese – behave like men. It is more to Eric's liking; there is more defiance, more energy. They soon learn that the camp is 'a little Chicago' in which every form of corruption and money-making scheme is possible. This incipient gangster culture inevitably brings violence in its wake: black sailors gang up on white sailors, who fight back with baseball bats, which in turn prompts an arms race as their black counterparts scramble to find weapons of their own. There are too many feuds to keep up with, and the safest thing you can do is keep your head down and try to avoid getting drawn in.

Sometimes it feels as if the violence is, as much as anything else, a defence against tedium. The camp's denizens – including Eric and John – remain as vulnerable to boredom as anyone else held against their will. At Milag, apathy and lethargy cover everything like a fine, suffocating dust. Eric soon learns that Saturday night is booze night, a moment of disproportionate importance within the week. If they are lucky, they drink raisin wine, but more often than not the men make do with hooch made from spirit gum or boot polish: the British camp doctor does not bother going to bed on Saturday nights. And there is another thing Eric cannot help noticing: the camp has a high suicide rate.

One day in May 1944 Milag receives a pair of visitors: Englishmen wearing the SS's distinctive uniform. Closer inspection reveals that in addition to the death's head badge adorning their caps, their uniforms display a number of unusual details: three leopards sit on their collar, one sleeve is adorned with a Union Flag, and the other displays in gothic script the legend 'British Free Corps'.

The British Free Corps (BFC) officially came into being on 1 January 1944. Though broadly inspired by John Amery's Legion of St George – which only ever really existed as a fantasy – it was created by the Waffen SS as a fighting unit in response to the urgent manpower shortage created by the bloodbaths of the Eastern Front. Amery has only a vastly diminished connection with the new organisation: one of its members claimed that his reputation was 'so unsavoury that I did not want him anywhere near me or the Corps', and in time the relationship will be almost entirely severed after someone else in the unit points out to the SS that Amery had Jewish ancestry.

Its existing recruits can crudely be divided into three groups: idealists – many of whom are former Mosleyites – who believe in the unit's stated mission; those who have been tricked or bullied into joining; and those who have sniffed the chance to 'have a grand time at the expense of the Germans'.

The war had left Oswald Mosley's movement in ruins, its members either condemned to detention or dispersed in the forces. The British Union of Fascists were bedevilled by their own many flaws, most of which were embodied flamboyantly by their leader, who did not learn, until it was too late, how quickly promise can curdle into something that looks far more like failure. In truth, Sir Oswald achieved nothing of consequence, and changed nothing that mattered. But if he bequeathed his supporters anything, it was a corrosive loss of faith in the British government and its institutions. An enormous amount of the BUF's energy was devoted to trying to hollow out the authority of those who ran the country. This made it easier for those committed fascists who had fallen into German captivity to convince themselves that the British government had in some sense abdicated its responsibility to the nation by taking them into a war in defence of Poland. The establishment was rotten; it had been humiliated during the fall of France, and it had entered into an alliance with the barbaric Bolsheviks, so what hold could it claim on the loyalty of its subjects, whom it had failed so badly? The terms of the social contract had been broken by the 'old gang' who had betrayed the trust that had once been invested in them, and those who had been formerly bound by it were now free to seek a new kind of settlement.

The idealists are not in a majority. 'He lived solely for the company of women and that was the only reason why he joined the B.F.C.', one of the men would later say of a former comrade. The unit's interpreter, Wilhelm Roessler, remembered of another that he had 'joined the B.F.C. merely to have a good time. Women were certainly a great attraction, and his conversation was almost entirely on this subject. I do not think I ever heard him discussing politics.'

The BFC's attempts at recruitment build on the lessons learned by John Amery. The arrival of Alfred Minchin and Kenneth Berry – who has swapped his lonely life as the sole member of the Legion of St George for the more amply populated BFC – had been anticipated by the delivery of a number of boxes of leaflets a couple of days earlier, the text crafted by Francis McLardy, the 'little Goebbels', who has volunteered to create the unit's propaganda. Some men are more assiduous in their preparation than others: one makes a point of speaking to the camp's commandant in advance in order to ascertain which men might be interested; he even starts keeping a card index listing potential candidates.

Although the leaflets generally contain a high-minded call to help protect civilisation against the depredations of the Soviet Union, as well as a reminder that it is a tragedy that Britain and Germany, two nations that historically have had so much in common, should be at war, in practice the possibility of swapping the dreary restrictions of life in a POW camp for the chance to sleep with local girls and drink yourself stupid appears just as regularly. Minchin, talking of the visit to Milag that tempted Eric Pleasants into joining, remembered that:

> When I recruited the four men I have previously mentioned for the Free Corps, there was no compulsion. I saw them separately and alone in an office at Milag and told them what a wonderful time they would have if they joined, with plenty of forms of pleasure and freedom. They had already seen the Free Corps pamphlets and they volunteered of their own free will. All I got out of it was a trip out across Germany.

The sour note on which he ends gives an indication of the lack of enthusiasm that characterises many of these recruiting trips: it is hard to persuade 'the average decent-minded Englishman [to] have anything to do with a scheme of this nature'. At best they can expect a sullen lack of cooperation, at worst they might end up in danger of physical attack.

This perhaps explains why they resort to lies. The strength of the unit is routinely overstated – men are told that 2,000 troops are waiting to join the corps – and convincing-sounding pieces of information about prospective commanders is included to give at least the appearance of truth. It is even suggested that the enterprise carries some kind of sanction from the British government: one putative recruit has been told by Amery that the unit will probably be joined by the Prince of Wales.

★

Eric Pleasants agrees about the threat of communism (though he tells Minchin and Berry that they are 'stupid bastards' if they think anyone would be foolish enough to sign up to fight on the Eastern Front), and that it is crazy that Britain and Germany should be at war, but he is less keen about the 'fighting shoulder to shoulder bit'. Though the leaflets make little impact outside the latrines, the arrival of the tall, thin, sickly-looking Alfred Minchin, who is obviously horribly nervous, and Kenneth Berry, who hangs back, doing his best to appear as inconspicuous as possible, prompts a flurry of interest, which swiftly becomes hostility.

In the face of this naked aggression Minchin fidgets, stammers and talks incoherently; he is, in Eric's estimation, 'a pathetic clown'. Berry simply disappears. The visit is brought roughly to an end and Minchin rushes out of the camp followed by knots of seamen keen to use their fists on a new target. Almost before the two men have disappeared, Captain Notman posts a sign on his office door warning that anybody who listens to the BFC's entreaties will be committing treason. When he finds out that Pleasants and Leister have talked with Minchin he confronts them; the pair deny that they are considering the possibility of signing up.

But, later that night, as the others sleep, Eric and John talk. They have both long since decided that they will not be taking sides in this conflict, and neither has any intention of collaborating; nobody, they reason, with a dubiously-founded confidence, can force them to fight. Yet they are dying here in this camp, of boredom, of bitterness – maybe this represents their opportunity to escape? They have both tried and failed a few times; now they have been offered a better chance. Of course, they could just sit things out and wait for the Allies to set them free, but they both pride themselves on having a constitutional preference for action. And then there is the good food they have been promised, and the absence of any kind of hard work, the chance to have a real good time, perhaps even female company. Surely nobody with half a mind, in view of their background and record – their troublemaking, their escape attempts – could seriously regard them as traitors. It is clear from the Allied planes that crowd the sky overhead that the Germans are losing the war. What would Eric and John have to gain by joining forces with the Nazis? They talk, and talk more. Pros and cons are weighed up, the consequences of their actions looked at from every possible angle. Finally, they make their choice.

Nearly sixty years later, as he writes his second set of memoirs, Eric will feel neither guilt nor regret at his decision. After all, his actions in 1944 are entirely consistent with the set of values he has constructed for himself: 'The first basic premise was that your life was your own, you were responsible for yourself and no one had the right to manipulate or use you for their own ends.' Let others follow orders like sheep; he will take his own path.

13

I'm sunk. I beg you only, just for my sake, give
us the address of Suzanne

Spring 1944

THESE DAYS SUZANNE Warenghem sleeps with a revolver under her pillow. She fears that some day Harold Cole, the man she used to call 'Paul', and to whom she was briefly married, will be given his freedom and hunt her down. If she sees his vulpine leer again, she knows she will not have long to live.*

There is an irony here, for if either of them is entitled to seek revenge, then surely it is Suzanne. She still remembers, with awful clarity, the events in Lyons, now almost two years past: how after months of evasion and unsettling, furtive activity that seemed designed explicitly to exclude her, Paul had informed her that they would be making a trip to the south together. 'Something went wrong in Paris . . . As for us, we've got to get out of occupied France – and quick.' Then he had handed her a thin piece of paper on which somebody had scrawled a plan of one of the main German fighter aerodromes outside Paris. 'If we can rush this to England soon,' he had told Suzanne, 'the R.A.F. will be able to bomb the airport and destroy dozens of Nazi fighters. I want you to take it, Suzanne, and when we get to Lyons I'll give you an address where you must deliver it.' And there was his other strange behaviour, which only makes sense to her now: the letter

---

* Although their clandestine union – conducted while Cole was in hiding after slipping the Gestapo's clutches – received a priest's blessing, they never went through the official civil ceremony. This must have been a disappointment to Suzanne at the time, but a source of relief very soon afterwards.

he had forced her aunt to write, chastising her for being a foolish and impatient girl; the way he had received the news that she was pregnant with his child with inexplicable passivity ('We'll take care of everything once we get south, Suzy dear'); his anxiety during the last night they spent together about the map of the airfield that was now in her possession: You will deliver it, won't you, darling? It's so important.

Next came the dawn raid by the Vichy police on the room they were occupying in the Hôtel d'Angleterre in Lyons – Harold had apparently been betrayed by an acquaintance to the French authorities, who took a dim view of German-sponsored activity on their territory* – followed by the terrifying solitude of a cold prison cell. And then, perhaps the greatest surprise: a French officer told her that her husband was a traitor, that he had ensured that the incriminating map would be in her possession so that when he gave her up to the Germans – don't you realise, *chérie*, that was always his plan? – he would be able at last to get rid of her.

Already five months pregnant, befuddled and frightened, she had refused to believe the Frenchman. Even after she was shown a dossier of Cole's statements in which he confessed, incontinently, to having betrayed the escape line, Suzanne remained convinced that it was all a lie, that somehow this was an attempt to entrap her . . . except that some of the things he said, some of the details he gave, rang false. And if he had lied about small things, is it possible he could have deceived her regarding larger matters?

It was then that her husband was brought into her room, handcuffed between two police officers. Suzanne had never seen a man behave like that. Hours ago – or was it days? It was hard to keep track of time behind the prison's walls – he had been a

---

* While in many respects Maréchal Pétain led a puppet government, certain pockets within it fought hard to preserve a degree of independence. Notable among these were former members of the Deuxième Bureau, France's military intelligence service, who had been reconstituted into a new organisation, which while nominally devoted to opposing communism and resistance activities, in fact spent much of its time pursuing German collaborators and engaging in clandestine counterespionage against the Third Reich.

dashing, suave British intelligence officer. Now he looked bowed and dishevelled, as if he had been a prisoner for many years already.

An officer stepped forward and slapped Cole twice – the blows were hard, she could see the sting on his cheeks.

'Now, you swine, tell this woman that you are just a dirty traitor. Go down on your knees and ask her to forgive you for what you have done to her.'

Suzanne went white as her husband began to cry. 'Suzanne, it's true, I am a traitor. Everything they say is true. I don't know why – I don't know why I did it. But you know I love you, really. I'll do anything, anything, if you'll only forgive me.'

Harold continued to babble incoherently, his voice tremulous and soaked in tears as the French guards grabbed him roughly and manoeuvred him towards the door. Long after he had been dragged out of the room she could still hear him beseeching her.

The last time she had spoken to him was in the anteroom of the French court just before his trial began. 'Good acting, wasn't it,' he had smirked, before assuring her that he really was a British agent – all she had to do was contact a certain man in Geneva, he would put her right. But by then she knew different.

In October of that year their son Alain Patrick Warenghem was born. The child had been sickly, even before Suzanne realised that the midwife to whom he'd been entrusted was selling his milk ration on the black market. And although she had tried to nurse him back to health, on 12 January 1943 he died in her arms in an unheated hotel room in Marseille. She had found out other things in the intervening period too: how to save his skin her husband had sent men such as the Abbé Carpentier and Dowding and Duprez to their deaths (on 30 June 1943 in a prison in Dortmund, Désiré Didry, Marcel Duhayon, Carpentier, Drotais Dubois, Bruce Dowding were all decapitated within minutes of each other; François Duprez died of exhaustion in April 1944); and how he had stolen money and jewellery from her elderly aunt.

All things considered, it is perhaps unsurprising that Suzanne has decided that if Cole comes to her door, she will shoot him before he has time to open his mouth.

★

One day in the spring of 1944 an urgent message from a *résistant* is passed to her: 'Paul Cole has been set at liberty by the Germans. We know he is somewhere in Paris and he is looking for Suzanne. Tell her to be very careful.' Next she learns that he has been visiting their old haunts, enquiring after her. It is plain that the Nazis have decided she should be arrested, though quite why they are so keen to bring her in is unclear: perhaps it is a test of the newly released Cole's loyalty? While the resistance try to arrange a safe passage to England for her she adopts an alias – Aline Le Gale – and passes from safe house to safe house, pursued continually by her terror at being caught.

As he hunts for Suzanne, Cole reprises the methods that had brought him so much success two years earlier. The Crépel family, who had long been an unstintingly generous source of lunches for Harold and Suzanne, and false identity cards for his escape network, are the recipients of one of his first visits.

When he arrives just after seven in the morning, the door is answered by a pyjama-wearing monsieur. Harold Cole looks different, Crépel notes; somehow less merry, lacking in the gallant confidence that had always been so much a part of his persona. The immaculate suits have given way to shapeless, unpressed trousers and shoes with a hole the size of a franc piece in their sole. He is accompanied by a man who Cole tells Crépel is an American officer.

'He's an agent of the United States Intelligence,' Cole informs the man at whose table he has sat so many times before. 'Can you help him in the same way as you've helped so many others, and get him false identity papers?'

Forewarned by Suzanne, Crépel plays dumb. What are you talking about, he asks, I don't know what you mean. Cole persists: 'But you can't leave this man in the lurch; you've simply got to help him to escape, like you always did before.'

The three men are joined by Crépel's daughters, Jeanne and Francine. As alert to the danger posed by Cole as her father, Francine pretends that Cole is asking about extra ration cards.

The American officer says little. Occasionally, when he thinks nobody's eyes are on him, he looks at his watch. Then he whispers something into Cole's ear. Crépel is only able to catch a fragment – '. . . the address of your wife' – but it is enough to confirm his suspicions.

'My dear Paul, the last time we saw her she was with you.'

'No, but you *must* tell me. It's terribly important.' There is something terrifying and empty about the raggedness of Cole's voice.

The doorbell rings – it is suddenly clear that the operation and its timings have been rehearsed many times before – and Jeanne opens the door to two men wearing long grey mackintoshes. Though they are both holding revolvers, Jeanne tries to shut them out, but they force their way in, brandishing their identity cards.

'You are hiding two spies here,' says one of the men as he brushes past them and, with a pantomime brutality, handcuffs Cole and the American.

Cole makes another plea, appearing oblivious both to how desperate he sounds and how transparent the attempt at deception has become. 'You see, it's all up with us now. But I am sure if you will just give us the address of Suzanne nothing will be done to you.'

Finally tired of the charade, the American shakes his handcuffs loose and begins to interrogate the family. For a moment it looks as if their attempts at obstruction will be rewarded with a trip to the Gestapo's cells, but eventually it is just the sullen Harold – still handcuffed – who is led away. In the moment before he ducks under the doorframe he turns to the Crépel family. 'I'm sunk. I beg you only, just for my sake, give us the address of Suzanne.'

A few days later, it is Eugène Durand's turn. Cole watches as the Gestapo arrive at the restaurant and arrest the waiter Georges Croisé before forcing him to take them to Durand's home. There are few preliminaries this time and within seconds the sixty-year-old proprietor of the Chope du Pont Neuf is bundled into a waiting black Citroën. Cole gives Croisé a bashful smile: 'Sorry, old man, it's just the luck of the war, you know.' They speed off to the Avenue Foch, where Durand is introduced to the wide range of methods of persuasion kept there by the Gestapo. Again and again – as his head is submerged in icy water, as a soldering lamp is applied to his skin – they ask him the same question: 'Suzanne – where is she now?' After eight days, he is released. Durand's body is bloodied, bruised and broken, but he has told them nothing.

As if stung by the failure of his visit to the Crépel family, Cole moves quickly in the days after Durand's arrest. Julien de la Tour, a waiter who had been at Cole's wedding to Suzanne, is sent, along with his wife, to a concentration camp. Agnes Kirman, who had bravely sheltered so many pilots in her apartment, is subjected to a brutal interrogation before being dispatched to Ravensbrück. The indefatigable, honourable Monsieur Besnard – another of the linchpins of the escape line – is snatched from his home in Saint-Martin-le-Beau and taken to a German prison. Both Kirman and Besnard will die in captivity.

Harold Cole is a busy man in the spring of 1944. During the intervals in his attempts to mop up what remains of the escape organisation he worked so hard to build, he returns to 84 Avenue Foch, an imposing house on one of Paris's grandest boulevards that has been occupied by the Gestapo since France's surrender four years ago.

Cole's new boss is Hans Kieffer, a policeman in Karlsruhe before the war who is now the head of the Sicherheitsdienst (SD) – the SS and Nazi Party's intelligence agency – in Paris. The stocky, curly-haired Kieffer is given to sentimentality, and is acknowledged to have a lively sense of humour (so much so that when three of the prisoners held at Avenue Foch go missing, leaving a note for him – 'As you will have realised when you get this, we are trying to escape. Now that I hope we shall not be meeting again, I should like to thank you for the good treatment we have received here, and to say that we shall not forget it. Wishing you the best of luck in the chase that will follow, but much better luck to ourselves' – he finds it hilarious and does not penalise them when they are recaptured), and yet he is also capable of acts of terrible ruthlessness, such as the murder in cold blood of Allied prisoners of war.*

Kieffer has particular responsibility for counter-espionage and is busily engaged both in infiltrating Allied intelligence and sabotage networks and in intercepting agents the moment they land in France. The task he seems to relish most is the *Funkspiel* (the wireless game), which involves playing captured radio sets and their operators back against the British. If London can be persuaded agents are transmitting of their own free will, then it can also be encouraged to parachute in still more operatives, who can then be turned themselves. The potential rewards are great, so too are the risks.

If a captured agent makes an error in his transmission, or something about the phrasing or tone of the communication jars with its recipients, then it will alert the British to the subterfuge and enable them to embark on their own deception. It is a game of deceit and trickery, where the slightest slip can prove fatal. Kieffer knows that having a native English speaker at his elbow, a man who plainly has a gift for slipping easily into the persona of another human being, will give him an incalculable advantage. The *Funkspiel* is complemented by the work of agents provocateurs, who pose as organisers in the French Section of Britain's Special Operations Executive (SOE), building up resistance networks, linking with others, arranging drops of weapons and supplies. Operating from his own room on the building's top floor, Cole gets to work.

With the same patience and skill that he had employed two years earlier in the north of France, he begins to construct a new chain of connections; designed to entangle and deceive, it is a negative of the organisation he once ran. Like him its recruits are marginal characters whose existence is uncertain; there is no place for the self-sacrifice and idealism that had infused the contributions of men like the Abbé Carpentier and François Duprez. Vodez de la Tour, a Swiss waiter at the Restaurant de la Taverne du Palais, specialises in infiltrating Gestapo agents into groups of British soldiers travelling back to England. Nicolas Pakomof, the Russian manager of the Cabaret NOX, is another Gestapo agent

---

* Kieffer will later be convicted of war crimes and hanged by Albert Pierrepoint.

who feeds Cole a steady stream of information. Mademoiselle Weiss lives in a *pension* in Rue du Languedoc, Toulouse; she claims to be a member of the Deuxième Bureau, but actually assists Cole in arranging the 'escapes' of British soldiers. Another Russian emigré, Helman, who lives in Auch, is the man Cole knows he can contact when difficulties arise.

Cole helps Kieffer as together they begin to lay traps, spread disinformation; soon their work bears fruit: *résistants* are woken at dawn to find a Gestapo officer standing at the foot of their bed; SOE agents parachuting into France are met by a welcome committee consisting of a squad of grim-faced German soldiers. Sometimes Harold himself participates, luring former contacts into indiscretions that are punished almost as soon as the words have left their mouths. He finds this work profitable in other ways: once an apartment's occupant has been hauled off what is to stop him and his colleagues from looting the premises?

The men and women brought to the Avenue Foch are expected to talk. If they are reluctant to do so, their interrogators employ a range of methods to encourage them to open up. After the war, one of their victims would itemise the Germans' techniques.

1. The lash.
2. The bath [*baignoire*]: the victim was plunged head-first into a tub of cold water until he was asphyxiated. Then they applied artificial respiration . . .
3. Electric current: the terminals were placed on the hands, then on the feet, in the ears, then one in the anus and one on the end of the penis.
4. Crushing the testicles in a press specially made for the purpose. Twisting the testicles was frequent.
5. Hanging: the patient's hands were handcuffed together behind his back. A hook was slipped through his handcuffs and the victim was lifted up by a pulley . . . The arms were often dislocated.
6. Burning with a soldering lamp or with matches.

Cole is often in attendance at these torture sessions, an onlooker as stubborn victims are subjected to the *baignoire*, and worse. While the cockney is at the Avenue Foch, Pierre Brossolette, a handsome French journalist and *résistant*, is half-drowned and beaten into unconsciousness several times but refuses to talk. In one of the brief interludes between his interrogators' visits he leaps from a fifth-floor window. He dies in hospital two days later, having preserved his silence. Brossolette's resilience is unusual; there is a reason why the Gestapo employ these methods: they work. While they are not sufficient to trap Suzanne, who in the early part of 1944 is spirited out of the country by the SOE, the net Cole casts over France does manage to sweep in Charlotte Leblanc, another stalwart member of his old network. During his interrogation in 1945 Cole will speak of how 'Mme. Leblanc had always been of great assistance to me and loved me deeply. I had been in touch with her from various prisons, by letter.' Harold rewards the patience and support she has offered him by arranging her arrest (although, inevitably, he can explain this: 'I had agreed to participating in her arrest and interrogation because I felt it was the only way to prevent her being deported and to get her liberty').

Whatever the truth, it is not long after he has helped arrange her release that they become lovers. The affair is attended by Cole's familiar evasions, half-truths and outright falsehoods. 'I am a German officer because I am German on my mother's side,' he tells her one day, which must come as a surprise to Charlotte, since for the previous three years she had been under the impression that he was an SOE agent; she has even borrowed 100,000 francs on his behalf to assist his endeavours. Before long he is boasting about the large houses he and his mother own in London and of the sizeable savings he has waiting for him in the British capital. On the faith of this they become engaged and in May 1944 he draws up a will made out in her favour. He undertakes to leave her £260,000, which he says is on deposit at the Westminster Bank, and a further £428,000 in shares, which are held at Barclay's. A John St Just McDonald KC is to be the document's executor. Amid the bluster there are flashes of something else too, brief moments where it is possible to detect human fragments stirring behind the endless stream of lies. Promise me you will never leave me, he beseeches her.

An intimate relationship with Harold Cole, *any* relationship with him, is bewildering, full of false paths and trapdoors. On the one hand there is his gallantry and his easy charm and his mountebank's gift for homing in with unerring dexterity on the things you value most, and on the other there is a welter of evidence that forces you to ask yourself terrible, uncomfortable questions: what a fool I am to be taken in so easily, how can I believe a word he says? But although it must be tempting to try to break away sometimes, he is skilful at quelling doubts, even at those moments when he has been caught in a lie. Skilful too at sending you tumbling off balance with a lachrymose display of vulnerability, or at reminding you of the hundreds of tiny hooks that he has sunk into you: you have been with me every step of the way, you have incriminated yourself too, if I am damned then so are you.

A year or so later, as he sits waiting for his death in a prison cell, Harold will exchange letters with his erstwhile lover. His correspondence to Charlotte does not survive, but her reply gives a startling insight into how curious, how tortuous, was their time together. There is something narcotic about Harold Cole: everything seems to make sense while you are in his company; it is only later, when his influence has left your veins, that you can begin to see things clearly.

> You make a great mistake if you think I am resentful because you gave me to the Gestapo . . . You saved me from Av. Foch; that is true. Why? I do not know it yet. Weakness perhaps? You took the decision to save me *after our first conversation* we had privately at Av. Foch; and this was possible only because of my attitude, and *after what I had told you*, facing the danger with a calm certainty in the ideal for which I was fighting. You felt very uncomfortable then and had a hard time to face me? The fact, that you saved my life, brought suspicion on me, from the French and British Intelligence and I was arrested for THE THIRD TIME. You do expect me to say THANK YOU? . . . I want to tell you one thing: although, you have always showed great respect for me, I reproach your attitude, as you should have been satisfied with my friendship only, if you really had the least consideration . . .

Her letter is followed by a list of questions that show how evasive Harold has been, how fractured and uncommitted his loyalties, how cynical his manipulations. Charlotte's tone is bruised and stupefied; it is clear that she no longer trusts a single word he has said to her.

. . .

4. Why have you played with my religious sentiments?

. . .

11. Why have you begged to visit me at Nexon's Camp?

12. Why have you insisted on having so much procuration and Will made, when they are of no value and you have not a bean to your name? Why? You knew I was not doing things for return of interest; I was only very anxious about the debts I was making for you, as you were always asking for more and there seemed no end to it.

. . .

18. What have you done with the papers and surgical instruments I was keeping and hiding in 1941, for the British Officers who escaped?

. . .

22. Why have you stolen my valise and my leather bag; did you really have the intention to come back to see me?

23. Have you nearly been through 'Court marshal' [sic] because of my iron box?

24. What is the reward you expected for me? Why did you say that you were proud of me at Av. Foch?

. . .

28. Have you ever made an effort to change from your black past and begin a better life? Why have you had such a life?

. . .

30. Will you really tell me the whole truth? What are you hoping or expecting from me anyway, after having deceived and robbed me?

If only the scoundrel would wake up! If you are not prepared to speak the truth, there is no need to answer!

Signed Ch. Leblanc

P.S. Oh! If you have not given me to the Germans, why were you leading the Gestapo men to my own flat? What a surprise to find me in?
C.L.

The abiding impression is of emptiness, as if Harold Cole were a tabula rasa; blank, ready to be inscribed by the worst that this tragic age has to offer. It would be easy – had he not left a trail of death and betrayal in his wake – to convince yourself that perhaps he had never existed at all.

Harold Cole is not the only curious English bird who has come to roost in the building. There is also Captain John Renshaw Starr. Starr, who reports to Cole, had previously been one of SOE's most prized agents, but in 1943 he was captured, tortured and then sent to the Avenue Foch. Here he plays a queer kind of role, somewhere between captive and court jester. The plump, avuncular Starr, whom the Gestapo agents there have taken to calling 'Bob', is a warm and friendly presence in this otherwise unlucky location. On Sunday mornings he visits each of the cells in turn, opening the door and exchanging a few cheerful words with the prisoners, before giving them biscuits, chocolates and cigarettes. When the guards learn that before the war he had been a poster artist, they start to ask him to paint their portraits. But there is something about his amiability, something about the freedom he enjoys at the Avenue Foch that does not add up.

Perhaps it is because the men he visits in their cells know that the liberties Bob enjoys –the whisky he is given at Christmas, those days when the Germans take him out to restaurants* – have been dearly bought. At Kieffer's behest he employs his artistic gifts to draw maps of resistance networks and, like Cole, he is brought in during interrogations of captured agents. It is not a good idea to confide anything in Starr that you would rather the

---

* In her book *The Starr Affair*, Jean Overton Fuller names a certain 'Placke' as a guest at one of these lunches. It is tempting to infer that this is John Amery's drinking partner Werner Plack, though I have not been able to determine any more either way.

Gestapo did not know as well. How strange it must be for recently apprehended agents to encounter, in this place of death and pain, Bob's compromised geniality. Uncomfortable too to find yourself, during your interrogation, watched by the cockney's tiny foxlike eyes.

But neither Harold nor Bob will be at the Avenue Foch much longer, for the Allies are coming closer. First Angers and Alençon fall; then Chartres. Those with keen ears claim to be able to hear gunfire in the distance. Suddenly the parks and squares of Paris fill up with soldiers returned from the front. Food supplies are dwindling rapidly, the electricity is only turned on once or twice a day and all the cinemas are closed. On 15 August the French police go on strike – the same day the last transport of Jews is sent to Germany: 2,453 souls.

The Germans heave countless crates of documents on to lorries; those they decide to leave behind are burned in huge pyres. Purple-faced generals, accompanied by elegant blonde women who look as if they are on their way to fashionable resorts, spill out of the city's smart hotels and decant themselves into expensive cars. A flotilla of ambulances, hearses and any other vehicle that can be commandeered at short notice drives off overloaded with four years' worth of plunder: medicines, Louis XVI furniture, works of art, rolls of carpets, food, machinery, bicycles. The streets and boulevards are so thronged with cars, trucks and artillery that it is difficult to believe that they will ever manage their escape – a stark contrast to the government buildings, which are empty now except for a few scraps of unwanted furniture and a forlorn chorus of unanswered telephones.

Harold Cole holds out until 19 August when at eleven in the morning he gets into a powerful red sports car and joins the column of SD vehicles heading out of the city in the direction of Nancy. Cole is, for once, wearing glasses, but perhaps this is less noteworthy than the fact that he is armed with a sub-machine gun and pistol and wearing a Gestapo uniform. It seems that at last he has decided where his loyalties lie.

14

It was all a big sham act

Summer 1944

ONE OF THE first things Eric Pleasants notices about the British Free Corps is that it has far fewer recruits than the posters had suggested. Perhaps seventeen, at most.* And if there is a shortfall in terms of quantity, it does not seem, at least at first, as if this will be compensated for by the unit's quality. In between handshakes Eric reckons he can tell pretty quickly which men are driven by fanatic belief and which are only quickened by a kind of moral squalor. There is a strange atmosphere too: a combination of guilt and bewilderment that leaves the men self-conscious and abashed, like schoolboys waiting outside their headmaster's office. This fantastic quality, which is perhaps enhanced by their surroundings – they are housed in the ancient cloisters of the Haus Germania, a former monastery in the small town of Hildesheim that had been converted into a 'political school' for training SS recruits from across Europe; a curious home for the British Free Corps, but they will stay here almost until the end of the war – will never be dispelled. Once the introductions have been made the men are forced to sit through a long, dreary stretch of propaganda, and, again, Eric is struck by the unit's lack of ardour. He looks around him and realises that none of the men believes a word of what they are hearing; but their fear of the Germans, and fear of one another, is driving them down strange paths. Years later he will reflect again on the

---

* At its largest, the unit consisted of twenty-seven men.

anxiety and lies that swirled around the volunteers: 'It was all a big sham act.'

The recruits are asked to sign a form. There is no pledge of allegiance to Adolf Hitler – whoever drafted it is evidently anxious to avoid including anything that will trouble those who have any doubts about the enterprise – but nonetheless a handful, including Berry, refuse to add their autographs. Nobody seems to care too much. The declaration reads:

> I am not of Jewish extraction, I have not been in prison and I will not in anyway help Germany against the English crown and commonwealth but I am willing to join the British Free Corps, composed entirely of English officers and men and under no way to come under German military discipline or become part of the German Army.

SS-Hauptsturmführer Hans Roepke, the German officer who is responsible for the unit – a gentle soul who knows that he is better off here than on the Eastern Front – also offers them all the chance to change their names; it is, he says, 'advisable'. Most follow his suggestion. Eric Pleasants himself assumes the name Erich Doran; he remains uninterested in any life the other men might lead beyond the boundaries of their assumed identities.

If any of them still laboured under the illusion that the unit has in any way been endorsed by the British Government, this small administrative step is a signal that they have stepped outside the law. They are renegades now. For some this is a central part of the unit's appeal, and they enjoy the thrill that comes with knowing they are outlaws. The men hang a photograph of Edward VIII – whom they recognise as their true king – on the barracks wall. They feel that he too is a rebel and they admire him for it. Whenever they have parties, the men always make sure to toast the Duke of Windsor, the man who in the aftermath of victory the Germans will return to the throne of an occupied Britain. Or so they have been told.

There is much about the corps that is familiar to those who were in the British Union of Fascists before the war: the same sense of being in an elite (self-selected, of course); the same sense of participation in a righteous crusade; even the uniforms are closer to the old black shirts than the battledress they discarded when they left their stalags. For others the BFC represents a beguiling lacuna in an otherwise tedious existence. Eric notes that Minchin – the man who had recruited him and John Leister – sometimes appears dazed by his luck at having found such a role.

There is a photo of Minchin posing with Berry and another recruit, taken for *Front Zeitung*, a German soldiers' paper. They seem relaxed, happy. Their peaked caps rest on their heads at a jaunty angle. Alfred Minchin has a kind of coiled, sharply tailored confidence and it is not hard to imagine him swaggering off once the shot had been taken. Berry does not give the impression of someone burning with shame or remorse. Rather, he looks like a boy who has finally been allowed to play with his older brother's friends. When he isn't complaining, Berry likes to tell people how proud he is to have been the first member of the Legion of St George.

The early days of the unit are characterised by a wariness, an instinctive lack of trust among the men; perhaps it is to be expected under the circumstances. The fanatics are a risk: who knows where they will take the unit? But they also offer an alibi: *it wasn't my idea, I was lost, he told me what to do.* After a week Pleasants reckons he has the measure of pretty much everyone there. One of the things that strikes him is that everyone is playing a role – and some seem to have difficulty in telling where the boundary between reality and fantasy lies. They have not just adopted new names, but new personalities too. Although Eric imagines himself the superior of the men around him, even he is not immune to the desire to tinker with certain elements of his past. He boasts about his time as one of Mosley's chucking-out gang and then, when questioned, withdraws this claim, explaining he had only made it to curry favour with McLardy and Roepke. Perhaps nobody here is really who, or what, they say they are.

Certain patterns swiftly emerge at Hildesheim. The first is that, outside the formal structures of authority laid down by the

Germans, a kind of oligarchy has asserted itself, an uneasy hierarchy that reflects wider divisions. The ringleaders are known as the 'Big Six', a swaggering, defiant appellation that belies the shrill assertions many of them will later make of their innocence. The strange and intense Thomas Cooper, who has already seen action on the Eastern Front with the SS, is nominally its 'boss', but his authority is not unchallenged. Two other men in particular seem keen to obtain greater power within the unit.

One is the rakish, slippery New Zealander Roy Courlander, a tea planter turned petty thief turned corporal in the intelligence corps. He is an adventurer and a cynic who can make being out only for yourself seem like a noble pursuit. His stories are wild and full of life. There is the one about how in a Cairo bar he met some White Russians: once he'd got some drinks inside him he told them he was one too, born in Riga (this is not true, but his first stepfather had been a Latvian Jew 'so the deception was easier than it might have been'). They made a 'terrific fuss' of him and gave him membership of the White Russian Club. Or how after he was captured in Greece and, having made several failed attempts to escape, he was 'trussed up with barbed wires, hands behind back and hands tied to feet' and thrown into the guard's van with a Jew who'd been tied up in same way.

Sometimes, when in his cups or just over-excited, he will concede that he is liable to play fast and loose with the truth – then he stares, wonderingly, as if he cannot believe that anybody would be foolish enough to fall for his tall tales. He has a high opinion of his own abilities, and a correspondingly low view of the gifts of others. It rankles with him that despite his education he was never made an officer; maybe things will be different in this new unit. Courlander understands that Hitler has promised that if the unit secures 5,000 recruits, he would be willing to support the formation of a 'provisional British Government' based in the Channel Islands, with the Duke of Windsor held ready for when London is captured. After the invasion, Sir Oswald Mosley will serve as the newly conquered country's prime minister, William Joyce as minister of information and John Amery as foreign minister. But in the meantime the bumptious Courlander is planning to 'run the show' here at Hildesheim.

By contrast, Francis McLardy is a shy, unhappy and lonely young man who had been training as a chemist before the war. McLardy was also the district treasurer and district leader of the BUF's Waterloo Division in Liverpool. Effeminate and small in size, with 'curly brown hair, a shifty look, and hesitant in speech', he keeps himself to himself most of the time, but can talk for hours about National Socialism when the mood takes him. He is one of the few in the unit who has read *Mein Kampf* and is not afraid to show off his erudition, but though the others acknowledge his intelligence, few respect him. McLardy had been serving in the Royal Army Medical Corps when he was captured in France in 1940, and the word is that he gave himself up willingly: 'He was about the most fanatical of them all but regardless of this was a big coward both physically and morally. He was a sneak and a tell tale . . . He told me he came over to the German side at the fall of France, that he had no intentions of trying to get away at Dunkirk.' His cowardice: that is something they all agree on.

Thomas Cooper is the most sinister man in the ranks of the British Free Corps. In the uncanny mugshot taken by the British authorities in 1945 his head is shaved – he looks like a precursor to the skinheads of the late seventies – but what really strikes you are his eyes. Or, rather, the way in which the shadow from his brow almost obliterates them. His gaze is steady but almost hidden by two crude daubs of black.

In 1943 he still has dark hair, which he brushes straight back to frame a sallow, clean-shaven face. Cooper's pimpled cheeks suggest that he is barely out of adolescence but his greasy skin and gauche demeanour are partially offset by his immaculate SS sergeant's uniform, and a mannered air of supercilious authority. Some of his eccentricities are harmless. When he first met the other members of the BFC he pretended he was German, and spoke to them in a curious, broken English. One day Eric notices Cooper taking a small slip of white paper from his pocket and reading it softly to himself. Cooper explains that it is a Latin quotation he is learning by heart because, 'It's easy to lead a conversation into the required direction where such a quotation can be used to impress your listeners with the extent of your learning.'

His intensity and sheer strangeness spook many of the others in the corps, but his position ensures that he remains an unavoidable presence in their lives. In his free time – when he is not associating with the Germans – he roams into the other men's rooms, like a garrulous but unsavoury apparition, hoping to engage them in conversation about one of his many obsessions. Sometimes he loses his temper and screams that he is fed up with England and Germany and will go to Japan as they are probably the future rulers of the world. Behind his back, the others call him the 'Mikado'.

As they eat in the mess he boasts how he had been forced to flee England after killing a Jew in a street fight. And that while serving with the SS in Poland and Russia he 'had himself shot over 200 Poles and 80 Jews in one day – by merely lining them up against a wall and shooting them down'. On one occasion, Cooper tells the others, with something that sounds like pride, he was surrounded by so much gore that he was up to his ankles in blood. He talks too of another time, in Warsaw.

> He said he was at that time in charge of a squad of Ukrainian volunteers and they were conducting a purge through the ghetto. His attention was drawn to a house by reason of loud screams issuing from the back of it. On going inside the house he found in the top flat a bunch of these Ukrainians holding at bay with pistols some twenty Jews. On asking them what the noise was about they told him in broken German that they had found a new way of killing Jews. This was done simply by opening the window wide and two men each grabbing an arm and a leg and flinging the Jew through the open window. The small children and babies followed their parents because they said they would only grow into big Jews.

While the rest of the men are somewhat awed by Cooper's gruesome braggadocio, Eric remains sceptical, regarding it as yet another piece of playacting. Cooper is certainly a perplexing, insecure creature perfectly capable of adopting a piece of barrack-room gossip as his own in a perverse attempt to impress others. Whether his boasts are true or not they are a reminder that while Hildesheim must feel as if it exists in a different world entirely to the horror of the Russian Front, or the cold-blooded cruelty of the Holocaust, by joining the BFC the men have linked hands with the same organisation that has been – and will continue to be until the war's end – responsible for cruelty and murder on a scale perhaps unparalleled in human history. Men wearing their uniform have killed Poles, Germans, Estonians, Russians, Latvians, Dutch, Norwegians, Frenchmen, Ukrainians in their thousands. They have also killed Britons – perhaps friends, neighbours or family of the Englishmen at Hildesheim. While some in the BFC might claim that they have only joined to drink and fuck girls, or to escape from the grinding discomfort of the POW camps, their motives are irrelevant: they are part of the Third Reich's machinery now.

Their days blur one into the other; sometimes it seems as if the constant quarrelling, the unseemly battles for power and favour, are just ways of passing the time. He might affect to keep a distance from the unit's turbulence, yet Pleasants is frequently drawn into the arguments that ensure an atmosphere of squalid mistrust reigns continually over the camp. Perhaps this is a price one pays on becoming a traitor – a corrosive suspicion of other men's motives that descends like a fog and guarantees that you will never again be able to see anything, or anyone, clearly. Amid the ennui there is a fluidity about life at Hildesheim. Such loyalties as exist are in a state of perpetual flux, alliances are broken almost as soon as they are formed, and whether through accident or design your status can change from one moment to the next. For a while Eric is a PT instructor at Hildesheim and one of the unit's policemen, and then in the time it would take you to blink everything has changed and he finds himself in trouble, charged with insubordination and fomenting discontent. But in the charged, claustrophobic yet curiously weightless atmosphere in the camp the disgrace does not endure and is soon forgotten.

What structure there is to the days comes with the dispiriting sham of the eight o'clock parade, which is supervised by another of the Big Six, 'Tug' Wilson, who lives half his life in a strange world full of bumptious dreams of power and glory. His alias at Hildesheim is Montgomery and he likes to give the impression he is related to the hero of El Alamein, bristling with pleasure if anyone makes the connection. From time to time a puzzled German will ask Eric what such an eminent figure is doing in the BFC.

When he is not fantasising about being a celebrated general Wilson spends his time trying to seduce local girls. Sometime he sits on the steps of Haus Germania delivering raucous renditions of ribald English songs – the highlight of his oeuvre is an extraordinarily filthy version of 'My Girl Salome'.*

On a good day they can expect perhaps half the men to attend the parade; the others might still be scrambling over a wall at the back of the barracks, or will simply decide to stay with whatever company they'd found the night before. They can always plead accident or illness, and almost always get away with it – Eric Pleasants only ever attends half a dozen during his whole time in the unit. There is no need even to go to pay parades, for it is possible to make so much money selling cigarettes and chocolate from their Red Cross parcels on the black market that collecting a salary is rendered quite pointless.

Wilson calls to attention those men who have bothered to turn up, and then Cooper carries out his inspection. Cooper concludes events with a rousing 'Heil Hitler' before they all march to the dining room for breakfast and to collect their daily ration of sausage and bread or substitute cheese.

They had been told by Roepke that in the German Army every rank from corporal upwards should be greeted with a salute. The men are as wary of this as they are of any other forms of discipline, only saluting NCOs and officers if it is unavoidable. They carry this reluctance into the dining hall, where they are also expected to give the Nazi salute if Germans are present. So

---

* Eventually Tug caught gonorrhoea from a Danish SS girl. He refused all advice and offers of help and instead attempted to cure himself. When he failed – he alone was surprised by this – he announced that he had done so deliberately as part of a scheme to infect as many people as possible, and thus undermine the German war effort. He was, he said, combining business with pleasure.

they try to go before or after their nominal comrades, but even this is not enough to prevent regular disturbances in the dining hall and complaints about food. They all miss English tea and cigarettes.

Back in their billets, each day stretches out before them: endless, empty, futile. There are attempts at improving the men through a series of lectures. Tug Wilson speaks on British Field Craft, Heighes on the mechanism of the German rifle, their interpreter Roessler instructs the BFC on the German language and Courlander lectures on politics. Pleasants himself gives lessons on health and efficiency, though he rarely bothers to attend any of the other sessions. When he is not delivering speeches on Nazi ideology, McLardy locks himself away to read Schopenhauer and Liam O'Flaherty. There is a recreation room with a dartboard, and games of table tennis with Danes and Norwegians, but most of the men are just waiting for the moment when the whistle is blown for tea.

Sometimes they speculate about what will happen when Germany wins the war – they prefer not to think about the alternative. One day one of the recruits asks Cooper about Britain's fate. 'We'll just make a little garden city out of the place,' comes the reply. 'All being well, I hope to become a Gauleiter over there, and to meet some of the swine who made me work for nothing.'

Eric establishes a daily routine that allows him, as much as possible, to avoid the rest of the men. This antipathy is reciprocated. The other recruits quickly learn that the supposed pacifist has a vicious temper and that he is a bully inclined to use his fists to get his own way. Many are afraid of him, so by and large they leave him to his own devices. When the weather allows, he and John sunbathe, otherwise there is a shed they can use to exercise in, filled with a range of equipment. They discover that life, at least compared with the rigours of their former camp, has become almost pleasant.

In truth, the men all live for the evenings, when they can head into Hildesheim, a small, respectable town that reminds Eric of Bath. They sprawl loutishly in its cafés and swagger around its streets, where they belt out the BFC's marching song, sung to the tune of 'Bless 'em All!':

> It's onward to Moscow we go.
> Up to our cobblers in snow,
> Digging slip trenches through six feet of ice,
> Living on sauerkraut and tortured by lice;
> Oh, we'll never get rid of them all,
> As over our bodies they crawl,
> They don't give the shits to the Red Russian Blitz,
> As they do to the British Free Corps.

The availability of women represents a welcome advance on masturbating furtively in a barracks room shared by thirty other men, and most embrace the opportunity with lubricious enthusiasm. They drink until they are sick and then fight over girls, before stumbling home to nurse their wounds. It is perhaps unsurprising that many suffer from agonising and repeated doses of the clap.*

But perhaps there is something else too. Many have been away from home since 1939. They have been parted from wives and girlfriends, starved of conversation with women, of the affection and tenderness that they took for granted in peacetime. It is a reminder, if one were needed, of the extent to which the conflict has torn a jagged hole in what is supposed to be the prime of their lives.

Eric has a steady girlfriend, Anneliese Nitzschne, an SS secretary whom he fondly refers to as 'My Dear Little Enemy'. Though he does not think her particularly pretty he admires her hazel eyes, which meet his without wavering, and her voice's soft cadences, and the way a hint of mischief always seems to hover at the edges of her smile. She has, he says, 'a gigantic soul and enormous courage', and, looking back on their relationship many years later, he will decide that all the many miseries he endured were a price well worth paying for the privilege of having known her.

---

* The only member of the BFC ever to be admitted to hospital was a man with a particularly uncomfortable sexually transmitted disease.

Eric and John had rationalised their decision to join the BFC by telling themselves that they were only doing so to enhance their chances of escape. But a combination of the pleasure he takes in Anneliese's company, and the imminence of Germany's defeat, means that they agree that there is little point in going on the run – far better to sit out the war in the relative comfort of Hildesheim. Why not make the best of the situation?

The tensions and resentment that course through the unit are never far away. One day, during a lecture on economics by McLardy, Wood, an Australian, is asked what he thinks about the subject. He replies that we are 'not interested in economics or anything to do with Germany; we are here for a good time and anyone who stops in this racket are not Englishmen but bastards.'

Roepke, who is still nominally in charge of the corps, is a popular figure at the Haus Germania. He had studied law in America before the war and speaks perfect English; now, having served on the Russian Front, he is keen to make the most of what should have been a soft posting. His new charges, however, seem almost wilfully determined to make his life as tricky as possible. It is not just the drunken chaos they are so fond of causing in town, though Roepke becomes accustomed to fielding the burgomaster of Hildesheim's complaints about BFC behaviour. The relationship between the recruits and Roepke is instructive, and emblematic of the BFC's vexed attitude towards the Germans.

On the one hand Roepke is a likeable personality. On the other, although in joining the unit they have allied themselves with the Nazis, there remains a squeamishness about being perceived as being too close to them – as if proximity risks moral contagion. When McLardy demands that Roepke intervene during his disputes with Cooper or Courlander, it draws contempt from the others. Another man, Reid, is accused of 'running tales to Roepke'. One night the well-meaning Roepke organises a friendship evening in which British and German soldiers are supposed to mingle. The Englishmen quickly get drunk and start running their mouths off. Fists begin to fly and a despairing Roepke is forced to wade in and pull the men apart.

The recruits try to insist that they should wear British battle-dress and be led by British officers; as if these things will be guarantors of their independence and integrity rather than a fig leaf designed to obscure the truth: that they are Britons in the service of their country's enemy. There is a word for men like that, but nobody much likes to use it.

15

John Amery n'est peut-être pas 'quite right in the head'

Summer 1944

HERE HE GOES again. 'My target is a minimum of five thousand ex-prisoners, and I am quite confident of getting that number very easily, as I told Himmler this morning . . . Those who are already members will go canvassing round the camps under the supervision of Tom Cooper, and once the prisoners realize what a wonderful time they will have outside, what with women and wine and the opportunity to work for our Führer, I'm sure the rush will be so great that we'll have to refuse applicants . . . You just watch out for the publicity we're going to give the Corps, and you will see at once I'm the right man to run the scheme. I told Himmler this morning it is my intention to turn what has been a near-failure into a resounding success. In fact five thousand is a conservative estimate, and we can't go wrong.'

John Amery is busy helping to loop a hangman's noose around his own neck. He is being handed the rope by the broad-shouldered, heavy-boned figure of Quartermaster John 'Busty' Brown, to whom he has been introduced by Thomas Cooper. With Michelle Thomas sitting beside him, John, who has plainly been drinking – he begins the meeting by producing two bottles of French brandy, which he boasts he has bought cheaply on the black market – harangues him for forty-five minutes. He is loquacious, boastful and drifts constantly into delusion: he did not spend the morning with Himmler, there are not thousands of men waiting to join the British Free Corps, and any influence he might have had over the unit has long since been prised out of his hands.

As Amery tells him how he had been working with Jacques Doriot to help him set up the LVG, Brown primly notes Michelle's strong scent and perfectly manicured hands, and that though she is dressed smartly, very little is left to the imagination. Amery goes on to assert that in truth he deserves most of the credit for the French organisation's success. He is committed to ensuring that its British equivalent enjoys the same fortune and claims to be paying close attention to the matter.

Brown is of the opinion that Amery's fervour is of the kind that one usually finds at the bottom of a bottle, but he keeps this to himself. And there is something else that Brown omits to tell Amery: every word from this conversation will find its way back to the intelligence services in London. Brown has carefully cultivated a reputation as a German sympathiser, in the process courting opprobrium from his fellow POWs. He is also one of MI6's most valued operators. A committed Christian (which helps steady his nerves) and a former member of the BUF (which is a useful way of securing the Germans' trust), he was approached by the secret services during the chaos of the fall of France and taught how he could establish a line of communication to them in England, even from within the barbed-wire fence of a POW camp. ('If you get taken prisoner, you can probably be of very great use to us – in fact more use than you are now.')* Through a combination of sycophancy, cunning and ostentatious cooperation he has obtained a position of responsibility within his camp, which in turn has allowed him a certain amount of freedom. Because he has won the trust of the German hierarchy, Brown is able to travel almost at will (a privilege he has used to establish a far-reaching black-market operation, which he soon learns is as useful for bribing Nazi guards as it is for obtaining intelligence).

Since then he has sent a steady stream of information on troop

---

* There is a discrepancy here between his memoir and the statement he gave after the war, in which he claims that he began sending intelligence back to Britain only at the end of 1942. It has been argued that Brown's motives were not quite as pure as he would subsequently portray them in his posthumously published book. Roy Courlander, writing from his prison cell, was a vigorous proponent of this theory.

dispositions and the locations of important buildings, while also keeping an eye on the real traitors. Can he, he has been asked by London, confirm Amery's identity beyond all possible doubt? Is the man who claims to be the son of a member of Churchill's Cabinet really who he says he is? As their conversation about the BFC comes to an end Amery asks Brown if he has a copy of his book and whether he knows if it is read much in the camps. Sensing an opportunity, Brown replies that it does not really matter if it is read avidly or used as loo paper; what is important is that nobody really believes he is the son of a Cabinet minister – the rumour is that the book was actually written by some German. 'But that's a bloody silly thing to say,' replies Amery. 'Ask Tom [Cooper] whether I wrote it or not.'

Still indignant, he produces his British passport, and throws it across the table to Brown. 'Well, see if that will satisfy the buggers.'

Brown inspects it. 'There's no doubt it's your passport,' he says blandly, happy to have accomplished his mission with a minimum of fuss.

Brown is not the only man who has been put on the tail of renegades like Amery. As Allied troops sweep across mainland Europe, they are followed by men intent on finding out everything they can. Soldiers newly released from prison camps are button-holed by harried-looking intelligence officers and asked to revisit encounters they can only dimly recollect. *What did he look like? What did he say? What did he promise you? Was he carrying a gun? Was he wearing a uniform? Please, try to remember. Tell me everything you can.*

Many of those still living in occupied territory begin to collect information on Cole and Joyce and Pleasants too: they know that a reckoning will soon come, so they make notes of everything the traitors say, take pictures of them surrounded by German officers; all ready for the day when Britain will want an accounting.

John Amery is frequently called on to speak at rallies in Paris. His speeches do not appear to have a proselytising function – who, by now, has not made up their mind about which side they are on? – rather they seemed to be part of an attempt to stiffen the spirits of an increasingly embattled portion of the French population. The near certain prospect of an Allied landing has instilled a quiet dread in the hearts of those Europeans who have thrown in their lot with the Nazis, while emboldening the previously quiescent. In France particularly the resistance grows notably more active as the year wears on.

In June 1944, in the dazzling art deco surroundings of the Gaumont Palace cinema in Paris, Amery addresses 2,000 people at the invitation of the Groupe de Collaboration and the Légion des Volontaires Français contre le Bolschevisme. The audience is drawn from these organisations, as well as from members of the Rassemblement National Populaire (Déat's party) and the Partie Populaire Française (Doriot's party).

John Amery stands up, a frail, nervous figure. As he walks to the podium his right leg drags fractionally behind him, the legacy of a car accident; and then he is there, speaking his queer, demotic French.

> First of all let's get things straight . . . you must not expect me to have come here today to say a lot of bad things against my country, because I adore my country like all of you adore yours . . . What I detest and what I have been fighting against for the last ten years are the clique of people in London who pushed the British Empire into this crazy war when not a soul menaced us.

He moves quickly to try to silence any suggestions that his treachery has been bought. I am rich, he tells them; though the price of whisky and cigarettes has risen, it is no concern of mine . . . except, he concedes, 'Mr Churchill has taken my money but I hope I will get it back off him with interest.' (This is a lie, but it will be among the smallest of his untruths today.)

Warming to his theme, he begins to rail against those who he claims have dragged the British flag and British honour in the mud by conducting a terrorist war against women, children and invalids. He idles for a moment, long enough to insult Neville Chamberlain's 'old undertaker's face' (the poor man has been dead almost four years), and to take a further swipe at 'Winston Churchill, and his syphilitic boy friend Roosevelt' (which is rich coming from a man who contracted the disease working as a rent boy). They are feeble insults, but it seems to be what the crowd expects. He returns once more to his main argument:

> And that's why I am fighting . . . because if we had the sense to come over to the side of civilisation and Europe now we could save most of our Empire . . . and even if Germany occupies England we can save something but if ever Churchill wins there will remain just nothing at all.

Changing tone, he addresses the uncomfortable reality that, even as he speaks, the bridgehead around Normandy is getting exponentially larger, and that Soviet troops are swarming into Belorussia – pushing closer and closer to the Third Reich's borders with every passing day. In the face of this, Amery is able to summon a surprising level of confidence: 'the sand glass is running out,' he tells the crowd, his voice notably rougher now than it had been during his radio broadcasts.

> I am no military expert, but I am convinced that when a few more months have gone by, something is going to happen and that the invaders of our Europe are going to receive a most terrific and shattering smash on the nose . . . We are sure that the invasion of Europe is going to be paid for by an unbelievable disaster, a thousand times worse than Gallipoli. And that, at that moment, the morale of our population is going to break because at last they will have understood. We are waiting with impatience for that to happen.

Does Amery, a man who styles himself as a 'student of reality', believe what he is saying? Does anyone in the audience? Everyone assembled here knows that if the Nazis lose they can expect little mercy from their countrymen; they will have no home in the new Europe. These are desperate times, and what are needed now – more than any disheartening dose of reality – are sustaining lies. And anyway, the world has experienced so much that is strange and new over the last decade that perhaps expecting some radical realignment of the Continent's loyalties is not so unreasonable: who could have predicted Hitler's 1939 pact with Stalin?

For the men and women collected in this cinema, the wickedness of the Soviet Union, the danger it poses to the rest of the world, is self-evident. It cannot be long before the British wake up to this and demand change.

Swaying uneasily and gripping the lectern as if he needs its support, he finishes on a rousing note. 'We know that if we wish to save civilisation it can only be done with the German Army and with Adolf Hitler . . . we stand unreservedly with the revolutionaries of Europe.' Loud applause breaks out.

For Amery this is just another waypoint on his lonely and restive drift around what remains of occupied Europe, a journey that seems to have been designed by his German masters to keep him as far away from Berlin as possible. Accompanied by his 'wife', an SS bodyguard, a representative of the Foreign Office, and, more often than not, Plack, he visits Belgrade, Slovakia, Hungary, Italy, Croatia, the Bohemian protectorate, Norway, Ghent, Bordeaux, Oslo, Rennes.* After a while his destinations blur into one: the theatre or concert hall draped in swastika flags; the 'Heil' for the

---

* In a letter his mother claims that he visited Russia too. There is also a note in the file MI6 kept on him that suggests he may have become embroiled in assisting the Abwehr in its operations against the SOE and French resistance. An agent operating in the Nice area reported that 'his chiefs had learned that . . . Amery has formed an organisation of British subjects living in France and Germany who were to make contact with the French Resistance groups as British Officers and then turn them over to the Gestapo. This organisation had possibilities of sending personal messages over the BBC, but could not send arms.' Amery's name also appears on a card discovered in the Abwehr's index system. In a letter to Captain G.M. Liddell, Lt Col Lord Rothschild notes that 'although the card is unfortunately lacking in details it must I should think constitute evidence of a very grave nature against Amery.' This discovery was supplemented by information that Amery met with Captain Konrad Ameln and Major Abshagen of the Abwehr for lunch in June 1944 at the Château Chevreloup in Roquencourt, a village seven miles from Paris. It was eventually decided that the material available would not be admissible as evidence, and if further enquiries were made, their results did not make their way into Amery's file. The matter remains an intriguing, and potentially highly incriminating, footnote.

victory of German weapons and the future Führer of Europe, Adolf Hitler; the small reception attended by representatives of the German diplomatic corps and prominent local collaborators; the drunken stumble later that evening – with or without Plack and Michelle – to a brothel.

Sometimes he is greeted with enthusiasm (the appearance of 'Sir John Amery' in Ghent is heralded by posters, radio announcements and a reception at the Flemish Club), more often he can expect to be the object of a kind of sceptical curiosity (a Parisian noted that his friend went to see Amery speak because he had a reputation as a 'comique'), and there are even occasions when he is booed off stage (in Oslo 'the whole audience got up and made a terrific noise so that for the next ten minutes he could not speak'). Few regard the contents of his speeches as anything other than hackneyed, but there is a mild frisson to be had from hearing them delivered by an Englishman, and the son of a Cabinet minister to boot.

John Amery had once been a headline act, now he is a novelty turn on a never-ending tour of the provinces. Having being relatively insulated in Paris and Berlin by his friendships with Déat and Doriot and the support of the Nazi hierarchy, his grand tour of the Continent also exposes him to scalding doses of opprobrium. One Frenchman remarked how 'None of my friends went to the speeches, it would have been a dishonour.' Amery has now entered the strange half-world that inevitably traps all traitors. Hated in your own country, but also despised, and perhaps feared, certainly mistrusted, by the majority of the nation with whom you have thrown in your lot. The charge of being a traitor hangs above you constantly – an accusation written in crimson letters. During a speech in Paris he tried to anticipate the audience's questions by posing one of his own: 'Why are you here, instead of being in England. Are you a traitor?' His answer was unambiguous. 'No, I am not a traitor; the traitors are those who have led their country into this disastrous war for England.'

Twenty years later, Guy Burgess and Kim Philby will live out lonely, drink-soaked lives in Soviet Russia. Philby, famously, is banned from even entering the headquarters of the KGB, whom he had served so faithfully for over thirty years. Amery's experience looks remarkably similar, held at arm's length by his German handlers, condemned to an ambiguous existence by his treachery. As another Frenchman said of him: 'He was regarded as a person who was not nice to know, even by the Germans who knew him. The Germans also considered him a traitor. His only motive in working for them was the financial one, he often did it for money and to have a good time.' Although Amery undoubtedly benefited materially from his actions, conducting a life of comparative extravagance that would have been unimaginable to most Europeans who lived through the war, it would be unfair to characterise this as the sole, or even primary reason for his treachery. It is, however, indicative of the transgressive nature of his crime. To be capable of betraying one's country is, in many people's eyes, to render oneself equally capable of any other kind of violation. It occludes the possibility that you might have been motivated for the 'right' reasons, that idealism might have any part to play in your decision-making process.

But what is remarkable is that Amery does not stop. His life thus far has been a litany of abandoned projects and broken commitments, but now he reveals an inner strength that few could have suspected he possessed. He seems fired by a burning sense of mission, talking endlessly about saving civilisation, and showing no sign of discontent at the life he has made for himself. 'What I have done I shall never regret,' he tells the Norwegian audience when they try to jeer him into silence. And in a report to Fritz Hesse at the Foreign Office about his visit to Scandinavia he argues that:

> The trip caused a most extraordinary sensation in this country . . . Not only were we able to give heart and courage to the members of Quisling's party, the National Sammling, but the fear of Bolchevism [sic], the fact that an Englishman of a well known family also esposed [sic] the cause of 'the defence of civilisation in collaboration with Germany', brought to our side many so far neutral persons, mainly among the shipowners, the herring kings and so on.

This cheery account of a triumphant visit reads like a fabrication designed to convince the Germans of his continuing value to them. It might also be attributable to what his psychological report described as a 'persistent tendency to grandiosity of thought and action of a mildly megalomaniac type'. His peregrinations are in one sense a living hell; in another they represent a test of the purity and endurance his faith demands. Each step he takes round the Continent takes him closer to the man he wants to be – fascism is now as much a part of him as his lisp, his limp and his thin face.

It is unfortunate that despite his sense of heroic purpose he is still attended by many of his old flaws. Although one part of his brain has been gilded by august conceptions of his own destiny, the other appears to treat degradation as his just deserts. In his mind he inhabits both palace and sewer. His drinking has continued, even accelerated. A French collaborator writing a memo in 1944 to a colleague during the war observes that the cognac Amery absorbs abundantly from the morning onwards does little to help his moral or mental equilibrium. He slips into English as he tries to make sense of the man he has just met: '*A ce sujet, je dirais volontiers que John Amery n'est peut-être pas "quite right in the head"*.' Another collaborator, who only knows him by reputation, feels able to claim confidently that 'The German authorities had expelled him because of his bad habits, and that he was disliked in Germany.' This is not technically true, but for many the rumour has the heft of fact. Although Amery may think he is the bearer of an urgent warning, to his audiences he might easily come across as the mephitic drunk who tells the same tedious story over and over again.

John Amery has joined William and Margaret Joyce's race to the bottom of the bottle, his body and soul alike slowly being eroded by the alcohol he pours down his throat. He appears in a photograph taken after he'd given a lecture in Antwerp (in which he'd been introduced by a local dignitary, who had stressed that Amery was no traitor, simply a man dedicated to serving Great Britain). It must be after dinner: brandy, coffee and cigars are on the tables. Amery occupies the middle of the picture, turning slightly awkwardly towards the camera. He is surrounded by uniformed German officers and officials from the Flemish collaborationist VNV. Two of the men are grinning foolishly. The other two seem more circumspect, as if they're asking themselves whether there might be a price to pay for being captured in this picture. John's suit looks good, his hair carefully parted, but his face – thin before – is now gaunt, almost cadaverous. Gone is the confident glare of ten years ago, his eyes are raddled, afraid; he seems to be barely keeping things together.

In the winter of 1942 a young Austrian diplomat called Reinhard Spitzy escorted John Amery and Jeanine Barde from Berlin to Paris. As they had drunk and talked and laughed, Spitzy was struck forcefully by John's courage and determination: 'For him there was no turning back. Perhaps the whole thing would not last very much longer and come to a bitter end. His own conscience was clear. Whichever way things might turn out he intended to stick at it and enjoy life to the full.' A year and a half after they met, Reinhard Spitzy runs into Amery again at an evening reception at the Foreign Press Club. The Englishman with whom he'd formed such an immediate connection is helplessly drunk, incapable even of conducting a reasonable conversation. Spitzy is told by others at the party that as the war situation has deteriorated, Amery has been suffering from increasingly frequent and profound bouts of depression. He learns too of the tragic circumstances surrounding Jeanine Barde's death. The horrified young Austrian leaves the room; it is far from clear whether Amery has even recognised him.

16

I am causing my Mother the greatest agony she as ever felt

Autumn 1944

ON A SATURDAY morning towards the end of the summer of 1944 the war finally comes to Hildesheim. In the space of five minutes, a town that had looked like a storybook illustration is devastated by an Allied air raid.

Something shifts in all the Britons there, and it is clear that the good life at Haus Germania is over. Insubordination and indiscipline settle like cobwebs upon the camp. Petty incident follows petty incident, tempers fray, and the relationship between the BFC and their German handlers sinks still further into acrimony.

Even young Kenneth Berry – whom the rest of the men look on as a kid, who says ridiculous things, who nobody takes seriously – is emboldened by the obtuse defiance that has become the unit's governing spirit. He begins to go out of his way to be awkward and difficult with the Germans and, far too late, comes to understand that he had been tricked.

> I was only 14½ years old when I was taken prisoner and it was Amery who influenced me into all this and he gave me some books to read, 'Fire over England', 'England Faces Europe', and 'The Root of the War' written by him. I also thought when he spoke to me that he was Foreign Secretary of England. I had got into this thing so deeply that I couldn't get out and had been warned that the penalty for leaving the Free Corps was death.

For a while he tries to make the best of the situation, perhaps to prove he is not the innocent the others take him for. He dabbles in selling Red Cross parcels on the black market, and gains a reputation as a racketeer. Sometimes he claims to be a National Socialist, but the suspicion lingers that he is just a fool.

Eventually Berry gives in to his distress. On a recruiting visit to Milag he approaches Captain Notman – the man whom John Amery had once tried to threaten – to confess about his role in the BFC, and to tell him that he does not want to stay in. Notman encourages Berry to make a statement.

> but its not been for the last month that I am a traitor to England and by what I am doing I am causing my Mother the greatest agony she as ever felt, so I implore you not for my sake but for me Parents sake to help me out of the mess I am in. Ill face anything if I can get out, but if it is possible to see Brigadier Major Fortune I think he will see that I don't go down the mines. Because I am scareded for my health and I would I have realised like to come to Milag with Real Englishmen, I thank you Sir.

Berry is not alone in realising that unless he acts soon, his actions are likely to catch up with him. When they had first joined up it was hard to imagine that their decision would have any consequences; they were working-class men who were used to being ignored, why would this be any different? But now a reckoning is in sight. Hildesheim is seized by a passion for writing fiction as the men begin to construct explanations for their presence in the BFC: *I joined only so I could escape; I joined only so I could sabotage it; I joined only so I could gather information.*

Thomas Cooper had once dreamed of the British Free Corps growing to such proportions that they would be sent to the Russian Front to link up with the SS, and that when the people of Britain got to know that so many divisions were fighting the Russians, they would call off the war with Germany and fight the Reds. He had put all his faith in the final victory of the Third Reich; now he has been forced to contemplate the hideous likelihood of its defeat. After the D-Day landings, he becomes visibly upset, and soon afterwards he approaches Quartermaster John Brown to see if he can assist with his intelligence-gathering activities. Cooper tells him that 'he had come to the conclusion that he had been a bloody fool, that England would win the war, that Germany was bound to lose and that he wanted to do something to make his own situation better if he got captured.'*

Eric Pleasants does not appear overly troubled by his own act of treachery. Because, of course, according to his own moral code, he has committed no such crime. How can a man who answers only to himself, who feels no allegiance to any country, or any creed other than frank self-interest, be a traitor? Who, precisely, has he betrayed? The fact that he is a member of Hitler's army has no political or moral significance for him. Why should it?

But if he is not obviously bothered by the ethical dimension of his behaviour, then it is nevertheless still clear that he will have to face its practical consequences. In 1940 he had been determined to escape the war, to prove that no government could stamp on him, drag him around or grind him down until his life was no longer his own. But, now, almost absently-mindedly, the implacable force of the war is beginning to draw him to its breast. As the autumn of 1944 drags on, and the number of Allied planes flying unchallenged in the skies above Hildesheim multiplies, he comes to realise that, whether or not he himself recognises the legitimacy of the case that would be built against him, the British government would be sure to take a close interest in his actions if he fell into its hands.

Time passes, nothing happens at Hildesheim. And then, suddenly, it does: the men discover that plans are afoot to send the unit to the Eastern Front. At the backs of their minds they have always known that this was a possibility; nevertheless the news comes as a great shock. It would not do to display any visible signs of alarm, but from now on the threat hangs above them constantly, intruding into every corner of their lives. The soldiers in the BFC act differently: some lose themselves in drinking and fucking, others retreat into themselves, and one or two simply remain

---

* After the war Cooper would claim, with impressive chutzpah, that he had joined the BFC in 'the capacity of an Intelligence man' out of a desire to serve his country.

oblivious. Sometimes men discover that they cannot suppress the tension that roils inside them: Wilson collapses to the ground with his mouth foaming, seized by an epileptic fit. For his part, Eric Pleasants withdraws into himself, reacting violently at the slightest encroachment on his personal space. In the course of one trivial disagreement, he strikes out and shatters another man's jaw.

In the lull before their deployment, Berry writes to the man who had lured him into this mess. 'Well Mr Amery it is a long time since I saw or heard from you last and I sometimes wonder how you are getting on. I hope you are in good health the same as this leaves me.' Berry goes on to say that he is still in the BFC, and that though there are rumours that they are to be sent to the front in two weeks, 'I don't think there is anything in it.' Berry chatters on in the manner of a boy writing home from school, the misery apparent in his statement to Notman seemingly banished: 'we are doing Pioneer training for the Past six weeks and I like it very much . . . I speak a Great lot of German now, so I can tell a few were to get of . . . I must close know because it is time for me to go on Garde duty. all the Boys sends there Best Regards. so goodbye for the time.'

Amery does not reply.

Proximity to 'Tug' Wilson can be uncomfortable, but he has the authority to issue papers that enable them to travel by train to Berlin at weekends, and John and Eric take advantage of this perk whenever possible; it is a relief from the pettiness and alienation of barracks life. The German capital is becoming an ever stranger, wilder city, and it is not always easy to predict how their trips will turn out. The metropolis, so different from the bucolic calm of Hildesheim, is now bomb-torn and filled with gruesomely wounded men. On one visit, Eric finds himself helping to deliver a baby.

Sometimes they are entrusted with messages for Major Vivian Stranders, another of the oddballs to have been drawn into the BFC's orbit. Stranders was born in England but came to Germany long before the war. He took Germany nationality, became one of Hitler's earliest adherents, and has enjoyed a distinguished academic career. Now he is a major in the Waffen SS and has been attached to the England Committee to liaise with the BFC. Eric considers him 'a funny little man . . . small, overbearing and theatrical' and, like the rest of the unit, he chooses to avoid 'the Gnome', whenever possible.

After one visit to his office on Fehrbelliner Strasse in June 1944 the Gnome offers to give Eric and John a lift back to their lodgings. Eric thinks it is probably so Stranders can show off the car the SS have just given him, but if that means they don't have to take tea with him in 'the English manner' – a burlesque of home they have all come to dread – then that is no bad thing.

En route, Stranders suggests dropping by the Rundfunkhaus; neither Eric nor John demurs. They are waved in by the SS sentries at the entrance and descend what feel like countless steps to a room where a party is taking place. The atmosphere is overwhelming, surreal, though they will learn later that celebrations – though perhaps that is not the correct word – like this take place here almost every day. Eric is struck by the air of 'desperate gaiety, the defiant bravado that hung with the smell of alcohol and cigarette smoke'. Something about the crowded room repulses him.

There is a flurry of hurried introductions. Eric shakes hands with a host of new acquaintances, but has no time to take in any names. Later he will remember how he found himself standing next to a small man in a frayed blue serge suit when he heard Major Stranders say, 'William Joyce.' 'I took a small, weak, clammy hand in mine. It left a cold patch in my palm for minutes afterwards. The sad, pale face was scarred from cheek to chin down one side. The man seemed to me a corpse, a walking, talking corpse.'

Eric cannot believe that this is the infamous Lord Haw-Haw. Cannot believe that one of the most notorious men on the planet should remind him so strongly 'of the owner of a dirty bookshop, continually washing his hands with invisible soap and water, putting up a futile struggle to make an impression of importance with the person to whom he was talking'. It strikes him that perhaps Lord Haw-Haw's mesmeric voice has gained its strength by sapping the vitality from his body. Joyce's eyes look wild, tired and a little mad.

Eric retires to a chair in the corner of the room where he remains for a while, happy to stay on the party's margins. He feels out of place here and is beginning to regret agreeing to come. Across the room he can see the slight figure of John Amery, who is perched on a sofa between two young women, clearly struggling to hold their attention. When it is clear he is not going to get anywhere, Amery, with a bottle of champagne in one hand, shambles over to Eric, who is unimpressed by his fellow renegade's pathetic attempts to appear carefree and debonair.

'Have a drink, old chap,' Amery drawls.

Pleasants has just enough time to say that he doesn't drink before the ear-splitting noise of the air-raid siren interrupts. Within seconds the sky is ablaze and buildings are toppling around them – a sight that fills Eric with awe. He stands, stock-still, noting that nobody else looks as if they're going to abandon the party for the comparative safety of the Rundfunkhaus's bomb cellar.

Eric's reverie is broken by Amery's thin, funny, insistent voice. 'Every time I drink champagne from now on, I am going to ask for an air raid as well. It makes the good old "champers" taste better.'

How strange to be here with these two notorious traitors. Both gaunt; both plainly physically and mentally diminished. They should have done more to look after their bodies, like Eric, who has carried his through the war as carefully as he might a cup filled to the brim with water across a crowded room. There is such a vivid difference in their respective situations – their raddled features seem as much a mark of guilt as they are a consequence of dissipation – that Eric finds it hard to acknowledge that he too has betrayed his country, even as he has stayed faithful to the promptings of his own conscience.

He can count twenty people in this smoke-filled room; all, as far as he can see, horrifically drunk. A small space has been cleared for use as an impromptu dance floor, and in between pawing at each other, a handful of couples make clumsy but determined attempts at the foxtrot. He watches drink spill everywhere as with an air of desperation glasses are filled by men and women who are trying, and failing, to pretend that they are not scared.

Again he drifts off into his thoughts, and again they are interrupted. Someone touches his shoulder. He looks up into the pleasant, smiling face of Margaret Joyce: 'We are having a cocktail party to-night. I suppose we will have to have it in the cellars. There are a lot of our guests who don't like bombs with their drinks. You *will* come, won't you?'

Why isn't he drinking, she asks, waving a bottle of Scotch in front of his face. Before he can think to tell her that he simply doesn't feel like it she passes him a glass and sits beside him.

'Oh, come on, darling,' she says in a loud, intoxicated voice. 'Drink and be merry for tomorrow we hang.'

Eric does not reply. After a short silence William Joyce re-enters the conversation, leaning forward and lugubriously observing that they can't hang us, we're Germans.

A somewhat desultory discussion follows in which they discuss who precisely the Allies could hang. John Amery, who is still cradling his champagne, makes his own, rather hesitant, contribution: 'I suppose I'll be all right, I'm Spanish.'

Eric looks across to where a minute or two before there had been dancing; now couples lie on the floor, kissing and fondling each other. A girl takes off her dress; everyone else claps and cheers.

Eric is alone with Margaret now, the others departed in search of drink or cigarettes. He notices her long, shapely silk-stockinged legs. Something passes between them: for a while they continue to make small talk, and ask each other trivial questions, but it seems they both know what they want. Eric is aware that outside this room tonight, hundreds will be killed or injured by the cascade of steel being hurled on to the ravaged city. Yet for the moment he has found another way to escape the conflict that has raged around him for the last five years. They turn off the radio before the evening's propaganda broadcast can begin, before that voice can fill the air around them and hurl them back into the war.

★

One day, soon after the attack on Hildesheim, Eric, along with seven others, manages to dodge fatigue duty and instead sunbathes in the cloister. They stretch out on the stone, practically naked, close their eyes and talk lazily among themselves.

The idyll is broken by the appearance of a group of Germans, led by a stocky, bull-necked officer whose chest is covered with rows of medals. For a second the sight of eight barely clothed Englishmen is enough to reduce the officer to an enraged silence, and then he erupts, screaming, '*Stehen Sie auf, Lumpen!*' at the prone forms in front of him. He receives no response. There is another pause, and then finally one of the Englishmen turns indolently around. 'Please keep quiet or fuck off!' he screams back.

The Englishmen are sent for two months to a punishment camp, where they work on a road-making gang and the food is so bad that they are forced to supplement their diet by stealing potatoes, peas and a pig, which is cleaned with a safety razor then stewed – the worst eight weeks of Pleasants's war, he will later say. Their misery is such that, having previously demanded to be released from the BFC, Eric and the others end up petitioning to be allowed to return which, eventually, they do, to SS Wildemann Kaserne, Dresden, where the unit has been redeployed. Eric is promoted to Rotenführer and in February 1945 he even travels with Leister on a fruitless recruiting mission to a civilian intern-ment camp. The official line now is that the time for dissipation is over. But, in truth, little or nothing has changed.

For his part, Eric chooses to spend as much time as possible in the gym. So much time in fact that along with another member of the BFC – William Alexander, a tough Glaswegian – he is sent as part of a group of boxers from Wildemann to Prague to fight a team drawn from the occupying army there. He is tickled by the thought that they are probably the only Britons who will ever represent the SS in a sporting competition. It is this image of Eric Pleasants that endures. Well-fed, well-watered, sweat plas-tering his curly hair to his brow as he happily exchanges punches with blond troopers in a well-heated gym. His unyielding self-involvement allows him to ignore the fact that by this point in the war, several thousand German soldiers are dying each day;

many of these casualties are old men, or boys too young to shave. In the Battle of the Bulge men from both sides sit shivering in frozen holes scraped out of the ground. Eighty per cent of Russian males born in 1923 will not live beyond 1945. And Eric plays. When bad news intrudes, he is able to dismiss it as yet another example of the madness and futility of war.

Refusal can be an act of bravery in itself. In *The Missing of the Somme*, Geoff Dyer speculates that 'Perhaps the real heroes of 1914–18, then, are those who refused to obey and to fight, who actively rejected the passivity forced upon them by the war, who reasserted their right not to suffer, not to have things done to them.' By this calculation Eric Pleasants's actions are infused by a kind of heroism: he has refused to participate in what he knows will be a bloodbath. He will not fight other men's wars for them. But while his arguments – that he recognises no difference between nations; that he 'couldn't see any justification for killing people with whom I had no personal argument merely because I was ordered to do so' – may sound admirable, the particular nature of the slaughter and cruelty of the last five years has rendered these sentiments obsolete. They are like the cavalry regiments who realised, almost overnight, that they had no place amid the trenches and machine guns of the Great War.

Can Eric really believe that there is some kind of moral equivalence between the armies charged with making Hitler's murderous visions manifest, and those committed to stopping them? And if he does not want to live in a world governed by the Nazis, is he happy to leave the task of defeating the Third Reich to other people? Surely now he must understand that he will not be forgiven for putting on his field-grey battledress each morning. For almost every day over the course of the last years, men wearing that uniform have dropped bombs on to British streets, driven bayonets through British throats, driven tanks over broken British bodies. They have suffered and sacrificed and lost while he has been sparring cheerfully with members of the SS.

17

I can't bear to see the city dying. She is dying
and will never be saved

Early spring 1945

THESE CIGARETTES ARE poison. It is the beginning of March, and William Joyce is taking the bus to work. He has been sleeping badly for longer than he cares to think, baths have become a rare luxury, the heating has long since given up the ghost, his knee is giving him hell and he has more work than he can cope with. Even after five and a half years of war his blessed superiors (who do little or no productive writing themselves, he cannot help but note) do not understand that a man like William needs certain amenities; they treat writing as if it were plumbing. When was the last time he had a proper smoke, one that didn't leave him gasping and sick and yet still strangely desperate for another lungful?

Like almost everyone else in Berlin, William and Margaret have seen their rations steadily but inexorably reduced. William is thin now, threadbare, scar-faced and lame; he claims to be nearly starving: 'Hunger is a terrible master,' he observes, with something approaching objective fascination. He is not always so sanguine: 'I could almost eat the fucking bunker,' he snarls on another occasion. Once upon a time his chest was terrific, his waist was small, his legs and arm muscles terrific too. But recently an old acquaintance spotted him and was shocked to note that the Irishman's appearance has descended to that of an 'Apache'.

William's work has deteriorated in tandem with his body. He

knows that neither his scripts nor his performances bear any comparison to those he delivered at the beginning of the war. Where once Joyce used to spend weeks on end at the Rundfunkhaus, it has become rare for him to be there for even an hour each day and he arrives in the studio at the very last possible minute. Sometimes there are flashes of his old high spirits and he banters cheerfully with the girls on duty, but more often than not he cuts a feeble figure, a man shivering with anxiety and exhaustion.

It is drinking that fills his time now. He has adopted a system of writing out his scripts two days in advance, so that should he be incapable of coherent thought before his broadcast, he will still have something to read out. Perhaps this does not matter so much any more. At the beginning of the war his talks were fed on a rich diet of crushing victories; nowadays they subsist on the thinnest of gruel: rumours, hope and fantasy. How can he be expected to deliver six consecutive *Views on the News* without actually knowing any news? It is hard to believe that he lives in the same country that once tore through Europe in a matter of months.

The Joyces have become used to living amid destruction. In 1933 Hitler had boasted of Berlin that 'In ten years nobody will recognize the city.' It is one of his few predictions that have come true. The Royal Library, the imperial palace, castle after castle, Tempelhof, the buildings along Unter den Linden, are all tangled piles of twisted metal and savaged bricks. Even the zoo has been largely reduced to rubble, its only survivors a bull elephant named Siam, a bull hippopotamus and a few apes.*

White-faced, eyes ringed red with exhaustion, covered in brick dust that clings to them like a suffocating second skin, Berliners now live like ghosts in a world of ruins. Bodies are left to rot in devastated buildings: the sight of a putrefying corpse is now an everyday occurrence. In some streets burst pipes gush water,

---

* One minor positive from the zoo's destruction was that in its aftermath there was a sudden glut of exotic meat in the city – bear sausage was particularly popular.

flooding them to create a mournful parody of Venice. Stinking greasy clouds of smoke float across what remains of the rooftops, occasionally casting the capital into a ghoulish darkness. In houses whose façades have collapsed, passers-by can see the pictures hanging on what had once been a sitting room wall, or a piano exposed on the remnants of the floor.

To the east, the sky appears tinged blood red and from that direction comes the ominous rumble of the Soviet heavy artillery (William dismisses those who tell him that they can hear the guns as 'suffering from auditory hallucinations'). Barricades – disused trams, rail carriages filled with rubble, railway sleepers stacked three metres high – are erected wherever possible, and William and Margaret watch as trenches and tank traps are dug outside their apartment.

Every day refugees from the east flood into Berlin, bringing with them terrible stories of rape and blood. They talk with horror of the Russians burning their churches and other old buildings; the Soviets, they say, are intent on obliterating every trace of their way of life and history. As the city contemplates its own destruction, an atmosphere of 'febrile exhaustion, terrible foreboding and despair' descends on it; the Heil Hitler has been replaced by *bleib übrig* – 'survive'. For some, life becomes unendurable. Four thousand suicides are registered in Berlin in April 1945; many more go unrecorded.

One afternoon, as William and Margaret attempt to pick their way through a heap of twisted metal girders in the street, he stops and says sadly, 'I can't bear to see the city dying. She is dying and will never be saved.' It seems as if the apocalyptic visions that once tore his sleep to shreds have been made flesh. Everything William has hoped for, the system in which he has invested so much emotional energy, and for which he abandoned a country that he loved to his very marrow, is disintegrating. That his grim prophecies have been vindicated gives him no relief.

William tells himself that he has been proved right. Germany is destroyed and communism stronger than ever. It is all right for him, he has the courage of his convictions, can stand up to the consequences, but he feels an immeasurable sorrow as he contemplates the likely fates of the men and women alongside whom he has lived for the last six years. 'Oh Lord! I pity them in the awakening that is coming. Trouble is that so many decent and innocent people have to suffer.'

These days his mind is turning with increasing frequency to the past, using it as a refuge so he doesn't have to face up to the truth of the present. When he can he repeats the morning rituals he had enjoyed so much in London: tea, bread (he longs for toast and butter) and a cigarette in bed as he reads the newspapers (which have nothing in them). William thinks about long-lost lovers (he has been, he believes, 'luckier in the marriages I did not contract than in those I did. Exception was Mary, with whom I am sure success would have been certain. Too *late* now! Anyway, Margaret and I pull together, if not always in the same direction'), and returns again and again to the events that led to his departure from England. He still loves the country, dearly – perhaps only now can he admit this to himself – and the thought that he might be regarded as a traitor burns at him. Who, now, will appreciate the sacrifices he was willing to make for the sake of that nation? He writes, with some anguish: 'Those who have never felt for England as I was taught to feel, those who have never suffered for England as I was made to suffer during long years, will not know or under-stand what that decision meant.'

In March 1945 the SD produce a report on the morale of the German people, as they have done throughout the war. It concludes that the population are not, as the Nazi hierarchy have often feared, about to embark on insurrection, but they do discover 'deep-seated disappointment at misplaced trust, a feeling of grief, despondency, bitterness and growing rage, above all among those who have known nothing in this war other than sacrifice and work'.

This is an uncannily accurate description of William Joyce's emotional topography. He too is prostrate with horror at the way matters have turned out. He has always combined a fanat-ical loyalty to the principles of National Socialism (nothing will dim his belief that it remains 'a splendid doctrine') with a

healthy disdain for those who he feels have prostituted its ideals
– men like Hermann Goering, with his lacquered nails and
rouged face, and ludicrous uniforms with epaulettes the 'size
of a fruit tart', who washes cocaine down with Dom Pérignon
and treats the Third Reich like a milch cow. And he has always
been privately scathing about the abilities of the Germans
around him: one of the main reasons he has never joined the
Nazi Party is that he has seen how incompetent so many party
stalwarts are. A single glance at the men surrounding Josef
Goebbels will tell you all you need to know: they look like
Yids or idiots and might as well be in the enemy's pay. 'We
have made a complete balls of it,' he reflects ruefully, and his
frustration is sharpened by the knowledge (obvious to him, but
sadly to nobody else) that it could all have been so different.

If only he had been allowed to speak with the old man, his
fond name for Adolf Hitler, the war might have been over four
years ago. It is almost too much to bear, but the idea of deserting
his post, or breaking in any other way with the Third Reich
is anathema to him; even as Berlin collapses around him, he is
still faithfully paying his income tax. (Looking through his
accounts he realises that his financial situation is not as good
as his income tax payment might suggest. 'But, does it matter?'
he asks himself. It is a question that seems to hover over
everything they do these days.)

It is now that William begins to keep a record of what remains
of his despoiled life. 'I regret having kept no diaries in the past
fifteen years. They would have been full of interest today, however
conceited their tone. Just now and then I realise how full my life
has been.' His entries are disjointed and oddly tentative in places,
as if he were only very slowly coming to terms with the demands
of self-reflection.

He also has a new game. He will sit in his office, bleak with
drink – it seems he no longer has any tolerance for alcohol, it
hits his system and deranges him almost instantly – and lays bets
with colleagues on the most likely way he will be killed.
Assassination is considered a possibility and, in view of his reluctance to take cover, air raids are reckoned the odds–on favourite,

but, if pushed, Joyce would put his money on a death at the end of a hangman's noose.

Drunk, lonely and brimming over with a barely suppressed bitterness, William's behaviour outside the Rundfunk is increasingly erratic. He limps through the streets of the city after dark, so intoxicated that falls and scrapes become a nightly occurrence. The consequences of what he sardonically refers to as his 'little habits' are writ large on his body: his knee is bent, his ankles are twisted and his face is a mess.

During the worst attacks on the city, while most others shiver in shelters, Joyce has been known to stand alone on the top of the Reichsportsfeld making a recording of the raid.* There is an ostentation about William Joyce's fearlessness, as if he were trying to prove something to the world at large, and also himself. John Amery too is sanguine in the face of falling bombs; a little over a year ago he was awarded a medal for his work in the rescue operation that followed the destruction of the Kaiserhof Hotel (and with it most of his possessions) in an air raid. Both men are avid for martyrdom, a desire firmly in keeping with the Third Reich's degraded cult of sacrifice; both men want to take the chance to be brave and glorious that the war, for a number of reasons, has denied them. There is, they learn, an intoxication that attends the discovery of where the outer limits of one's courage lie. Given William's conviction that he is already on his way to the gallows, however, it is possible that he considers death by any other means a form of escape. For John there is a joy in having overcome the cowardice that honeycombed his childhood. 'It's funny fear,' he will write in his last hours. 'I used to be so frightened and since I have had one occasion when I have been so frightened that I have thereafter no more feared anything like being sea-sick there is a kind of moment when it is so extreme that thereafter it no longer occurs or recurs again.'

---

* Though his sangfroid can inspire bravery in others, Joyce appears to have little concern for their well-being. It is known that he has sent a strongly worded note to his superior, Dietze, criticising him for being over-considerate to his underlings and providing comfortable air-raid shelters.

When William does deign to take shelter, he fills the bunkers with raucous singing before collapsing into fits of hysterical laughter. One evening he tries to teach Jean, a Frenchman who is having an affair with Margaret, a clutch of English songs. When the grim, mountainously tall air-raid warden tells him to stop singing, Joyce turns to him, a pugnacious leer on his battered face. Why should I?

'Because, you are annoying your fellow citizens.'

'Why? Are you all *that* frightened?'

'Leave the cellar at once!'

'Fuck off.'

There is a scuffle, which leaves William with a bleeding lip – another scar – and the warden with a black eye. Joyce turns and shouts incoherently at the other occupants of the crowded and stifling bunker, who are staring at him in horror. Then he doubles over and collapses on to the ground, laughing so frantically that his breaths come in desperate gulps.

As March wears on the Joyces are informed that they, along with the rest of the employees at the Rundfunkhaus, must decamp to the bucolic environs of Apen, a small town close to the Dutch border. Both are devastated by the news, not least because they are concerned that they will not have enough to drink out in the country but Margaret, more even than her husband, is inconsolable. 'Poor Margaret is crying, she could not believe that it would ever come to this. Poor darling has worse surprises in store for her. Now we are going to reap the whirlwind. But, thank God, the Burgundy was very good today.'

They had always intended to stay in the city, whatever happened. Earlier in the year an official had told Margaret that some foreign employees were arranging to have false passports made in anticipation of the inevitable. Perhaps she and her husband would like to do the same? When Margaret mentioned it to William, the words had barely escaped her mouth before she saw him beginning to quiver with anger.

'Soldiers can't run away, so why should I?' he spat.

Margaret said nothing; she had lived with him long enough to be able to recognise the signs of one of his feverish rages. He had often raved about staying to man the barricades – he would save two bullets, one for each of them.

'If you want to clear out, go.'

Margaret remained silent. Over the last two years they have divorced and remarried, taken lovers, split up and eventually arrived at a kind of fractious modus vivendi. He has told her that she is a wife unworthy of a great man, that she is too old even to become a prostitute. She has used her affairs – Nicky von Besack, the handsome, dissolute German officer who was the cause of the couple's first divorce, has been joined by Pieter, R., Eddy, Pablo, Jean – to humiliate 'Fat Will' in as public a fashion as she can. But they have continued to see each other: sometimes they meet as many as three times a day; they eat together, go on walks, play chess. Ugly rows ('dinner early at Funk Eck. W banged my head & made it ache so I went home') are interleaved with moments of tenderness and affection. In June 1944 they even decide to try for a baby. William might tell Margaret that he has 'never had such a shameless whore on my hands as you' (the insult underlined in red in Margaret's diary, and scribbled over an earlier entry, obliterating it), and yet the couple know that their fates are bound together; who else could understand the particular quality of the bitter loneliness they both carry within them? She will stay by his side, come what may.

Other departments have already been ordered to leave, and dismantled teleprinters, typewriters and packing cases litter the entrance hall. Secretaries bustle past William with their arms full of paper. He watches as boxes of scripts and gramophone recordings all disappear into waiting lorries, then returns to his diary, which is becoming a source of increasing comfort to him. 'I loathe to think that these might be my last hours in Berlin – a city which I love, despite its swine, and despite the heartaches it has brought me. Berlin is a composite part of my life, and I do not yield it up lightly.'

William Joyce will not return to his office again. Over 67,000 tonnes of explosive have been hurled at the city by the Allies, and the Rundfunkhaus is covered by a 'shroud of plaster dust, broken glass and shrapnel', yet that room – with its sign warning visitors to knock before they enter; a regulation he has always enforced with notable punctiliousness – has escaped any direct hits and is mostly intact, save for a few windows that have been covered with plywood. Joyce wanders around the building for the last time. He looks into forlorn offices where plaster detaches itself from the crumbling ceilings and drops with a soft sootfall to the floor. Sometimes, befuddled, as if he has temporarily forgotten that the Third Reich is being dismantled around him, he opens a familiar door, ready to greet one of his colleagues – only to be met by debris, abandoned files and chairs that are already beginning to be submerged by dust.

He leaves behind, for fascinated British intelligence officers to discover, a couple of rifles, a German–English dictionary, an American detective novel and cuttings from English papers (including one heavily underlined piece urging clemency for collaborators after capture). There is also a copy of the collected works of Goebbels with an inscription written by an English-speaking staff member to another which includes a Latin phrase, *Morituri te salutant*: 'those who are about to die salute you'.

18

It is now time for our soldiers to issue their own justice

Late spring 1945

THE WORLD TURNS, and it turns, and everybody wants something different from it. William Joyce and John Amery want to make it spin in a different direction; Harold Cole does not really care which way it twists, as long as it is to his advantage; Eric Pleasants just wants the world to leave him alone. His desire for sanctuary is the direct opposite of the desperate urge for significance that drives Amery and Joyce.

He and Anneliese have slipped away from SS Wildemann Kaserne by using an illegally obtained pass that gives him permission to visit his dying grandmother. He has no intention of returning. They go first to her parents' house in Wilmsdorf, where they plan to spend a few days on 'leave' before going to Berlin. Every night she sneaks into his room and they talk about the future. How will they keep out of the hands of the Gestapo? What will they do when the Russians come?

Their days in the pine forests of the Sächsische Schweiz are idyllic, suffused with a blissful calm. As they wander arm-in-arm through the region's sandstone hills they are surrounded by flowers and birdsong and a sense of warmth and well-being that belies the late winter chill. Perhaps its sweetness comes from the knowledge that it will soon come to an end.

The end arrives in brutal fashion on the evening of 13 February 1945, when they stand on the porch of her house and listen to the deadly buzz made by wave after wave of bombers, heading for Dresden. Within half an hour the city is ablaze. Though they are twenty miles away, they are soon covered by scorched debris, a ghastly black snow that settles gently on to their shoulders.

A few days later Eric and Anneliese venture into Dresden's scorched remnants. The immolated city is covered by a suffocating blanket of smoke. Here and there buildings still burn fiercely. The couple, who are swiftly press-ganged into helping the relief effort, are surrounded by injured men and women, crying out with a frenzied pain that they are powerless to relieve. They struggle for five days, helping to drag the dead and the dying from the rubble, working themselves into an exhausted, hallucinatory stupor. Eric and Anneliese stack bodies into heaps and watch, horrified, as men wielding flamethrowers reduce them to ashes. Some streets are simply bricked up and the corpses in them left to decompose until the salvage teams find time to return. Eric works with a mask wrapped tightly around his nose and mouth, but the cloying, sickening stench of burning flesh and hair, of rotting bodies and slowly drying blood pervades everything. It soaks into your skin and your clothes and makes you think you will never be able to rid yourself of it.

At one point he picks up a baby's shoe from a snarl of bricks. It still has the child's foot in it.

When they arrive in Berlin they find that somehow Anneliese's flat is still standing, unlike its neighbours. The apartment is simple – just a small room with a bed and a washbasin and an even smaller kitchen – but even in these desperate times they make it a haven, a means of hiding away from the sordid world outside its walls. To begin with the couple rarely venture into the streets but slowly they learn about the administrative turmoil at SS HQ and realise that it affords them an opportunity. Eric puts on his uniform and heads to Fehrbelliner Strasse to claim his rations. Nobody asks him why he has been absent from his unit for several weeks. He starts to go back regularly and is surprised and delighted to run into his friend from Jersey, John Leister, who he thought had disappeared to Italy with the Kurt Eggers SS propaganda unit. Some days he goes into German officers' messes to fight exhibition bouts against the former heavyweight champion of the world, Max Schmeling.

To supplement his rations, Eric begins to forage in the back streets of Berlin, where it strikes him that he is reprising the erratic scavengers' existence of his life in Jersey. One day he and John Leister help an SS sergeant load a wagon with provisions and when the poor fool goes off on an errand they offer to look after it. As soon as the German's back is turned they steal his transport; they take rations, a pistol and an American revolver and then dump anything they cannot use.

There are other discoveries that do not immediately appear as useful as guns or food. One of the legion of urchins and orphans who roam the ruined city attaches himself to Eric. Beneath layers of grime a deathly pale waif's face stares back at him; the boy is endearing and vulnerable but already part feral. Every day they meet at a spot near the station that, without discussion, they have settled on as a rendezvous. Eric notices that if you have a child in tow, you can go straight to the front of queues for food hand-outs, and after a while he asks him if he would like to come and live at Anneliese's apartment; the boy refuses, he has lived on the streets so long by this point that he no longer feels comfortable enclosed by four walls. Nevertheless they force him to come home with them where they wash and scrub him until, for perhaps the first time in months, he begins to resemble a normal child.

One morning, Eric waits for him until it becomes clear that he has slipped soundlessly out of their lives. He is surprised to find how much he misses the boy. Not long afterwards Eric finds a more loyal companion in the shape of a dog they find yelping with distress in a bombed-out house.

On 9 April, his papers allowing him to escape Berlin finally having come through, John Leister leaves. Eric stands with him on the platform waiting for the train. They know that this will be the end of their partnership, perhaps the last time they will see each other. The finality of it all is oppressive, and they struggle to think of much to say to each other. Around them the station is in ruins. Even if they could find the right words, the mortar bombs crashing all around them would make it difficult for the other man to hear anything. It is a relief when the train, which is almost overflowing with wounded soldiers, pulls up. For a moment John hesitates, an agitated, anxious presence on the platform. His girlfriend Lena calls to him from somewhere within the carriage; then calls again, with increased urgency. Finally he follows her and disappears momentarily into the mass of disfigured and bandaged bodies crowded against the windows. As the train moves off, Eric can see his handsome blond head and a waving arm that he thinks is John's recede into the distance. They will learn later that this was the last service out of the city.

On a day garlanded by pink and white cherry blossoms that drift incongruously through the ruined city, Eric and Anneliese marry at the register office in Charlottenburg. The registrar proceeds calmly, unruffled by the bombs smashing into the buildings around them, until the groom gives his name: Reginald Eric Pleasants, born in Norfolk, England. An awkward silence follows, punctured by the crash of yet another explosion nearby and then the ceremony continues. As the happy couple step into the bright spring sunshine outside, Eric notices that for the first time since he has been in Germany, a German official makes no attempt to salute him in the Nazi manner.

It occurs to Eric that because of his refusal to take sides, he belongs nowhere. He considers himself to be unbound by time and place, and despite the destruction and chaos that surround him he feels a happiness and freedom so strong that it makes him light-headed. Whatever awaits him holds no fear: it will be a result of choices he has made. Nobody has forced him to do anything he did not want to. He has refused to 'be stamped on, dragged around and ground down until your life isn't your own'. Fleetingly, the thought of Hitler, hiding half-mad in a bunker somewhere beneath the ruined city, crosses his mind.

His thoughts are interrupted by an especially heavy salvo of artillery fire, and he and his new wife duck into a machine-gun post. Barricades are going up in every street, with housewives stacking their last remaining furniture in a futile bid to stop the Russian surge into the city. The flimsy structures are fortified by burned-out vehicles, iron palings and barbed wire. Some of the devastated houses they pass now bear messages from families to sons that they hope will be returning from the front; others carry more official communications: 'Looters will be punished with death!'

On the corner of Joachimstaler Strasse they pass a public notice announcing the execution of an officer and three soldiers. The men were deserters, caught with false papers, one of the many hundreds of Germans shot or strung up from one of the city's few remaining trees or lampposts as punishment for this 'crime'. Eric is unsettled by the strangely archaic, formal nature of these deaths amid so much chaos. It is another reminder – as if one were needed – of the state's jealous desire for control over its people. Even in its death throes, it refuses to let them go.

Life in Berlin now is characterised by many such vignettes signalling the ghoulish cynicism at the Third Reich's core: baby-faced members of the Hitler Youth handing out cyanide pills after concerts; hordes of party functionaries streaming out of the city, leaving the rest to their fate. The city stinks of smoke, rotting bodies, burned gasoline and gunpowder. Brick dust and plaster envelop everything like a fog and the roads, canals and sewers are clogged with debris. The dead lie everywhere, their corpses feasted on by fat blue flies and strewn with shards of glass and twisted metal. There is nobody left to treat the wounded. Night comes as a relief: in its relative cool the stench from decomposing bodies becomes almost bearable.

Eric and Anneliese are faced by a paradox: escape from Berlin will not be possible until the city falls, so they must wait for the Russians to come. Their flat on Rüdesheimer Platz is still somehow standing, but they know it will only be a matter of time before it shares the fate of the buildings that once surrounded it. This leaves the vast network of sewers and tunnels that lie like a honeycomb beneath Berlin – a negative of the city that few of its residents have ever seen – as their only option. Many others make the same decision to seek the dubious safety of an existence below ground: by the time of the surrender 3 million people will be trapped in bunkers, the cellars of the flak towers or their own homes.

It is with something like high spirits that they leave the flat for the last time (these days, there are so many things one does, so many people one sees, for the 'last time'); Anneliese locks the door carefully, and they both laugh at her caution. It has been yet another place of refuge for Eric, where he has been able to shut out what he calls, with some understatement 'the harshness of the world'.

They make their descent into the underworld through a sewer beneath the Reich Chancellery. The crash of bombs might be muffled and the risk of being blown up reduced, but they feel as vulnerable as ever. The sewer resembles a dilapidated tube system, populated by criminals, deserters, prostitutes and people who have escaped from concentration camps. There have been spasmodic attempts by the authorities to clear out the occupants of this underground fortress – one system was flooded by the SS to fight off the Russians; many Germans drowned, or were trampled to death in the panic to escape through the few ventilation shafts – but so far it has proved easy to defend.

Somehow they find a space on a concrete ledge among an unwashed mass of families. Two wounded men lie in a corner, covered with coats; they moan with pain as their blood trickles into the main channel below. Their neighbour is a dignified woman of about forty, nursing a toddler while a small boy plays with a ball beside her. From time to time bombs shake the cellar, sending chunks of concrete tumbling down the walls and flooding the catacombs with an acrid burning smell. Amid the cacophony they can hear the high reedy voice of the boy shouting 'Boom, boom', as he pretends his ball is an explosive. Someone puts on a portable gramophone. Three or four figures start to dance by the light of flickering candles and hurricane lamps.

Nobody dares venture anywhere alone; to do so is to make yourself a target for the gangs of hungry and desperate brigands who roam this subterranean hell, willing to kill for a scrap of food. A curious hierarchy forms: the strong protect the weak from the many predators who haunt this sepulchral kingdom. Occasionally the strong, including Eric, will venture up small iron-runged ladders and through manholes into the city to scavenge for food. Eric watches dispassionately as his new companions – young men aged prematurely by the war – machine-gun anyone who gets in their way. They return with oil, wine and Danish sausages, which are lowered by rope into the sewer. These sporadic excursions are their only chance to find out what is going on in the other world. Otherwise, down here, it is impossible to know.

There is little for them to do together other than to lie close, as if proximity somehow offers a kind of protection. Inexplicably, considering their current predicament, they both find themselves considering having children.

A few days pass, the bright flourish of their wedding day feeling increasingly distant. Then an explosion in a nearby tunnel is followed by a number of terribly burned men who stumble into the chamber inhabited by Eric and Anneliese. In between gasps they explain that the Russians are using flamethrowers to clear the sewers. Eric is sceptical. He knows how easy it is to cause an explosion underground, and he is surprised that there is no further noise or commotion. Yet if what the men say is true, then they must depart at once. Leaving Anneliese by herself – he only plans to be gone for a moment – he decides to track down one of the groups nearer the exits to see if he can find out any more.

As Eric returns he hears shrieks of terror, which cut through the rest of the noise. '*Nein, nein, bitte nein. Eric! Eric!*' He breaks into a run. Drawing the Walther he keeps hidden beneath his shirt he sees Anneliese struggling with a man clothed in a tatty uniform, while another scarecrow figure rifles through the bundle of their belongings on the ground; their neighbours watch without interest. He shoots the man who is bent over their possessions first, anxious not to hit his wife. The tunnel is briefly filled with the pistol's deafening crash – monstrously amplified in the tight space – and Eric watches as his adversary slumps against the wall. He then moves closer to the man holding Anneliese. The man lets go of her but then seems caught between standing his ground or taking to his heels. Taking advantage of his opponent's indecision, Eric springs. Wrestling the German to the ground, Eric begins pounding the back of his head with his pistol. It is a lightweight weapon and seems to be doing little damage, but Eric is engrossed in his task. So engrossed that he doesn't notice a sobbing and dishevelled Anneliese appear by his side, clutching a tiny Beretta. There are several whipcracks, and then the would-be thief jerks before going limp.

Anneliese collapses into a heap of sobs, clutching frantically at Eric's legs. In a mixture of German and English he tries to calm her. Eventually they cling to each other, taking comfort in their nearness. It is clear that they cannot stay here any longer; better to take their chances on the streets rather than die here like rats. Eric rifles through the pockets of the two corpses, looking for anything useful and then pushes them into the stinking water at his feet.

That night they return to the surface to find that Berlin has capitulated. Although the air is acrid with the smell of a city that has been reduced to ash, blood and rubble, they feel clear and clean.

They find their feet carrying them towards the flat on Rüdesheimer Platz, where they watch the building for a while before going in. Instantly, they regret returning; their refuge has been ransacked. Anything – like the furniture – that the despoilers have not been able to carry off has been smashed into pieces. Someone has shat and pissed in the corners, a mindless act of violation that will be repeated almost mechanically in thousands of homes across the city, but which also feels vindictive and personal. As if whoever had emptied his bowels knew that this small room was special, and resented the sanctuary it offered.

They make a makeshift bed on the kitchen floor and struggle to sleep amid the noise made by the clank and grind of tanks and the harsh unfamiliar cries of the triumphant Russian soldiers flooding into Berlin. The next morning they burn any papers that connect Eric to the SS and with their possessions in a rucksack, the dog perched on top, they leave the city. The behaviour of the Soviet troops seems to bear out Joyce and Amery's gloomiest prophecies. Like beasts they drink and rape and shoot anyone who tries to stand in their way. It is around this time that a senior Russian officer in the city receives a report from his chief of staff. 'Comrade Marshal,' he is told, 'the soldiers are not behaving themselves. They break furniture, mirrors and dishes. What are your instructions in this connection?'

The officer waits for a few moments. 'I don't give a fuck,' he spits. 'It is now time for our soldiers to issue their own justice.'

19

Come on in, gentlemen. Have a good gawp

Spring 1945

THE PARTY IS over. Bottles litter the floor, some smashed, their dregs seeping into the carpet. Until last night the room – in an elegant palazzo outside Milan – had acted as an impromptu radio studio. But then a host of young faces was forced, finally, to contemplate certain defeat; and pain, frustration and fear were transformed into a fury that kicked and punched and tore until every piece of radio equipment had been reduced to a tangle of wire and jagged plastic. The house is haloed by shards of glass, smashed gramophone discs and broken chairs.

When John Amery was a teenager, one of the hapless succession of private tutors his parents had employed to look after him decided to take his young charge to Iceland on a camping trip. John's luggage included a portable gramophone and twelve records, three of which were of the utmost significance to him ('Old Man River', 'Tea for Two' and 'I'm a Lucky Boy'). He played the discs with a manic, cracked persistence and gave the impression of being willing to guard them with his life, carrying them himself to ensure their safety.

In a taxi on their way to the docks in Edinburgh, where they were to catch their ferry, John became so consumed by emotion that he got up, put the records on the seat and jumped up and down, smashing them into tiny pieces. With his companion reduced to a perplexed silence he then proceeded to make the taxi stop at Leith to replace the records, which in the days that followed he would treat with the same neurotic care as he had before. Thinking back many years later to those queer seconds in the back of a Scottish cab, the tutor recalled how John did not speak once to justify his behaviour; he did not even flick an eyelash to acknowledge that he had been the author of such strange violence. John Amery's life has been marked by a series of such *actes gratuits*; frail fists waved fiercely at the world. The destruction of the studio is only the latest.

He has been a member of Benito Mussolini's lilliputian Italian Social Republic (assembled from scraps of Italy and foreign conquests) for several months now, following an invitation from the leader himself. Incoherent acts of destruction are the only means he has left of exerting any kind of control over his surroundings. When he is not drinking, or helping to smash a nobleman's ancestral home to pieces, he is an aide-cum-confidant to Il Duce, haunting his side during these melancholy, regret-soaked last days.

It is – as far as the gloomy circumstances will allow – a happy coalition, given the two men share the same plangent combination of delusion and bombast, and Mussolini, whose mistress Claretta Petacci thinks John 'the perfect English gentleman', even offers him a commission in his Brigarta Nera. Amery refuses – he is too much of a patriot, he feels, to wear another nation's uniform (like the fuss kicked up by the BFC about their own uniforms, this futile gesture appears to be an attempt by John to demonstrate that he is still his own man, that he has surrendered none of his power or independence to the men who pay his wages) and he worries that it might involve him firing on his fellow countrymen – but nonetheless he undertakes to 'dress myself in a manner that my opinions should be unmistakeable'. So he sports jackboots, greenish-grey breeches and a black shirt; some people think he looks like an Albanian shepherd. The talk at Gargano is of a last-ditch salient near the Swiss border from which Mussolini will sally out to launch 'peace initiatives'.

On 23 April 1945 John and Michelle set off in his car with the aim of reconnoitring the area around Como. Two days later, they are ambushed by partisans. Though they are spared Il Duce's gruesome fate (he and Claretta are shot dead, and then their corpses are kicked and spat on before being hung upside down on meat hooks from the roof of an Esso petrol station), the couple are roughly handled. John is dragged out of the vehicle, Michelle's fur coat is ripped off her back. In a photograph taken almost immediately after their capture he looks haggard and dazed, as if he can barely believe what has just happened to him. His suit is draped baggily over a frame so slender that it looks as if it could be carried away by a breath of air; from a distance you might mistake him for a child. Closer in you can see how wild and tired his eyes are. John has always been grubby – regularly going days without washing – but here he looks truly filthy. When was the last time he slept? When was the last time he ate?

He, like William Joyce, has long dreamed of a martyr's death, and that his war has ended in such an undignified fashion is an abject humiliation. The forlorn couple look on helplessly as the partisans gleefully relieve them of their possessions – '1 suit case (important documents and personal effects), 1 overcoat, 1 fur coat and two silver foxes, a 20 liter petrol tin full, 1 Lancia Aprilia motor car No 78410 M1 C. D. I.' – and then hand them over to the British authorities.

Extravagant clothes, a smart fast car . . . if nothing else his tastes have remained consistent. As soon as he is in British hands, Amery becomes agitated about their return, as if he is unaware of what lies before him. Does he really think he will be able to drive his car in prison, wear his overcoat on the gallows?

As the plane lifts into the air, John opens up to the avuncular Commander Leonard Burt of Scotland Yard, who has been charged with escorting him home. John stays cocksure. 'You know, everything I did – *everything* – was in the best interests of my country.'

He is only echoing the sentiments he committed to paper in the statement he produced after his arrest. 'I defy anyone,' he wrote, 'to find in my speeches, radio or otherwise, my conversations in private and what I have written one single solitary word against my country.' The same pages also contained his belief that in one form or another he would be able to continue his life's political work, work that would 'render very considerable services to my country'.

But his confidence seems to diminish the closer they get to England. While Amery still sees himself as England's friend, talking to Burt he begins to understand – perhaps for the first time – that others might not. In Great Britain, the country in whose interests Amery believes he has spoken, but in truth knows so scantily, he has been associated with an evil regime that seemed poised to extinguish Britain's freedom. How could he think they could forget that? For a heartbeat the policeman feels a surge of empathy for the befuddled boy-man before him – empathy he briskly tries to brush aside by thinking instead of the young, ignorant lads in the POW camps this Old Harrovian has led astray.

'Tell me, what were the air raids really like?' John asks him, as if the question has only just occurred to him. 'Were the casualties very high? Wasn't the bombing accurate? They were picking out military targets all the time, you know.'

John does not seem interested in Commander Burt's reply. He waits – not long, enough for the other man to finish his sentence – and then speaks again. For a moment the last ten years fall away and he is once again the belligerent young man who had pulled a gun on another driver, who behaved as he wished because he believed there would be no consequences.

'I don't suppose for a moment they'll bring a charge against me. But if they did, of course, my father would see that—'

'I wouldn't bring your father into it, if I were you,' replies Burt. 'I think he has suffered enough. Don't bring your father's name into it.'

'All right, I won't.'

Spring 1945

William Joyce's diary: 22 April 1945

I realised this morning so clearly that in the eyes of Englishmen, I have forfeited all claim to live in their land or consider myself English. I am sorry; for I have now nothing left. Long before Germany's defeat became certain, I knew that I could never be at home here. Has it all been worthwhile? I think not. National Socialism is a fine cause, but most Germans, not all, are bloody fools. England means so much to me, and now I am old. Well, in that spirit, I can take any punishment that is coming to me, but I am sorry for Margaret, whose outlook is quite different.

Joyce manages to slip away with Margaret, a false passport in the name of Wilhelm Hansen offering him a figleaf's protection. Against the odds they find a refuge in Flensburg, close to the Danish border. It seems they are safe. As April slides into May, William and Margaret begin to venture out more. Sometimes he plays a game he calls Russian roulette, accosting Allied soldiers in the street, addressing them in what he believes to be his unmistakable voice. None of them seems to know who he is. One day, as William takes a walk in the German countryside, he comes across two British officers who are looking for firewood. He approaches them – perhaps he is playing his game again, perhaps he is tired of this life that is no life at all – and opens his mouth: '*Il y a des morceaux ici,*' he says, gathering some kindling for them and placing it in their vehicle. Then, in English, he tells them where they might find more. This time he is recognised. 'You wouldn't be William Joyce, by any chance, would you?' he is asked. As the Irishman reaches for his papers, one of the officers shoots him in his buttock; in an irony that this instinctively humorous man will no doubt appreciate, his captor is Jewish, firing a Walther pistol confiscated only days earlier from a Hamburg policeman.

As the two officers gingerly approach William, who has been knocked to the ground by the force of the gunshot, he looks up at them and almost smiles. 'I suppose in view of recent suicides, you were expecting me to reach for a phial of poison? Don't worry, I'm not that sort of person. I ask for one favour, will you tell my wife what happened?'

Margaret is captured soon afterwards. 'We've been expecting this to happen for weeks, so we mustn't make a fuss about it now,' she says to the man who arrests her. A little later, in a British safe house in Lüneberg, Germany, she is locked in the cell recently vacated by Heinrich Himmler. There is a decaying mattress on the floor and a hastily scribbled sign on the door that describes the occupant as Mrs Hansen alias Mrs Joyce.

One of the guards enters abruptly and then stands, unspeaking, a distance away from her. Eventually he tires of his self-imposed silence. 'I just wanted to see what a traitoress looked like,' he tells her. Other soldiers follow his example and peer into the dirty cell. They are all curious and yet afraid, behaving as if the tired, hungry and frightened woman before them might be carrying a bomb, or be capable of black magic.

'Come on in, gentlemen. Have a good gawp.'

One soldier asks her whether she feels guilty about Belsen. Margaret answers that she, like the majority of Germans, knew nothing about it. (A lie, or at least an evasion of the truth.) The men staring at her are digesting her response when a major and an army chaplain enter the cell.

The major peers into the gloom, sniffs the air and tells her that she reeks. The chaplain asks her when she married Joyce – assuming that she had, he adds maliciously. Margaret wraps her fur coat around her and says that unless he puts his questions in a more becoming manner she will refuse to answer them. She then requests a glass of water. The major orders the guard to make sure it is laced with typhus, like the water the inmates of Belsen were forced to drink. Margaret looks at him and without thinking corrects him: 'Don't you mean typhoid?'

The major loses his temper, calls her a bitch and, moving close enough that his saliva lands on her face, shouts, 'I should knock your pretty teeth out for saying that.'

'I don't mind if you hate me,' comes the response, 'so long as you do it politely.'

She remains an object of fascination for the next few hours, visited and jeered at by a steady procession of soldiers. Somehow Margaret manages to hold back her tears until the last man has sauntered out of her cell; the only witness is the guard assigned to make sure she does not take her own life.

William is subjected to his own humiliations. A card is hung around his neck bearing the legend 'Lord Haw-Haw . . . Traitor'. Soldiers brandishing cameras crowd around the ambulance he is being carried in, hoping for a glimpse of one of the world's most

COME ON IN, GENTLEMEN

infamous personalities. They are disappointed to find a small sardonic man with sunken features – his false teeth have been confiscated – clad in blue and white striped pyjamas. Some amuse themselves by taunting him with shouts of 'Jairmany Calling! Jairmany Calling!' but he has a retort ready: 'In civilised countries wounded men are not used for peepshows.'

A couple of days later William is paraded in front of the Pathé cameras. He emerges from a car and then proceeds to stroll up and down a dusty stretch of track. He looks shrunken, weak and confused. He cannot possibly be drunk, but there is something about the queasy jerk with which he walks that makes him appear unsober. It is only when he turns around, and the livid slash on his face is revealed, that one remembers that this diffident-seeming man in a suit so large that it flaps around him like sails has long since surrendered his life to hatred and violence and rage.

Summer 1945

An excursion. On 11 June 1945 three men leave Paris at 6 a.m. The leader of the expedition is an Englishman, Major Peter Hope. He is accompanied by two bodyguards, Commissaire Pouzelgues and Inspecteur Feinte, and a chauffeur, Inspecteur Noel.

Although the conflict in western Europe officially ended over a month ago, their journey is neither quiet nor safe. The war's ravages have left the roads potholed and rutted and the tidy-minded Hope can barely believe the state they are in. The car suffers two punctures and a broken spring, but worse is to come.

As they approach Nancy a man emerges from a wood and discharges his rifle into a pipeline, creating a fountain of petrol that reaches 150 metres into the air. Hope had not expected his journey to be easy, but it seems that every development is a cause of fresh concern. His companions refer affectionately to Noel, a short, tough Corsican, as the Killer. Hope finds this less reassuring than the others evidently expect him to. He is equally ruffled by the way that, as soon as they enter Alsace, the three Frenchmen all produce revolvers, which they make sure are close to hand. Yes, we are in France, they explain, but one cannot trust the Alsatians.

So Hope feels some relief once they manage to cross the Rhine at Breisach without incident. This relief only lasts as long as it takes for his companions to locate three sub-machine guns in the back of the car, which they hold at the ready. They arrive at Tuttlingen at 9 p.m., just as darkness is falling. Here the French officers refuse to proceed further for fear of the Werewolves – it seems as if even the Killer's bravado has disappeared in the face of the threat of bands of Nazi fugitives.

When they reach Sigmaringen the following morning they eventually manage to locate a tired-looking French officer, Captain Preuzes, who, after a little prompting, confirms that 'Captain Mason' – their target – had been in his office that morning. Hope takes him into his confidence, and explains, to Preuzes's great shock, why they have been sent. Preuzes's surprise curdles into embarrassment as he launches into some explanations of his own. It emerges that the reason he appears so exhausted is that the night before he had been at a party hosted by Harold Cole, as he now knows his name to be, at his home in the country. There had been a guest of honour – Brigadier Nicholls of the British Parachute Corps – together with Major Smith, American liaison officer to the Allied Military Government for Occupied Territories, Major McGwyer, Lieutenant Dureng of the Sécurité Militaire, the chef de cabinet of General Bonjour, Commander Second Army Corps and a number of other American and French officers.

Preuzes warns them to approach the house carefully for it is surprisingly heavily populated. As well as Cole himself there are a number of German servants, the members of Cole's unit, and also its owner, a Nazi farmer. The French captain adds that, despite the farmer's political allegiance, he had not been arrested since Cole has signed a safe conduct for him, countersigned by the Sécurité Militaire.

Instead they decide to lure their quarry to the military government's offices. Preuzes's adjutant is dispatched to bring Cole back by telling him that a security matter with which he had been involved needs his urgent attention at Sigmaringen.

The plan is as follows: Preuzes is to sit at his desk, which faces the door, with Pouzelgues and Feinte, who are each armed with a Sten gun and revolver, seated either side of him. Hope, having discarded his distinctive battledress jacket, will occupy a chair behind the door, and the Killer is to station himself by the entrance to report their target's arrival.

Now, all they can do is wait in anxious silence. Preuzes is especially jumpy. He has been charged with shaking Cole's hand – the signal for the rest to leap into action – but what he has learned of Cole's personality this morning has, understandably, frayed his nerves. Finally, after twenty-five minutes, the Killer, who has got hold of a sub-machine gun for himself, reports that a large party of American and French officers are descending from a car outside the building. A few moments later the party enters the room, led by Cole, who walks in nonchalantly, a Tommy gun nestling in the crook of his arm, and two revolvers holstered around his waist. For an awful moment Preuzes remains motionless; it seems as if he will miss his cue. Then, finally, he extends his arm and the pair shake hands. Before Cole's face has time to register surprise, Feinte seizes hold of his outstretched right hand, and Pouzelgues grabs him round the middle. Rallying, Cole starts to fight back so fiercely that Major Hope feels it is worthwhile joining in the mêlée himself. For a few moments there is a lively scramble on the floor under the grand piano in the commandant's sitting room, which is only concluded when manacles have been fixed round Cole's wrists.

Hope turns towards his captive: 'You are Harold Cole, a British soldier who has deserted from the British Army.'

Belying the stern resistance he has just offered, Cole replies, 'Yes, I am. I am glad you have come and arrested me. I have been waiting for you as I realised this would come.'

'You understand you are being detained on suspicion of having worked for the Gestapo and for having given away to them the names of persons engaged in escape organisations as well as other things.'

'Yes, sir, I know all about that, and I will tell you the truth. I know I must die for what I have done and it is no use telling you lies now. I will tell you anything you want to know.'

★

It had been good while it lasted. Harold Cole had been the model of bonhomie as he emerged from the thick forest two months ago and introduced himself to a group of startled American soldiers: 'I'm a British officer. Captain Mason is the name. I've been acting as an agent here in Germany and just waiting for you chaps to turn up. Very glad to see you, I'm sure, and I may be able to be of service to you, I think. By the way, this man Kieffer has been very helpful to me, so I'd be glad if you can do anything for him.' It was the same winning combination of charm and confidence that he had used so many times before.

He cooperated with the Americans eagerly, denouncing local Gestapo chiefs and making himself so indispensable that he was given an official role. With a pair of French renegades and an authentic American hero – Captain Frank Lillyman of the 101st Airborne Division, the first paratrooper to land in Normandy on D-Day – in tow, he began conducting a number of what he euphemistically described as 'security enquiries', in the course of which he murdered at least one former Nazi officer, accumulated six motor cars, 200 gallons of petrol, US Army rations, hams, some 500 bottles of wine, and a quantity of personal baggage, weapons and ammunition. His munificence ensured that he became highly popular among the bored French and American officers stationed in the area, and he steadily began to feel confident enough to start contacting some of the people he had left behind in Paris. So confident that he risked sending the postcard to Charlotte Leblanc, his discarded lover, that finally alerted the authorities to his presence.

They strip him and remove his battledress, which they replace with an ill-fitting civilian suit. Mindful of the way in which Heinrich Himmler had, courtesy of a hidden cyanide pill, escaped justice after his capture the month before, they take the unpleasant but necessary precaution of removing their captive's false teeth and examining his mouth, as well as all his other orifices.

But any indignity is worth it. After four long years, Harold Cole is about to be brought to justice.

Summer 1945

Finally, after picking their way cautiously through a country that has been reduced almost to dust, Eric and Anneliese reach an internment camp. Here Eric assumes a new identity: Hans Sandau, of Sächsische Schweiz, a circus strongman before the war. By this point he has even started to think in German, and he is surprised to find how strange spoken English has begun to sound to him. The food here is good and the accommodation comfortable. In the camp they can for the first time live as man and wife in married quarters; there is also the chance to make some kind of a living. Eric gets a job as an interpreter, helping the stressed Americans try to organise the bewildering array of refugees – there are 17 million displaced persons in Germany alone – more of whom flood into their zone with every passing day.

Eric has always worked busily to ensure that his conscience is kept as clear as a well-swept front porch. It helps that he has never been called to account for his actions, and has thus never been faced by any more formidable interlocutor than his own conscience. But lately his broom's bristles are proving ineffective against the fears collecting before him in a menacing pile. The threat of an immediate death in the chaos of post-war Germany has receded, but Eric is assailed, with an urgency that is new to him, by the feeling that the decisions he has made will catch up with him. He knows that the Allies are searching relentlessly for all those renegades who have worked, in whatever capacity, for the Third Reich and the couple live in constant fear of someone denouncing him; all it needs is one mistake, or one act of malice, and their hard-won new life will be torn from them. Eric torments himself by wondering whether he will be shot or hanged. Even as he tries to rehearse excuses that will justify his actions, he knows that the effort is in vain: who will believe that he was motivated only by a desire to escape? (He doesn't ask himself whether his fellow countrymen will sympathise with this, even should they believe it.) How will he explain his marriage to a member of the SS? Eric resolves to submerge himself into Hans Sandau as thoroughly as possible.

For a while it appears as if his vanishing act has succeeded. He develops a profitable sideline in selling Nazi memorabilia to gullible officials in the camp. First he gets hold of a few dozen copies of *Mein Kampf* and persuades an 'adept' German prisoner to write inscriptions by Hitler and Goebbels. Americans will pay the princely sum of $50 for one of these. Soon copies of 'Hitler's' inkwell, 'Goering's' watch, and 'Himmler's' dagger find their way across the Atlantic to sit on mantelpieces in Kansas, New Mexico and Pennsylvania.

Eric and Anneliese watch the strain of the last few months fade from each other's faces; they begin to wonder whether perhaps everything is going to be all right. There are very few awkward questions asked in the camp, and nobody seems interested in interfering in their lives, and they are just beginning to feel settled when the Russians are given responsibility for taking over the running of the camp. The couple know that there will be another round of purges, and that plausibly as Eric has come to inhabit the persona of Hans Sandau, his paperwork might not survive close inspection.

Leaving the camp they find an evacuated cottage, and ransack other abandoned houses to furnish it. Surrounded by what seems to them the height of luxury, the couple start to plan their future in earnest. They will stay in Germany; Eric likes it here and there is nothing waiting for him back in England, even assuming he will not have to face some kind of reckoning if he returns. A beguiling vision of buying a farm in the mountains of Bavaria emerges from their conversations: they can take in tourists in the winter; he can work as a ski instructor; she will take the guests to and from the nearest railway station; all they need is money.

Eric sets himself up as a people smuggler, ferrying desperate people out of Soviet territory and across no-man's-land into the American zone. He sets about discovering those remote paths where the patrols that criss-cross the area do not stray. Being as discreet as he can, he approaches people in local inns; his price is high, but everyone pays.

It is a risky trade, one that becomes riskier the longer you do it, but circus work – the only other kind of employment on offer

– will not buy their farm. Eric makes trip after trip, and slowly they creep closer to the total they need. But then one night in August 1946 Eric opens the door to a pair of huge Russians speaking heavily accented German. One of them brandishes a pistol that looks as if it could serve as an artillery piece. The other thrusts forward his identity card. 'Russian State Police,' he says. Eric asks them to leave the room while Anneliese gets dressed; they snigger and crowd in. 'Now, we want a complete confession of your espionage activities on behalf of Great Britain,' they tell him. His first response is to laugh at the sheer ridiculousness of the situation and the accusations that have been levelled at him. A ringing blow to his head and a sharp explosion in his ribs convince him they are serious.

It is exactly a year since peace was declared, and Eric's freedom is at an end.

20

Cheer up, the worst is yet to come

Autumn 1945

FOR A TIME it seems as if, against all odds, John Amery will not have to answer for his actions.

His trial is adjourned while his brother Julian secures from 'Heli Rolando de Tella y Cantos, General Commanding the Legion and the 63rd Division of the Navarre Army Corps, Knight Laureate of the Royal Order of San Fernando and of the Military Medal etc. etc.' what looks like irrefutable confirmation that John had 'taken the oath of the flag . . . after applying for Spanish nationality, renouncing the English nationality which he previously had'. But MI5's investigations prove that Amery had been at sea, many miles away from Spain, on the day that he had notionally received citizenship, so he must take his place in the dock after all.

After only eight minutes Amery, his slight figure encased in a well-worn double-breasted suit, roughly laundered shirt and soft collar, pleads guilty to all charges and is sentenced to death. On learning his fate, Amery smiles gently, bows to the judge and disappears below ground. Before then he had been a faint, impassive presence, his composure only breaking when a reference was made to his 'beloved friend and brave political revolutionary Jeanine Amery-Barde' – he buried his delicate, lined face on his arm for some moments and then recovered himself, looking wonderingly at the judge as if he had forgotten altogether that he was in a courtroom where a decision was about to be made as to whether he would live or die.

While John appears resigned to his fate, even to welcome it,

Leo makes another attempt to save his son's life. He commissions a historical psychological report (it must be based on testimony about his behaviour in the past, because an examination in the present is denied them), which diagnoses 'a severe and long standing case of psychopathic (mental) disorder or a near psychotic (insane) type'. The conclusion is endorsed unreservedly by four 'of the foremost psychiatrists in Britain', but the government's doctors, having made their own assessments, decide that 'These findings do not constitute any significant abnormality and should in my opinion be regarded as within the bounds of normal.' The sentence holds.

William Joyce's defence centres on the proposition that he cannot be accused of committing treason against Great Britain because, since he was born in Brooklyn, to a father who had taken US nationality, he has never actually been a citizen of the country. The prosecution argue successfully that the fact that William possessed a United Kingdom passport (whether deviously obtained or not) meant that he was entitled to the Crown's protection, and as such owed it loyalty.

When Joyce learns the result of the Amery trial he knows that he too will die (the fact that the judge, Mr Justice Tucker – or Ucker, as the Irishman calls him – has, in a court of law, already described him as a traitor, does not fill him with optimism; Joyce observes that the man presiding over the trial cannot be said to be in a state of 'mental virginity'*). He has long understood, in a way that Amery cannot, that their personas are both soaked in six years' worth of loathing and fear, that they have become symbols both of treachery, and of the Nazi regime. What they

---

* This was in the context of the tangled, compromising set of charges brought against the White Russian (and secretary of Archibald Ramsay's Right Club), Anna Wolkoff and Tyler Kent, a cypher clerk at the US Embassy in May 1940. They were accused of stealing sensitive information and, among other things, sending a coded letter to William Joyce. Colin Holmes argues compellingly that this letter, authored by Angus Macnab, was an extension of the plot he had conceived with Joyce to undermine the British war effort. Oswald and Diana Mosley are also incriminated – a reminder of their naked sympathy for the Nazis, which contradicts the couple's post-war attempts at obfustication.

represent is something that must be expunged from the planet
– and they cannot expect sympathy or understanding. There has
been little talk recently of the sanctity of human life, which has
led to some strange equations: a Jew is better dead than alive; it
is better that two cities in Japan are destroyed than any further
American blood be shed. In the last six years, 60 million lives
have been erased; what price two or three more? Cracked and
confused as he has been for so long, even John Amery knows
that after six years of brutal conflict the world has been so
profoundly disturbed that it may never be the same again.

Sympathy, mercy and forgiveness are values that are in short
supply in 1945. Where were they in Treblinka, or Belsen, or any
one of those anonymous corpse-stuffed ditches in Ukraine or
Poland? Or, indeed, in William Joyce's broadcasts, or the basement
of 84 Avenue Foch? Perhaps they are like muscles that need to
be exercised regularly if they are not to atrophy; certainly they
have not been used much in the last half decade. There is blood-
letting across the Continent: the *épuration sauvage*, where
collaborators are ruthlessly hunted down; in some case the attacks
are encouraged by local authorities, who recognise their value as
a means of providing an outlet for years of pent-up rage. Women
with their heads sheared as a punishment for sleeping with
Germans become, for a while, a familiar sight. And in France, as
in many other countries, hundreds of men disappear into prison
cells where swift and rough justice is served: rape, mutilation, even
enforced prostitution; few chastisements are considered too severe.

In England there is a chorus of outraged voices, each seeming
to compete to outdo the others' virulence. Some of the angriest
words come from those Conservatives who had been the keenest
advocates of appeasement in 1938, and the communists who had
argued for a peace settlement two years later. One could be
forgiven for wondering whether they hope that the justice they
are demanding for Britain's renegades and quislings will in some
way be an expiation for their own sins.* Perhaps if Joyce and

---

* Certainly Joyce's perfidy allows Mosley and many of his former followers to
obscure their own as they seek to make new lives after the war. By repudiating

Amery could have evaded capture for a few more months then, like the French novelist Louis-Ferdinand Céline, they might have emerged into a climate from which much of the poison had been drawn, and been given a milder form of retribution. But what could the post-war world offer them? Could either of them be happy in the New Jerusalem Clement Attlee is beginning to build?

Prison gives William Joyce, John Amery and Harold Cole – who is still waiting for his court martial – time and space to reflect on the destruction they have wrought. John asks his parents' forgiveness for the pain he has caused them, and William makes his own apology to Margaret, who has been forced to remain on the Continent. 'My beloved – do, I beg, forgive me for having spoilt your life. You know that it was fated to happen. That is my excuse.' Alone in his cell there is no longer any need for Harold to manufacture the fictions that have distorted most of his adult life. His tragedy has always been that a small but significant part of him wants to love and be loved in return, but his 'shabby make up' and his 'pshycologically [sic] complicated, unbalanced criminal' soul ensure that anything good and true in his life is soon drowned in betrayal and deceit. When he writes to Charlotte Leblanc, her response comes without the benediction he had sought.

> If you have sacrificed others to save your own skin, not for a very important mission as you pretended to, you know perfectly well you will not find human pity in me . . . Human justice, a firing squad and years of imprisonment would never alter the fact that you have to wake up, one day, to your real self and leave behind all this.

In their last weeks, something like grace descends upon both John Amery and William Joyce. John, who is still claiming he has consumption, lies indolently in his bed in the prison hospital all day. He reads the daily papers and smokes innumerable cigarettes but does not wash and rarely eats; it is as if after a life of always

---

Joyce, they are also able to implicitly deny the substantial sympathy for Hitler that existed within the movement.

wanting more than he can have, he has finally found a way of existing in his own skin.

William scribbles cheerful letters to Margaret (who, like Michelle Thomas, has not been allowed to leave the Continent) and Angus Macnab. He has adopted the habit of talking about the prison as if it were a high-class hotel 'while the NCOs, though they sound demented, are efficient just and conscientious. As a glasshouse, the place is AI . . . Summing my experience as a gaol-bird, I would say that prison is all right for a visit, but I wouldn't want to live there if you gave me the place,' and signs them off as Brixton Bill.

He enjoys the food, and his passion for order and discipline – mislaid temporarily in the dissipated last months in Berlin – is met by the routines of prison life. It is a pleasure, he has found, to be part of an organisation that functions flawlessly. William was always a favourite among policemen in his BUF days – they admired his ability to keep control of his men – and here it is no different. One guard is moved to say that 'Joyce is a wonderful man . . . smiling and courteous, never depressed, never out of temper, always thinking of others, apologising for causing us trouble. We all love him here – there has never been a prisoner like him.' His fellow prisoners do not share this affection: he is jeered at when he exercises alone in the yard, and sometimes at night he hears a chorus of whistles and catcalls he knows is directed at him. Occasionally unexpected communications from outside the jail serve as an unwelcome reminder of the mood of the remainder of the British public. One anonymous piece of correspondence simply reads: 'Cheer up, the worst is yet to come.'

John Amery's main concern is how he will be judged in future; he frets that anyone might think he was motivated by 'cheap political gain or money'. 'I have been too much an individualist to fit any society of peace,' he tells his father, 'but I have loved and fought with burning passion for what I thought right, and the possibility of my being a financial politician is absurd to all who, like you, know that money and I were made to be parted.' Despite everything he remains convinced that Germany alone has 'realised the immensity of her historic mission; all the rest of us Europeans, what shall we leave as a record, as a justification of our lives?' On the night before his execution in December 1946, Leo Amery pays John a last visit. As they part for the last time Leo turns to his elder boy. 'You have been very brave.'

John draws himself up from his bed: 'But I'm your son.'

The next morning he is hanged by Albert Pierrepoint, who has just come back from executing the 'Belsen gang' in Germany. Pierrepoint returns a little under a month later to perform the same service for William Joyce, who meets his death with a similar equanimity. Just before he leaves his cell he hands a note to his brother Quentin. Its defiant tone matters little, for the Irishman's last communication to the outside world is undermined by a hollowness that renders its words brittle and unconvincing. William Joyce has already been reduced to a cipher, his identity so completely defined by the act of treachery that there is little or no room left for any discussion of the motivations that had led to it. 'Without you at the centre . . . there is no empire,' William Joyce's mother had once whispered in his ear, and he might hope that what he is about to suffer will be a small price to pay if it ensures that his warnings are heeded – but while there are crowds outside the prison waiting for news of his execution, few are interested in what he has to say any more. His knowledge of pain and disappointment has increased exponentially, and yet his world-view remains exceptionally, almost parodically, narrow.

> In death, as in this life, I defy the Jews who caused this last war; and I defy again the power of Darkness which they represent. I warn the British people against the aggressive Imperialism of the Soviet Union. May Britain be great once again; and in the hour of the greatest danger to the West, may the standard of the *Hakenkreuz* be raised from the dust, crowned with the historic words *Ihr habt doch gesiegt* [You have conquered nonetheless]. I am proud to die for my ideals; and I am sorry for the sons of Britain who have died without knowing why.

By the time he writes this, the Soviets control half of Europe, and have begun a savage programme of subjugation. The people of Poland, Hungary, Bulgaria and Czechoslovakia have seen communists seize power in their countries using a cynical mixture of deceit and brutality; and for decades to come they will suffer at the hands of repressive regimes modelled on the system that has already butchered or imprisoned millions in Russia. Within a couple of months of Joyce's execution Winston Churchill speaks in a grieved, bitter tone of the Iron Curtain that has disfigured the Continent, and before long the cold war begins in earnest. In the years to come Britain will discover that even as it decried men like Joyce and Amery it had been incubating another kind of traitor far closer to home – men and women who had burrowed into the establishment and worked to orders delivered by their unsmiling masters in Moscow. William Joyce and John Amery betrayed their country, they were blind to the malignant horror of the Third Reich, they traded in the most grotesque forms of anti-Semitism imaginable, but they saw the Soviet Union for what it was. 'I tell you that's the *real* peril,' John had told Commander Burt on their way back to England. 'I know. That's why I did what I did. I should have thought that now the war's over they would be ready to look at this problem with clear eyes. Then they'll see that I was right. Either then or later.'

Five days after Joyce goes unrepentantly to the gallows, a tall, thin man, with a long, pale face, receding ginger hair and a prominent Adam's apple is tracked down to the apartment he has taken above a bar off the Boulevard Raspail in Paris. Over the past six years he has taken on and sloughed off many different identities: Sonny Boy, Paul Rook, Paul de Loebelle, Paul Anderson, P.R.M. Corser, Joseph Deram, Paul Christin, Richard Godfrey. He has played a heroic part in the French resistance and collected intelligence for MI6, but the men on his trail are more interested in his work as an agent provocateur and interrogator for the Gestapo.

Harold Cole has done remarkably well to evade justice since he escaped from the Allied prison – he walked out wearing the coat of an American sergeant, and with the typewriter on which he claimed he was writing his memoirs under his arm – but now he has joined the millions of people drifting across Europe, a continent in which law and order has almost disintegrated. For a while it seems as if the Allied agents tracing him will be left to grasp uselessly at phantoms. They hear of sightings of a man matching Cole's description in a Parisian nightclub; they learn about how an unknown person speaking French with a strong British accent telephoned Dr Rodocanchi's apartment (where Cole had been so humiliatingly confronted by O'Leary) and asked to speak to him: on being told the doctor had died at Buchenwald the anonymous caller had said, '*C'est très bien fait*,' and hung up. It should have been easy for Harold Cole to stay at large, but now at last his luck has finally run out. He hears the proprietor call 'Monsieur Harold' as she comes up the stairs. He hears too that her steps are accompanied by other, heavier, ones. Harold grips his pistol and opens the door, firing wildly at the two detectives who push into the room. Several answering bullets thud into his body, slamming him across the shabby room and back on to his bed. Blood soaks into the dirty sheets.

A few months later a former circus strongman from a small village in Norfolk sits impassively as a Soviet court sentences him to twenty-five years of hard labour for 'espionage, sabotage and demoralisation of Russian troops'. When the judge asks Eric Pleasants, through his interpreter, if he has anything he wishes to say in response he surprises the men and women who have been assembled to pass judgement on him by saying, 'Can you give me something to eat? I'm hungry.'

The next years will be hard and strange; perhaps even more so than the hard, strange years that preceded them. Eric is moved from prison to prison, from Sachsenhausen to the Lubyanka, and, finally, on to an Arctic gulag. His life becomes one of sleeping six to a cell, sheep-dip bathing and rotten potatoes. Very few Britons will ever be able to say that they, like him, have had first-hand experience of Russia's nightmare century, but it does not feel like a privilege.

In the strict hierarchy of the camp he is treated with casual disdain, either ignored or referred to dismissively as *Anglichanin*, the Englishman, and to begin with he is almost always alone and afraid, existing in fear of the day when he is found face down in the latrine, several inches of homemade knife sticking out of his back. Eric learns to avoid crossing the Blatnoys, a gang who exert murderous power in the camp. Fortunately it is easy to tell when you are in their company, for their torsos reveal complex arrangements of tattoos: it is not unusual for a crucifix with a Madonna kneeling at the foot, with the words 'Do not forget mother' to be juxtaposed with a naked woman fucking the devil while he blows a trumpet. To those who deign to talk to him he teaches a smattering of English in return for food or clothing. It amuses him to think that perhaps one day someone else from his country will encounter a Russian speaking the language in a broad Norfolk accent.

For month after month Eric works long, brutal hours in coal-mines and watches the men around him die or fall into insanity. Once, in a life that seems so distant that it might as well be another century, he had looked after his physique with almost fanatical care, observing with disgust those who poured cigarette smoke into their lungs and whisky into their mouths; who sat in stifling atmospheres, or spent hundreds of pounds on pep-pills and dope to clog up their already bloated bodies. Now he fights impotently against hunger, exhaustion and scurvy, and can only suffer in horror as his teeth fall out, his gums bleed, and his legs become cratered with ulcers. He kills a man in a fight over a crust of bread and it is only later that he notes, coolly, that he feels no remorse.

Another casualty provides a turning point. The Blatnoys are impressed when he beats a Ukrainian strongman to death. Before long Eric is initiated into their ranks and given a nickname: *Anglissy kuwaldo*, the 'English Sledgehammer'. Everything becomes easier – although easy here is a relative concept. Whatever favour they might enjoy, everyone in the camp remains at the mercy of a cruel and unrelenting system that despises them, even as it appears to clutch them jealously to its breast.

It is no surprise that while everyone here talks endlessly about the past, there is nobody who wants to discuss the future.

★

Eric Pleasants would lose seven years of his life in Stalin's prison camps. On his return to Great Britain in 1952, the authorities chose not to take any action against him, feeling that he 'had suffered enough'. Pleasants went back to Norfolk where he married – he was never able to track down Anneliese, nor even learn anything of her fate – taught judo and physical education, and became a respected member of the local community. He wrote two memoirs before his death in 1998, one of which was published posthumously. While he made no secret of his past, nor did he choose to dwell on it.

Michelle Thomas moved to Switzerland after the war, where she married an insurance salesman and wrote affectionate letters to John Amery's family. Margaret Joyce would never achieve the same kind of contentment. The British authorities declined to prosecute her and she remained for a number of years in Hamburg, where she worked for Deutsche Maizena Werke, a food company. She re-established her relationship with Nicky von Besack, but finally broke it off when his wife became pregnant. In 1955 she reapplied for British nationality and returned to London. Seven years later, at the age of fifty-two she was married. Her new husband was the rackety Donald John May, a man eleven years her junior whom she met in a pub. In 1972 she died, from hepatic cirrhosis brought on by her chronic alcoholism. Suzanne Warenghem, after her escape from France, trained as a radio operator and continued to perform valuable work for the SOE. She anglicised her name to Suzanne Warren.

Epilogue

Treason doth never prosper

W<small>E DO NOT</small> always mark the moment when failure enters our lives. It can sit there unheeded, for years even, until the day when finally we turn around and there it is in front of us, so sprawling and undeniable that we wonder how we ever could have missed it. William Joyce could never really see straight, but he knew this. As the war drew on he was increasingly fond of quoting an epigram that seemed to speak to his circumstances: 'Treason doth never prosper: what's the reason? Why if it prosper, none dare call it treason.' By 1945 all four men – Joyce, Amery, Pleasants and Cole – had come to feel the weight of that couplet's meaning. The moment they entered the Third Reich's service they passed on to the wrong side of history and ensured that everything that followed in their lives would consist only of wasteful variations on ignominious defeat.*

Ultimately, each of these men's fates was tied to the fortunes of the country Hitler led to disaster. Eric Pleasants was never able

---

* The fact that a person might have ended up on the 'right' side of history does not necessarily endear them to their compatriots, especially if those compatriots were on the 'wrong' side. Both Marlene Dietrich (who renounced her German citizenship in 1939) and Thomas Mann (who left Germany for Switzerland in 1933, and then moved to the USA in 1939), for instance, were both vocal opponents of the Third Reich, but were openly described as traitors on their return to their homeland. There is much to examine in this attitude, but it does suggest that a public who has suffered is not inclined to be sympathetic to someone who they believe has not shared their experience; absence alone can become another form of betrayal.

to keep the war at arm's length, and mired himself in a swamp of moral compromises in his attempts to do so. Neither Amery nor Joyce ever really understood that the accumulation of notoriety does not necessarily translate into the multiplication of one's significance. Words matter. In wartime they can become weapons – why else would each of the competing nations devote such resources to their propaganda operations? They can wound and they can destroy and they can burrow deep into your opponents' skin: guileful voices that warn of defeat and chaos and a price that must be paid in blood. But by most metrics Joyce and Amery were rotten propagandists. They could hector, rant and threaten, and yet they were never able to persuade; their combined efforts were only sufficient to prise a handful of men away from their loyalty to the Allied cause. Worse, for a man of his pride, Joyce's ability to instil fear in the hearts of the British people was in direct proportion to the success enjoyed by the Wehrmacht; as the threat of invasion receded and the tide of the war slowly began to turn in the Allies' favour, so Lord Haw-Haw's potency leaked away and became once more the comic, hollow caricature he had been at the start of the conflict.

The only man in this book whose actions had a measurable impact on the war was Harold Cole. He did not simply help send over 150 men and women (the figure is necessarily an estimate, and it could possibly be higher) to an early grave, he also substantially undermined the work of an organisation that had played an important role in both helping downed airmen and straggling members of the BEF escape the clutches of the Germans, and collecting desperately needed intelligence on the Continent. It is not for nothing that he was described by some of the MI6 officers handling his case as 'the worst traitor of the war'. Cole seemed to believe that he would always find a way to stay one step ahead of justice, and yet the old lag was unaware that he was caught up in events far bigger, complex and more serious than he could ever understand.

That is not to say that Cole and his fellow renegades ended their lives without coming to understand a few new things. They learned that patriotism is a contested territory, and that it is all too easy for it to become tangled with your own ambition and resentment. They discovered that they carried within themselves unforeseen strengths, but also learned about the devastating flaws that lurked beside them. They learned how quickly the champagne thrill of success can be replaced by the sour taste of defeat. And over the course of six years in which the world was consumed by a horror they learned, to their cost, how hard it is to truly shape, or escape, one's fate.

Acknowledgements

I RECEIVED IMMEASURABLE AMOUNTS of help from a host of people as I wrote this book. Needless to say, any mistakes or errors that remain within its covers are my own alone.

The Traitors stands on the shoulders of those people who have written brilliantly before me about these fascinating men. Adrian Weale's *Renegades* was a pioneering account of the lives of the British men and women who worked for the Third Reich and, along with his *Patriot Traitors*, which tells John Amery's tragic story, remains the definitive book on the subject. Colin Holmes's excellent *Searching for Lord Haw-Haw* is the product of a lifetime's scholarship and puts paid to a number of the lingering myths that have surrounded William Joyce, as well providing a valuable historiographical essay tracing the ingenious attempts after the war by Joyce's friends and relations to launder his image. Biographies by Mary Kenny, Nigel Farndale, Francis Selwyn and J. A. Cole have each contributed valuable information and research, and all offer useful insights into Joyce's character. The interviews Brendan Murphy conducted with many of the key players in Harold Cole's story in the course of writing *Turncoat* help make it a very fine book, but they have also preserved essential testimony about the war's 'worst traitor'.

Everyone who I encountered at the National Archives, Imperial War Museum, Churchill College, Cambridge and the British Library has been, without exception, unfailingly helpful and patient.

Wise and generous early readers included John Bew and Lindsay Duguid; both made comments that improved the text, and I'm so grateful that they gave their time to do so. I was incredibly grateful too to receive a grant from the Society of Authors, which allowed me to travel to Paris and Berlin to conduct essential research. I would also like to thank Anthony Clavane for pointing me in the direction of a couple of key references.

My agent, Jon Elek, and Mark Richards, my editor, have been huge sources of advice and encouragement from the very beginning. I don't know if they are aware how much the faith they showed in my writing has meant to me, but I feel lucky to have worked with them. They're both brilliant.

I would like to thank everyone at John Murray, notably Caroline Westmore who brought supreme order and good sense to the project, and Juliet Brightmore, who found a number of excellent and surprising photographs. Morag Lyall copy-edited the book and I can only wince at the number of times her unerring eye saved me from making foolish mistakes.

My parents, John and Tessa Ireland, have provided three decades of unstinting support and inspiration. My wife, Victoria, is a phenomenal human being, and anything I say here will only ever be the smallest drop in the ocean compared to what I owe her, so I will confine myself to this: none of it would have been possible without you.

Illustration Captions and Credits

Prologue: John Amery and Una Wing in Paris.

Chapter 1: The British Cabinet, August 1931. Back row (*left to right*): Sir Philip Cunliffe-Lister, Jimmy Thomas, Rufus Isaacs, Neville Chamberlain and Sir Samuel Hoare. Front row (*left to right*): Philip Snowden, Stanley Baldwin, Ramsay MacDonald, Sir Herbert Samuel, John Sankey.

Chapter 2: Sir Oswald Mosley flanked by Blackshirts.

Chapter 3: William Joyce recovers in hospital.

Chapter 4: William Joyce: a new wardrobe signals a shift in his allegiance.

Chapter 5: An exultant William Joyce strides through Berlin.

Chapter 6: Harold Cole, in and out of disguise.

Chapter 7: Defiance in a Marseille café.

Chapter 8: John and Una take a drink.

Chapter 9: Paris adjusts to occupation.

Chapter 10: Jacques Doriot, John Amery's mentor.

Chapter 11: Kenneth Berry and Alfred Minchin (*left and centre, respectively*) of the British Free Corps.

Chapter 12: Eric Pleasants on display.

Chapter 13: A French *résistante* returns to the room in which she was subjected to a torture known as the *baignoire*.

Chapter 14: Eric Pleasants, wearing the BFC's uniform.

Chapter 15: John Amery poses with Flemish collaborators.

Chapter 16: Dresden in ruins.

Chapter 17: William Joyce is paraded for the cameras after his capture.

Chapter 18: Berlin during the last days of the Third Reich.

Chapter 19: John Amery and Michelle Thomas after their capture.

Chapter 20: Notice outside Wandsworth Prison announcing William Joyce's execution.

Alamy Stock Photo: Chapter 5. Cumbria Archive and Local Studies Centre, Whitehaven: Chapter 6. Getty Images: Prologue and Chapters 1, 2, 3, 7, 9, 13, 16, 17, 18, 20. Mike Gunnill/REX/Shutterstock: Chapter 4. © Imperial War Museums/HU131886: Chapter 19. National Archives Kew/HO45/25773(7): Chapter 15. Private Collections/photographer unknown: Chapters 11, 12, 14. Süddeutsche Zeitung Photo: Chapter 10. TopFoto/EUFD: Chapter 8.

Every reasonable effort has been made to trace copyright holders, but if there are any errors or omissions, John Murray will be pleased to insert the appropriate acknowledgement in any subsequent printings or editions.

Notes

Chapter 1: Hush! Do not awaken the dreamers

9 'Oswald Mosley is surrounded': Stephen Dorril, *Blackshirt: Sir Oswald Mosley and British Fascism*, Viking, 2006, p.139; Francis Beckett, *The Rebel Who Lost His Cause: The Tragedy of John Beckett MP*, London House, 1999, p. 55.

9 'All around him sit': Arthur Kenneth Chesterton, *Portrait of a Leader*, Action Press, 1937, p. i.

9 'In his election address': Dorril, *Blackshirt*, p. 118.

10 'He is decent, reassuring': Robert Skidelsky, *Oswald Mosley*, Macmillan, 1990, p. 212.

10 'Not so long ago': Ibid., p. 73.

10 'Yet they are not': Robert Skidelsky, *Politicians and the Slump: The Labour Government of 1929–1931*, Macmillan, 1967, pp. 12, 162.

10 'What I fear more': Skidelsky, *Oswald Mosley*, p. 215.

11 'This bitter soul': Robert Boothby, *I Fight to Live*, Victor Gollancz, 1947, p. 106; Skidelsky, *Politicians and the Slump*, p.85; Dorril, *Blackshirt*, pp. 83, 104.

11 'Mosley's gaze takes': Sir Oswald Mosley, *My Life*, Nelson, 1968, pp. 218, 219, 222, 235.

11 'Sir Oswald can barely': Dorril, *Blackshirt*, pp. 146, 155.

12 '"I was always suspicious"': Skidelsky, *Oswald Mosley*, p. 80.

12 'He has long been': Dorril, *Blackshirt*, pp. 25–6.

12 'Great things, he says': Mosley, *My Life*, p. 227.

12 'The mind can be': Ibid., p. 166.

12 'He was a poor': Skidelsky, *Oswald Mosley*, pp. 152, 165; Chesterton, *Portrait of a Leader*, p. 41; Dorril, *Blackshirt*, p. 41.

12 'Sir Oswald has taken similar': Mosley, *My Life*, p. 6.

13 'If truth be told': Skidelsky, *Oswald Mosley*, p. 133.

13 'Sir Oswald has also': Mosley, *My Life*, pp. 9–10, 104.

13 'He has no gift': Nicholas Mosley, *Rules of the Game/Beyond the Pale: Memoirs of Sir Oswald Mosley and Family*, Pimlico, 1998, pp. 68, 112.

13 'One day he gives': Ibid., p. 248.

13 'Sir Oswald is, in': Dorril, *Blackshirt*, p. 107.

14 'Mosley had been born': Skidelsky, *Oswald Mosley*, pp. 30, 32; Dorril, *Blackshirt*, pp. 3–5.

14 'in May 1915, having': Skidelsky, *Oswald Mosley*, p. 63; Dorril, *Blackshirt*, pp. 23–5, 29.

14 'Shortly after the peace': Dorril, *Blackshirt*, p. 34.

14 'There are many things': Ibid., p. 36.

14 'He claimed their hopes': Mosley, *My Life*, p. 110.

15 'Although he stood as': Skidelsky, *Oswald Mosley*, p. 69; Dorril, *Blackshirt*, pp. 30, 32.

15 'Sir Oswald's temperament is': Skidelsky, *Politicians and the Slump*, p. 190.

15 'John Beckett, a maverick': Beckett, *The Rebel Who Lost His Cause*, p. 55.

16 'In an exchange of': Mosley, *Rules of the Game*, p. 126; Mosley, *My Life*, p. 234.

16 'Oswald Mosley is perhaps': Skidelsky, *Politicians and the Slump*, p. 82; Dorril, *Blackshirt*, p. 113.

17 'Thomas has long since': Skidelsky, *Politicians and the Slump*, pp. 87, 105, 112, 159; Dorril, *Blackshirt*, pp. 121, 129.

17 'His comic turns': Egon Ranshofen-Wertheimer, *Portrait of the Labour Party*, G. P. Putnam's Sons, 1929, p. 182.

17 'Previously, on his good': Skidelsky, *Politicians and the Slump*, p. 171.

17 'While Thomas has floundered': Mosley, *Rules of the Game*, p. 122.

17 'Doctrinaire socialism has only': Mosley, *My Life*, p. 172.

17 'He is convinced that': Skidelsky, *Oswald Mosley*, p. 135; Dorril, *Blackshirt*, p. 124.

18 'Thomas is unaware of': Skidelsky, *Politicians and the Slump*, p. 192.

18 'Snowden, incensed by his': Dorril, *Blackshirt*, pp. 122, 131, 133, 136.

18 'He is offered a': Ibid., pp. 137–8.

19 '"It was easy enough"': Mosley, *My Life*, p. 260.

19 'So it has come': Dorril, *Blackshirt*, pp. 139–40.

19 'He is struck by': Boothby, *I Fight to Live*, p. 91.

19 'Mosley stares at him': Dorril, *Blackshirt*, p. 140.

20 'As early as 1922': Skidelsky, *Oswald Mosley*, p. 117.

20 'You can "do more"': Mosley, *Rules of the Game*, p. 152.

Chapter 2: I'm glad that I haven't a son

23 'Coal and cotton, which': Skidelsky, *Politicians and the Slump*, p. 21; Juliet Gardiner, *The Thirties: An Intimate History*, HarperPress, 2011, pp. 26, 47.

24 'I'm glad that I': Gardiner, *The Thirties*, pp. 31–2.

24 'In some of the': Beckett, *The Rebel Who Lost His Cause*, p. 47; Gardiner, *The Thirties*, pp. 71, 210, 263, 265–6.

25 'Years later, during the': William L. Shirer, *Berlin Diary: The Journal of a Foreign Correspondent 1934–1941*, Little, Brown, 1941, p. 368.

25 'Ministers from both parties': Skidelsky, *Politicians and the Slump*, pp. 25–6.

25 'Richard Reynell Bellamy': Richard Bellamy, *We Marched with Mosley: The Authorised History of the British Union of Fascists*, Black House Publishing, 2013, pp. 2–4.

26 'Sir Oswald had once': Dorril, *Blackshirt*, pp. 109, 213.

26 'He moves swiftly to': Mosley, *Rules of the Game*, p. 229.

26 'Those who refused tended': Martin Pugh, '*Hurrah for the Blackshirts!': Fascists and Fascism in Britain Between the Wars*, Jonathan Cape, 2009, pp. 51, 69.

26 'Fascism was, in origin': Mosley, *My Life*, p. 287.

26 'We count it a privilege': Chesterton, *Portrait of a Leader*, p. i.

27 'It is the kind': Arthur Kenneth Chesterton, *Creed of a Fascist Revolutionary and Why I Left Mosley*, Steven Books, 2003, p. 3; Pugh, '*Hurrah for the Blackshirts!*', p. 139.

27 'The old parties cannot': Dorril, *Blackshirt*, p. 217.

27 'They are against the': Chesterton, *Portrait of a Leader*, pp. 113–14; Dorril, *Blackshirt*, p. 219.

27 'When one of the': Nigel Farndale, *Haw-Haw: The Tragedy of William and Margaret Joyce*, Macmillan, 2005, p. 81.

27 'The fascists have certain': Chesterton, *Portrait of a Leader*, p. 30; Bellamy, *We Marched with Mosley*, p. 9.

28 'Mosley had insisted': Skidelsky, *Oswald Mosley*, p. 292.

28 'The BUF provides': Mosley, *Rules of the Game*, p. 289.

28 'There is a Blackshirt': Farndale, *Haw-Haw*, p. 91.

28 'Membership of the party': Ibid., p. 73: Mosley, *Rules of the Game*, p. 309.

28 'Mary Ormsby-Gore remembered': Dorril, *Blackshirt*, p. 422.

29 'An excited belief grows': Bellamy, *We Marched with Mosley*, p. 77.

Chapter 3: If my mother is going to Hell, then so shall I

33 'Every time the propaganda': Farndale, *Haw-Haw*, pp. 55–6, 69; Mary Kenny, *Germany Calling: A Biography of William Joyce Lord Haw-Haw*, New Island, 2004, p. 10; Francis Selwyn, *Hitler's Englishman: The Crime of Lord Haw-Haw*, Penguin, 1993, p. 19; Leonard Burt, *Commander Burt of Scotland Yard, By Himself*, Heinemann, 1959, p. 19.

34 'Or, at least, that's': Selwyn, *Hitler's Englishman*, p. 29.

34 'Other, better, witnesses could': Colin Holmes, *Searching for Lord Haw-Haw:The Political Lives of William Joyce*, Routledge, 2016, pp. 52–3.

34 'An attempt was made': Farndale, *Haw-Haw*, p. 55.

34 'It's not clear when': Ibid., p. 2.

35 'William appears to have': PRO KV2/245.

35 'William Joyce was always': Farndale, *Haw-Haw*, p. 47.

35 'Bright blue, sardonic eyes': Selwyn, *Hitler's Englishman*, p. 22.

35 'He hero-worshipped Napoleon': Kenny, *Germany Calling*, p. 63.

36 'William also came to': Farndale, *Haw-Haw*, p. 48.

36 'They were also fervent': Kenny, *Germany Calling*, p. 58; Peter Martland, *Lord Haw Haw: The English Voice of Nazi Germany*, National Archives, 2003, p. 10.

36 'William and the rest': Holmes, *Searching for Lord Haw-Haw*, p. 64.

36 'Joyce began to spend': Farndale, p.49; Selwyn, *Hitler's Englishman*, p. 17.

36 'A building leased by': Holmes, *Searching for Lord Haw-Haw*, p. 19.

37 'On another occasion': J. A. Cole, *Lord Haw-Haw & William Joyce: The Full Story*, Farrar, Straus & Giroux, 1965, p. 22.

37 'Over the following years': Burt, *Commander Burt of Scotland Yard*, p.1 8, HO45/25780.

37 'The British Union of': William Joyce, *Twilight Over England: The Path to Democracy is the Road to Oblivion*, private printing, 1940, pp. 47–9.

38 'At university Joyce had': Farndale, *Haw-Haw*, p. 53; Kenny, *Germany Calling*, pp. 121–2.

38 'While his boxer's frame': Cole, *Lord Haw-Haw & William Joyce*, pp. 31, 57.

38 'His birthplace can lurch': Holmes, *Searching for Lord Haw-Haw*, p. 11.

38 'He can even blame': Adrian Weale, *Renegades: Hitler's Englishmen*, Pimlico, 2002, p. 12.

38   'His new pre-eminence': Farndale, *Haw-Haw*, p. 72.

39   'Though for the moment': PRO KV2/245.

39   'It is said that': Holmes, *Searching for Lord Haw-Haw*, p. 16.

39   '*Good*: Boundless physical and': PRO KV2/245.

39   'Although it has always': Dorril, *Blackshirt*, pp. 238, 302–6, 324.

40   'He is already another': Selwyn, *Hitler's Englishman*, p. 48.

Chapter 4: Margaret and I are making a little trip to Deutschland in the morning

43   'He claims to find': Farndale, *Haw-Haw*, pp. 6, 99–102.

44   'Margaret Cairns White smiles': Ibid., p.88; Cole, *Lord Haw-Haw & William Joyce*, pp.49–50; Kenny, *Germany Calling*, pp. 125, 211–12.

44   'She is good at': PRO KV2/253.

45   'Margaret will remember for': Cole, *Lord Haw-Haw & William Joyce*, pp. 61–4.

46   'Soon after William and': Ibid., pp. 98–9.

47   'Almost immediately the Irishman': Holmes, *Searching for Lord Haw-Haw*, p. 113.

47   'Beckett is an irresponsible': Beckett, *The Rebel Who Lost His Cause*, pp. 10, 11, 17, 20, 33, 42.

47   'In public Mosley can': Bellamy, *We Marched with Mosley*, pp. 134–5.

47   'He thought Mosley was': Beckett, *The Rebel Who Lost His Cause*, p. 146.

48   'In the moments after': Farndale, *Haw-Haw*, p. 94.

48   'One day he might': Cole, *Lord Haw-Haw & William Joyce*, p. 53.

49   'His anti-Semitism continues': Beckett, *The Rebel Who Lost His Cause*, p. 151.

50   'One former colleague in': Kenny, *Germany Calling*, pp. 147, 149; Selwyn, *Hitler's Englishman*, p. 68; Beckett, *The Rebel Who Lost His Cause*, pp. 146–51.

50   'He speaks on street': Burt, *Commander Burt of Scotland Yard*, pp. 22–3.

50   'They are rebuilding': Kenny, *Germany Calling*, p. 30.

51   'William Joyce is not': Dorril, *Blackshirt*, pp. 424–5, 446, 470; PRO KV2/616, KV2/617; Holmes, *Searching for Lord Haw-Haw*, pp. 135–6.

51   'Many of Britain's leading': Martin Gilbert, *The Roots of Appeasement*, Weidenfeld & Nicolson, 1966, pp. 142–3.

51 'David Lloyd George returns': Volker Ullrich, *Hitler: A Biography, Volume I. Ascent*, Bodley Head, 2016, p. 634.

52 'The tutoring business run': Cole, *Lord Haw-Haw & William Joyce*, p. 80.

52 'He talked aloud about': Cole, *Lord Haw-Haw & William Joyce*, pp. 77–8.

53 'When, in the summer': Farndale, *Haw-Haw*, p. 113.

53 'I hope that all': PRO KV2/245.

53 'In his revulsion': Cole, *Lord Haw-Haw & William Joyce*, p. 83.

54 'Long walks have always': Farndale, *Haw-Haw*, p. 78.

54 'But Joyce, a man': Cole, *Lord Haw-Haw & William Joyce*, p. 83.

55 'Joyce knows that both': Ibid., pp. 85–9.

56 'With something approaching confidence': Farndale, *Haw-Haw*, pp. 114–17.

56 'The following evening, after': Cole, *Lord Haw-Haw & William Joyce*, p. 83.

56 'William and Margaret keep': PRO KV2/245; Farndale, *Haw-Haw*, p. 117.

Chapter 5: Bombs will speak for themselves

61 'In those first, gilded': Farndale, *Haw-Haw*, p. 149.

61 'The early days of': PRO KV2/346; Martin Amis, *Koba the Dread: Laughter and the Twenty Million*, Jonathan Cape, 2002, p. 195.

61 'There is food from': Nicholas Stargardt, *The German War: A Nation Under Arms, 1939–45*, Bodley Head, 2015, p. 131.

62 'William has much in': Alexandra Richie, *Faust's Metropolis: A History of Berlin*, HarperCollins, 1999, p. xviii.

62 'It is perhaps indicative': Cole, *Lord Haw-Haw & William Joyce*, pp. 123–4.

62 'He also has started': PRO HO45/25780, KV2/246.

63 'Adolf Hitler once wrote that': Martin A. Doherty, *Nazi Wireless Propaganda: Lord Haw-Haw and British Public Opinion in the Second World War*, Edinburgh University Press, 2000 pp. xv, 3, 38, 129; Selwyn, *Hitler's Englishman*, pp. 8, 92.

63 'Washable silk frocks are': Farndale, *Haw-Haw*, p. 140.

64 'Early on William discovered': Cole, *Lord Haw-Haw & William Joyce*, pp. 123–4.

64 'The unprecedented potency': Doherty, *Nazi Wireless Propaganda*, p. 3.

65 'He has 6 million': Cole, *Lord Haw-Haw & William Joyce*, p. 127.

65 'His voice is better': Selwyn, *Hitler's Englishman*, p. 16.

65 'And how satisfying it': PRO KV2/884.

65 'As 1938 rolled into': Dorril, *Blackshirt*, pp. 384, 432, 436, 441, 503, 505.

65 'Hitler's ambitions were modest': Mosley, *My Life*, p. 365.

65 'Supposing every allegation were': Mosley, *Rules of the Game*, pp. 414, 429.

66 'Our members should do': Ibid, p. 424.

66 'After the war, in': Mosley, *My Life*, p. 371.

67 'The preface is usually': Joyce, *Twilight Over England*, p. 9.

67 'The names of downed': Selwyn, *Hitler's Englishman*, p. 110.

68 'It is said that': Kenny, *Germany Calling*, p. 311.

68 'Even the phlegmatic Commander': Burt, *Commander Burt of Scotland Yard*, p. 12.

69 'Astrology, spiritualism and séances': Kenny, *Germany Calling*, p. 205; Doherty, *Nazi Wireless Propaganda*, p. 134.

69 'And it is in': Cole, *Lord Haw-Haw & William Joyce*, pp. 155–8.

69 'Though he speaks as': Kenny, *Germany Calling*, p. 204.

69 'Much the same might': Cole, *Lord Haw-Haw & William Joyce*, p. 162; Kenny, *Germany Calling*, p. 200.

70 'against the Conservative Party': Burt, *Commander Burt of Scotland Yard*, p. 19.

70 'So the very fierceness': Joyce, *Twilight Over England*, p. 114.

71 'Whenever Margaret tries to': PRO KV2/346; John Brown, *In Durance Vile*, Robert Hale, 1981, p. 72.

71 'There must be a': PRO KV2/346.

71 'In the midst of': PRO HO45/25780.

71 'One evening he turns': PRO HO45/25780.

71 'From time to time': Ibid.

72 'Questioned after the war': PRO KV2/826.

72 'It appears that even': PRO KV2/346; John McCutcheon Raleigh, *Behind the Nazi Front*, George G. Harrap, 1941, p. 266.

72 'Margaret fears the city's': Cole, *Lord Haw-Haw & William Joyce*, pp. 130–1; Roger Moorhouse, *Berlin at War: Life and Death in Hitler's Capital, 1939–45*, Vintage, 2011, pp. 34–40; Raleigh, *Behind the Nazi Front*, p. 24.

73   'Like all Berliners': Shirer, *Berlin Diary*, p. 487.
73   'The first air-raid': Cole, *Lord Haw-Haw & William Joyce*, p. 170.
74   'Hitler, by contrast, never': Albert Speer, *Inside the Third Reich*, Phoenix, 1997, p. 409.
74   'Before long William Joyce': Kenny, *Germany Calling*, p. 223.
75   'It is only some': PRO KV2/346.
75   'Schnapps, white wine, champagne': PRO KV2/50, KV2/346.
75   'In the first year': Farndale, *Haw-Haw*, p. 184.
76   'Margaret is lonely and': PRO KV2/346.
76   'She has lost her': Cole, *Lord Haw-Haw & William Joyce*, pp. 160, 186; Farndale, *Haw-Haw*, p. 35; PRO KV2/346.

Chapter 6: In the name of my King and Country I thank you

79   'It had started with': Gordon Young, *In Trust and Treason: The Strange Story of Suzanne Warren*, Edward Hulton, 1959, pp. 57, 69; Airey Neave, *Saturday at M.I.9: The Inside Story of the Underground Escape Lines in World War II*, Coronet, 1985, pp. 19, 20, 22, 24–5; Brendan Murphy, *Turncoat: The Strange Case of Traitor Sergeant Harold Cole*, Macdonald, 1988, pp. 50, 72.
80   'He was born in': Murphy, *Turncoat*, pp. 24–7, 41; PRO KV2/415.
81   'Though Cole was bright': PRO KV2/415, KV2/416; Young, *In Trust and Treason*, p. 58; Murphy, *Turncoat*, pp. 24–7.
81   'It is clear': Neave, *Saturday at M.I.9*, p. 309.
81   'In the service of': Ibid., p. 83.
82   'I don't care a': Murphy, *Turncoat*, p. 41.
83   'Instead, he has let': Young, *In Trust and Treason*, p. 58.
83   'Sometimes he uses the': Murphy, *Turncoat*, p. 62.
83   'He speaks such bad': PRO KV2/417.
83   'The people in the': Young, *In Trust and Treason*, pp. 58–60; Vincent Brome, *The Way Back: The Story of Lieut. Commander Pat O'Leary*, Cassell, 1957, p. 44; Murphy, *Turncoat*, pp. 58, 59, 78.
84   'He loves the secret': John Bulloch, *The Traitors*, New English Library, 1970, p. 62.
84   'At the same time': Murphy, *Turncoat*, pp. 76–7.
85   'The eighteen-year-old': Ibid., p. 59.
85   'There is Cole in': Iain Adamson, *The Great Detective: A Life of*

Detective Commander Reginald Spooner of Scotland Yard, Muller, 1966, p. 141.

86 'It is Lepers who': PRO KV2/416; Murphy, *Turncoat*, p. 66.

86 'Garrow reports enthusiastically': Murphy, *Turncoat*, pp. 82–3.

87 'Meanwhile, Garrow looks on': Neave, *Saturday at M.I.9*, p.109; Murphy, *Turncoat*, p. 76.

87 'Whereas others in the': Mark Mazower, *Hitler's Empire: Nazi Rule in Occupied Europe*, Allen Lane, 2008, pp. 438–40; Brome, *The Way Back*, p. 20; Murphy, *Turncoat*, pp. 89, 91.

88 'One recent recruit is': Young, *In Trust and Treason*, pp. 21, 30, 51, 62, 63, 64, 67.

88 'Harold gives the impression': PRO KV2/416.

89 'It is another of': PRO KV2/416.

89 'In Paris, among others': Ibid.

Chapter 7: I've got the Germans in my pocket

94 'If he had a': PRO KV2/415.

94 'Recently it has mostly': PRO KV2/415, KV2/416; Young, *In Trust and Treason*, p.95; Neave, *Saturday at M.I.9*, p.309; Murphy, *Turncoat*, p. 128.

95 'From Marseille they learn': PRO KV2/415; Murphy, *Turncoat*, pp. 62, 112, 113, 129, 130–4, 138.

97 'In Marseille, Garrow has': Murphy, *Turncoat*, p. 107.

98 '"Hello, Paul"': PRO KV2/416; Murphy, *Turncoat*, pp. 74, 148–9, 151; Brome, *The Way Back*, p.39; Neave, *Saturday at M.I.9*, p. 84.

100 'Cornelius Verloop': Young, *In Trust and Treason*, p.98; Murphy, *Turncoat*, p. 156; PRO KV2/415.

102 'François Duprez is the': PRO KV2/415, KV2/416; Murphy, *Turncoat*, p. 153.

103 'Five days later, Harold': Young, *In Trust and Treason*, p. 103; Murphy, *Turncoat*, pp. 165–6.

104 'De Fliguë realises': PRO KV2/417.

104 'Cole has held off': PRO KV2/416; Young, *In Trust and Treason*, pp. 74–80, 80–1.

107 'I, a priest, would': Murphy, *Turncoat*, pp. 107, 163.

Chapter 8: We are not ordinary people. You can't do anything to us

111 'John Amery has a': Burt, *Commander Burt of Scotland Yard*, p. 28.

111 "'I am myself,'": PRO KV2/79.

112 'By the age of': PRO HO144/22822, Adrian Weale, *Patriot Traitors: Roger Casement, John Amery and the Real Meaning of Treason*, Viking, 2001, pp. 98–100.

112 'It was as if': Martin Pugh, *We Danced All Night: A Social History of Britain Between the Wars*, Vintage, 2009, p. 192.

112 'He dressed like a': David Faber, *Speaking for England: Leo, Julian and John Amery, the Tragedy of a Political Family*, Free Press, 2005, p. 190.

113 'Although Amery asserted that': Weale, *Patriot Traitors*, p. 110.

113 'Aged eighteen and armed': Private Papers of D. W. A. Mure, Imperial War Museum.

113 'History does not record': PRO MEPO3/616, Weale, *Patriot Traitors*, p. 117.

114 'Amery's undoubted charm': Faber, *Speaking for England*, p. 278; Mure, Private Papers.

115 'He had become the': PRO HO144/22822, KV2/79; Mure, Private Papers.

115 'Despite his parents' attempts': John Barnes and David Nicholson (eds.), *The Leo Amery Diaries*, Hutchinson, 1988, pp. 254, 288.

115 'If only Jack behaves': Faber, *Speaking for England*, p. 295.

115 'For all the effort he': PRO HO144/22822, Weale, *Patriot Traitors*, pp. 115–17.

116 'John did not recognise': Ibid.; Faber, *Speaking for England*, p. 196.

116 'We are not ordinary': Bulloch, *The Traitors*, p. 36.

116 'Amery vanishes almost completely': Faber, *Speaking for England*, p. 294; CC AMEL 7.34.

117 'He is big and': David Pryce-Jones, *Paris in the Third Reich: A History of the German Occupation, 1940–1944*, Collins, 1981, pp. 54, 66.

118 'According to an interview': PRO BT/271/104, KV2/80.

118 'John had also been': Barnes and Nicholson, *The Leo Amery Diaries*, p. 428.

118 'until the end of': PRO HO144/22822, BT/271/104; Burt, *Commander Burt of Scotland Yard*, p. 27.

118 'John's passport records, however': PRO KV2/81.

118 'He was undoubtedly intoxicated': Emmanuel Carrère, *My Life as a Russian Novel*, Metropolitan Books, 2007, p. 63.

119 'He was reputed to': Burt, *Commander Burt of Scotland Yard*, p.27; Mazower, *Hitler's Empire*, p. 424.

119 'Jeanine Barde was another': PRO KV2/79.

119 'Before long he was': Burt, *Commander Burt of Scotland Yard*, p.29; PRO KV2/78, KV2/79.

Chapter 9: Simply as an Englishman

123 'In September 1939 the': Weale, *Patriot Traitors*, p. 121.

123 'Writing from the Hotel': PRO KV2/80.

123 'Later, during the war': PRO KV2/78.

124 'For the first year': PRO KV2/81.

124 '"Russia! Our ally!"': Burt, *Commander Burt of Scotland Yard*, pp. 27–8.

124 'He is maddened by': John Amery, *In His Own Words*, Historical Review Press, 1997, pp. 7, 8, 15, 26–7.

126 'It is a pygmy': Pryce-Jones, *Paris in the Third Reich*, p. 16; David Drake, *Paris at War, 1939–44*, Belknap Press, 2015, pp. 107, 139–40; Antony Beevor and Artemis Cooper, *Paris: After the Liberation 1944–1949*, Penguin, 2007, pp. 11–13.

126 'Amery's commitment to radical': PRO KV2/81.

127 'They are not much': PRO KV2/81.

127 'The visa to leave': PRO HO144/22822; Faber, *Speaking for England*, p. 440.

127 'He can tell as': PRO KV2/79.

127 'There is something else': Weale, *Patriot Traitors*, p. 138.

127 'A couple of months': PRO KV2/80, KV2/79; Drake, *Paris at War*, p. 239.

128 'Amery follows this up': PRO KV2/81.

128 'John, sporting a neat': Reinhard Spitzy, *How We Squandered the Reich*, Michael Russell, 1997, pp. 353–4; PRO KV2/79.

128 'To begin with John': PRO KV2/826.

128 'At the suggestion of': PRO KV2/3550, KV2/79.

129 'While his taste for': PRO HO45/25781.

129 'it was Plack': PRO HO45/22385.

129 'The MI5 report into': Ibid.

129 'Over the next couple': PRO KV2/81.

129 'The problem, as he': Selwyn, *Hitler's Englishman*, pp.125–6; Faber, *Speaking for England*, p. 450; PRO KV2/79.

129 'Baillie-Stewart (who': PRO HO45/25787; Kenny, *Germany Calling*, pp. 210, 247, 261.

130 'Hesse, a suave operator': PRO KV2/81.

130 'And if they can': PRO KV2/79.

130 'A pulse of excitement': PRO KV2/826.

130 'All his adult life': CC AMEL 6; PRO KV2/81.

131 'With his lordly entitled': Bulloch, *The Traitors*, pp. 25, 39.

131 'Nobody would claim that': PRO HO45/25776.

131 'Sitting in his suburban': Cole, *Lord Haw-Haw & William Joyce*, p. 206.

131 'Many Englishmen who share': NA BT/271/104.

131 'Amery's speech is to': Faber, *Speaking for England*, p. 453.

131 'Listeners will wonder what': PRO HO45/25773.

132 'His voice is well-bred': PRO HO144/22822, KV2/80, KV2/81.

132 'Five hundred miles away': Barnes and Nicholson, *The Leo Amery Diaries*, pp. 843–5; CC AMEL 7.36., Weale, *Patriot Traitors*, p. 96.

133 'Julian, who is busy': Faber, *Speaking for England*, p. 488.

133 'His brother's actions may': Ibid., p. 440.

133 'He writes of the hurt': CC AMEL 7.36.

Chapter 10: It was our one hope. It still is, if you could only realise it

137 'He is still seen': PRO HO45/25780.

137 'There are also whispers': Faber, *Speaking for England*, p. 453.

138 'The feeling persists that': Spitzy, *How We Squandered the Reich*, p. 353.

138 'He speaks French fluently': PRO WO204/12691, HO144/22822; KV2/78; KV2/80; Burt, *Commander Burt of Scotland Yard*, p.24; Faber, *Speaking for England*, p. 181.

138 'Hitler believes that': Mazower, *Hitler's Empire*, p. 432.

138 'They swiftly check into': PRO KV2/80.

138 'If you know the': Pryce-Jones, *Paris in the Third Reich*, pp. 19, 24, 26, 29, 30, 36, 43, 77, 84, 87, 99, 136, 140–1, 143, 144; Drake, *Paris at War*, pp. 92, 99, 117, 124, 165, 262.

141 'There is Marcel Déat': Pryce-Jones, *Paris in the Third Reich*, pp. 67–8, 117; Drake, *Paris at War*, pp.161, 195–8; Beevor and Cooper, *Paris*, p. 64.

141 'All are invested in': Pryce-Jones, *Paris in the Third Reich*, p. 66.

141 'But the Third Reich': Speer, *Inside the Third Reich*, p. 182.

143 'Among them are wild-eyed': Drake, *Paris at War*, p. 198.

143 'In December 1942, Doriot': PRO HO144/22822; Burt, *Commander Burt of Scotland Yard*, p. 28; AMEL 6.3.15.

144 'Lurid rumours instantly': PRO HO45/25780, KV2/79; KV2/80; Spitzy, *How We Squandered the Reich*, p. 355; Weale, *Patriot Traitors*, pp. 195–8.

144 'On the way home': PRO HO45/25781, KV2/279.

145 'As with Jeanine, he': PRO KV2/78; KV2/79.

145 'Years later, Michelle, married': CC AMEJ 3.1.49, AMEJ 3.1.51, AMEL 6.3.15, AMEJ 3.1.42.

Chapter 11: Don't wait until the truth stabs your eyes out

150 'On the day Amery and': PRO KV2/79; KV2/81.

150 'He is joined by': PRO KV2/80; KV2/79.

150 'After a few minutes a': PRO KV2/81.

152 'Suddenly, a disturbance in': PRO HO144/22822; KV2/81.

153 'John emerges into a': PRO KV2/80, KV2/79.

154 'Over the next two': PRO KV2/81.

155 'Kenneth Berry is a fresh-faced': PRO HO45/2580, KV2/255.

156 'When he was a': Mure, Private Papers.

157 'Berry spends his': Sean Murphy, *Letting the Side Down: British Traitors of the Second World War*, Sutton, 2003, p.125.

157 'When he needs money': PRO KV2/255.

157 'Some of the men': Brown, *In Durance Vile*, pp. 12, 48; Adrian Gilbert, *POW: Allied Prisoners in Europe 1939–1945*, John Murray, 2007, pp. 79, 83–4, 92, 94, 97.

157 'He had grand plans': Barnes and Nicholson, *The Leo Amery Diaries*, p. 1072.

158 'When the senior British': Burt, *Commander Burt of Scotland Yard*, p. 30.

Chapter 12: The average decent-minded Englishman

161 '"Be strong, boy"': Eric Pleasants, *I Killed to Live: The Story of Eric Pleasants as Told to Eddie Chapman*, Cassell, 1957, p. 9; Eric Pleasants

(ed. Ian Sayer and Douglas Botting), *Hitler's Bastard: Through Hell and Back in Nazi Germany and Stalin's Russia*, Mainstream, 2003, pp. 29, 75.

161 'The son of a Norfolk': Pleasants, *I Killed to Live*, pp. 16–17, 18; Pleasants, *Hitler's Bastard*, pp. 49, 54, 81.

161 'An officer who passed': PRO KV2/251.

162 'Eric has always prided': Pleasants, *Hitler's Bastard*, pp. 13, 32, 74, 177–8.

163 'In a manner that': Pleasants, *I Killed to Live*, pp. 18, 20–1; Pleasants, *Hitler's Bastard*, p. 82.

163 'I have my own': Pleasants, *I Killed to Live*, p. 9.

163 'Instead of joining the': Pleasants, *Hitler's Bastard*, p. 16.

164 'The BUF itself was': Mosley, *My Life*, p. 381.

164 'In the weeks before': Pleasants, *I Killed to Live*, pp. 24–5, 28.

165 'Since the only legal': Pleasants, *Hitler's Bastard*, pp. 19, 21, 28.

165 'Another acquaintance during this': Pleasants, *I Killed to Live*, p. 24; Pleasants, *Hitler's Bastard*, p. 47.

165 'Eric had never broken': Weale, *Renegades*, p. 124.

165 'The appeal of this': Pleasants, *I Killed to Live*, p. 29; Pleasants, *Hitler's Bastard*, p. 57; Weale, *Renegades*, p. 124.

166 'Dijon prison was a': Pleasants, *I Killed to Live*, p. 30.

166 'Their freedom did not': Pleasants, *Hitler's Bastard*, pp. 66–74.

166 'A perverse sense of': Weale, *Renegades*, p. 124.

167 'Eventually the two men': Bulloch, *The Traitors*, p. 49; Pleasants, *I Killed to Live*, pp. 35–7; Pleasants, *Hitler's Bastard*, p. 78.

167 'But here at least': Pleasants, *Hitler's Bastard*, pp. 79–86.

168 'One day in May': PRO KV2/251, KV2/255, HO45/25817.

168 'One of its members': PRO HO45/25805, KV2/251.

168 'Its existing recruits can': PRO HO45/25817.

169 'The British Union of': Boothby, *I Fight to Live*, p. 91.

169 'The unit's interpreter, Wilhelm': PRO HO45/25835.

169 'The arrival of Alfred': PRO KV2/251.

170 'The sour note on': PRO HO45/25805.

170 'This perhaps explains why': PRO KV2/264, KV2/251.

171 'Eric Pleasants agrees about': Pleasants, *I Killed to Live*, p. 38; Pleasants, *Hitler's Bastard*, pp. 88–90; PRO KV2/251; Weale, *Renegades*, p. 125.

Chapter 13: I'm sunk. I beg you only, just for my sake, give us the address of Suzanne

175 'These days Suzanne Warenghem': Young, *In Trust and Treason*, pp. 110, 112, 118, 165–6, 178–80; Murphy, *Turncoat*, pp. 159, 163; PRO KV2/415.

180 'Cole's new boss is': PRO KV2/415, KV2/416; Jean Overton Fuller, *The Starr Affair*, Victor Gollancz, 1954, pp. 54, 76.

181 'The *Funkspiel* is complemented': Overton Fuller, *The Starr Affair*, p. 86; PRO KV2/415.

181 'Nicolas Pakomof': PRO KV2/415.

182 'After the war, one': Moorhouse, *Berlin at War*, p. 209.

182 'Cole is often in': PRO KV2/416.

183 'During his interrogation in': PRO KV2/416.

184 'You make a great': PRO KV2/417.

186 'Harold Cole is not': PRO KV2/416; Overton Fuller, *The Starr Affair*, pp. 14, 31, 55, 63, 84, 94.

187 'But neither Harold nor': Pryce-Jones, *Paris in the Third Reich*, pp. 192–9; Beevor and Cooper, *Paris*, p. 34; PRO KV2/415, KV2/416.

Chapter 14: It was all a big sham act

191 'One of the first': Pleasants, *Hitler's Bastard*, pp. 93, 96.

191 'This fantastic quality': PRO KV2/251; Pleasants, *I Killed to Live*, pp. 38–9.

192 'The recruits are asked': Pleasants, *Hitler's Bastard*, p. 93.

192 'a handful, including Berry': PRO KV2/255.

192 'I am not of': PRO KV2/251.

192 'The men hang a': PRO HO45/25817, KV2/251.

193 'There is a photo': Pleasants, *Hitler's Bastard*, p. 101.

193 'When he isn't complaining': PRO KV2/251.

193 'The early days of': Pleasants, *Hitler's Bastard*, p. 97.

194 'The ringleaders are known': PRO HO45/25817.

194 'The strange and intense': PRO HO45/25805.

194 'One is the rakish': PRO KV2/252, KV2/251; Pleasants, *Hitler's Bastard*, p. 100.

194 'Courlander understands that Hitler': Dorril, *Blackshirt*, p. 532.

195 'By contrast, Francis McLardy': PRO KV2/252, KV2/251; Pleasants, *Hitler's Bastard*, p. 100.
195 'Thomas Cooper is the': PRO HO45/25805.
195 'Some of his eccentricities': PRO KV2/264.
195 'One day Eric notices': Pleasants, *Hitler's Bastard*, p. 97.
196 'His intensity and sheer': NA CRIM 1/484, HO45/25805.
196 'He said he was': PRO KV2/264.
196 'While the rest of': Pleasants, *Hitler's Bastard*, p. 97.
197 'What structure there is': NA KV2/251; Pleasants, *Hitler's Bastard*, pp. 97, 98, 99, 101–2.
198 'Eventually Tug caught gonorrhoea': Pleasants, *Hitler's Bastard*, p. 99.
198 'They had been told': PRO KV2/251; Pleasants, *Hitler's Bastard*, p. 103.
199 'Back in their billets': PRO KV2/251; Pleasants, *Hitler's Bastard*, p. 103.
199 'One day one of': Brown, *In Durance Vile*, p. 99.
199 'Eric establishes a daily': PRO KV2/251; Pleasants, *Hitler's Bastard*, p. 101.
199 'In truth, the men': Pleasants, *I Killed to Live*, p. 39.
200 'It's onward to Moscow': Pleasants, *Hitler's Bastard*, p. 98.
200 'The availability of women': Gilbert, *POW*, p. 119; Pleasants, *Hitler's Bastard*, pp. 103–5.
201 'The tensions and resentment': PRO KV2/252, KV2/251.
201 'Roepke, who is still': PRO KV2/251.
201 'On the one hand': Ibid.

Chapter 15: John Amery n'est peut-être pas 'quite right in the head'

205 'Here he goes again': PRO KV2/80, HO144/22822, KV2/79.
206 'As Amery tells him': Brown, *In Durance Vile*, pp. 14, 40, 41, 75, 85, 109–15; Weale, *Renegades*, p. 105.
207 'Many of those still': Bulloch, *The Traitors*, p. 40.
208 'In June 1944': PRO HO144/22822.
208 'As he walks to': PRO KV2/78
210 'For Amery this is': Cole, *Lord Haw-Haw & William Joyce*, p. 213.
210 'Accompanied by his "wife"': PRO KV2/3550, KV2/79.
210 'In a letter his': PRO KV2/79, CC AMEL 6.3.15.
211 'the drunken stumble later': PRO KV2/80.
211 'Sometimes he is greeted': PRO KV2/80, KV2/84.

211 'One Frenchman remarked how': PRO KV2/80.
211 'During a speech in': PRO HO144/22822.
212:'He was regarded as': PRO KV2/80.
212:'What I have done': Ibid.
212:'The trip caused a': PRO KV2/81.
213 'It might also be': PRO HO144/22822.
213:'He slips into': PRO KV2/79.
213: Another collaborator, who only': PRO KV2/80.
214 'In the winter of': Spitzy, *How We Squandered the Reich*, pp. 353–4, 355.

Chapter 16: I am causing my Mother the greatest agony she as ever felt

217 'On a Saturday morning': Pleasants, *Hitler's Bastard*, pp. 121–3.
217 'Even young Kenneth Berry': PRO HO45/2580, KV2/255.
217 'For a while he': PRO KV2/251.
218 'Berry is not alone': PRO KV2/264.
218 'Tom Cooper had once': PRO HO45/25805.
219 'The fact that he': Pleasants, *Hitler's Bastard*, p. 13.
219 'At the backs of': Ibid., pp. 119, 141–2.
220 'In the course of': Ibid., p. 106.
220 'Well Mr Amery it is': PRO HO45/2580.
220 'Proximity to "Tug" Wilson': Pleasants, *Hitler's Bastard*, pp. 110–11; PRO KV2/1288.
221 'En route, Stranders suggests': Pleasants, *I Killed to Live*, pp. 49–52; Pleasants, *Hitler's Bastard*, pp. 113–16.
224 'One day, soon after': Pleasants, *Hitler's Bastard*, pp. 124–6.
224 'The Englishmen are sent': PRO KV2/251;Weale, *Renegades*, p. 129.
224 'But, in truth, little': Ibid.
224 'So much time in': Pleasants, *Hitler's Bastard*, p.136;Weale, *Renegades*, p. 153.

Chapter 17: I can't bear to see the city dying. She is dying and will never be saved

229 'William is thin now': Burt, *Commander Burt of Scotland Yard*, p. 11; PRO KV2/250.

229 'William's work has deteriorated': Cole, *Lord Haw-Haw & William Joyce*, p. 220.

230 'Perhaps this does not': Selwyn, *Hitler's Englishman*, p. 144.

230 'The Joyces have become': Moorhouse, *Berlin at War*, pp. 94, 323, 346, 365, 367.

231 'In houses whose façades': Antony Beevor, *Berlin: The Downfall 1945*, Viking, 2002, p. 1.

231 'To the east, the': Moorhouse, *Berlin at War*, p. 373.

231 'Every day refugees from': Beevor, *Berlin*, pp. 48, 56, 122, 173.

231 'William tells himself that': PRO KV2/250.

232 'In March 1945 the': Stargardt, *The German War*, p. 545.

232 'He has always combined': Speer, *Inside the Third Reich*, p. 358; Richie, *Faust's Metropolis*, p. 442.

233 'And he has always': Cole, *Lord Haw-Haw & William Joyce*, p. 177.

233 '"We have made a"': PRO KV2/250.

233 '"I regret having kept"': Ibid.

233 'He also has a': Farndale, *Haw-Haw*, p. 244.

234 'During the worst attacks': PRO KV2/346; Kenny, *Germany Calling*, p. 240; Shirer, *Berlin Diary*, pp. 491–2.

234 'Both men are avid': Michael Burleigh, *Sacred Causes: The Clash of Religion and Politics, from the Great War to the War on Terror*, HarperPress, 2006, pp. 114–15.

234 'Given William's conviction that': Cole, *Lord Haw-Haw & William Joyce*, p. 213.

234 'For John there is': CC AMEL 6.3.18.

235 'One evening he tries': Cole, *Lord Haw-Haw & William Joyce*, p. 220.

235 'Poor Margaret is crying': PRO KV2/250.

235 'They had always intended': Cole, *Lord Haw-Haw & William Joyce*, p. 222.

236 'Margaret remains silent': PRO KV2/250, KV2/346.

236 'Other departments have already': Cole, *Lord Haw-Haw & William Joyce*, p. 223.

236 'I loathe to think': PRO KV2/250.

236 'Over 67,000 tonnes': Farndale, *Haw-Haw*, p. 256; Moorhouse, *Berlin at War*, p. 333; Holmes, *Searching for Lord Haw-Haw*, p. 206.

Chapter 18: It is now time for our soldiers to issue their own justice

241 'He and Anneliese have': Pleasants, *Hitler's Bastard*, pp. 143–52.
242 'Some days he goes': Weale, *Renegades*, p. 160.
244 'Some of the devastated': Beevor, *Berlin*, p. 1.
245 'On the corner of': Stargardt, *The German War*, pp. 454–5; Pleasants, *Hitler's Bastard*, p. 153.
246 'They make their descent': Pleasants, *I Killed to Live*, pp. 55–62; Pleasants, *Hitler's Bastard*, pp. 154–7.
248 'It is around this': Beevor, *Berlin*, p. 33.

Chapter 19: Come on in, gentlemen. Have a good gawp.

251 'The party is over': PRO WO204/12691, KV2/79.
251 'When John Amery was': PRO HO144/22822; Faber, *Speaking for England*, p.198, Weale, *Patriot Traitors*, pp. 107–8.
252 'Amery refuses – he is': PRO KV2/81.
252 'So he sports jackboots': Burt, *Commander Burt of Scotland Yard*, p. 14.
252 'On 23 April 1945': PRO KV2/81.
253 'Closer in you can': PRO HO144/22822.
253 'The forlorn couple look': PRO KV2/81.
253 'As the plane lifts': Burt, *Commander Burt of Scotland Yard*, pp. 14–16; PRO KV2/81.
255 'Joyce manages to slip away': Cole, *Lord Haw-Haw & William Joyce*, p. 241.
255 'One day, as William': PRO HO45/25780; Cole, *Lord Haw-Haw & William Joyce*, pp. 244–9.
255 '"I suppose in view"': Farndale, *Haw-Haw*, pp. 17–21.
256 'A card is hung': Holmes, *Searching for Lord Haw-Haw*, pp. 321–2.
257 'An excursion. On 11': PRO KV2/416; Young, *In Trust and Treason*, p. 187.
259 'Hope turns towards his': PRO KV2/417.
260 'It had been good': PRO KV2/416; Young, *In Trust and Treason*, pp. 185–6.
260 'With a pair of French': PRO KV2/416, KV2/417.
261 'Finally, after picking': Pleasants, *Hitler's Bastard*, p. 172.

261 'In the camp they': Pleasants, *I Killed to Live*, pp. 69, 70; Pleasants, *Hitler's Bastard*, p. 172.

262 'Eric and Anneliese watch': Pleasants, *I Killed to Live*, p. 70; Pleasants, *Hitler's Bastard*, pp. 173–4.

263 'But then one night': Pleasants, *I Killed to Live*, p. 86; Pleasants, *Hitler's Bastard*, p. 187.

Chapter 20: Cheer up, the worst is yet to come

267 'His trial is adjourned': PRO FO372/4762.

267 'After only eight minutes': PRO HO144/22822, KV2/81.

268 'This was in the': Holmes, *Searching for Lord Haw-Haw*, pp. 291–308.

269 'In the last six': Amis, *Koba the Dread*, p. 252; Diana Souhami, *Murder at Wrotham Hill*, Quercus, 2012, pp. 256–8; Beevor and Cooper, *Paris*, p. 77; PRO KV2/84.

270 'His tragedy has always': PRO KV2/417.

270 'In their last weeks': Barnes and Nicholson, *The Leo Amery Diaries*, p. 1075.

270 'John, who is still': PRO HO144/22822.

270 'William scribbles cheerful letters': Farndale, *Haw-Haw*, pp. 27, 35.

271 'He enjoys the food': Cole, *Lord Haw-Haw & William Joyce* p. 254.

271 'One guard is moved': PRO HO 45/25780.

271 'One anonymous piece of': PRO KV2/247.

271 'John Amery's main concern': CC AMEL 6.3.18.

271 'Despite everything he remains': PRO HO144/22822.

272 'As they part for': CC AMEL 6.3.18.

272 'The next morning he': PRO HO144/22822.

272 'In death, as in': Cole, *Lord Haw-Haw & William Joyce*, p. 302.

273 '"I tell you that's"': Burt, *Commander Burt of Scotland Yard*, p. 16.

273 'Five days after Joyce': PRO KV2/417; Neave, *Saturday at M.I.9*, p. 309.

274 'A few months later': Pleasants, *I Killed to Live*, pp. 20, 95, 96, 116, 129, 133; Pleasants, *Hitler's Bastard*, pp. 192, 203, 210, 211, 214–15, 231.

Epilogue: Treason doth never prosper

277 'As the war drew': Pleasants, *Hitler's Bastard*, p. 116.

Sources and Bibliography

Archives

Imperial War Museum

Private Papers of D. W. A. Mure
Private Papers of Eric Pleasants

Churchill Archives Centre, Cambridge

The Papers of Julian Amery
AMEJ 1/7/50
AMEJ 2/1/132
AMEJ 2/1/147
AMEJ 3/1/2
AMEJ 3/1/14
AMEJ 3/1/16
AMEJ 3/1/42
AMEJ 3/1/49
AMEJ 3/1/51

The Papers of Leopold Amery
AMEL 6/3/11
AMEL 6/3/15
AMEL 6/3/18
AMEL 7/33
AMEL 7/34
AMEL 7/36

National Archives

BT/271/104
CRIM1/1717

FO372/4762
HO45/22385
HO45/25776
HO45/25780
HO45/25781
HO45/25787
HO45/25805
HO45/25817
HO45/25835
HO144/22822
KV2/50
KV2/78
KV2/79
KV2/80
KV2/81
KV2/84
KV2/245
KV2/246
KV2/248
KV2/251
KV2/252
KV2/253
KV2/255
KV2/264
KV2/279
KV2/346
KV2/378
KV2/415
KV2/416
KV2/417
KV2/428
KV2/439
KV2/826
KV2/884
KV2/885
KV2/1288
KV2/2861
KV2/3550
MEPO3/616
WO204/12691

Books

Adamson, Iain, *The Great Detective: A Life of Detective Commander Reginald Spooner of Scotland Yard*, Muller, 1966

Amery, John, *In His Own Words*, Historical Review Press, 1997

Amis, Martin, *Koba the Dread: Laughter and the Twenty Million*, Jonathan Cape, 2002

Applebaum, Anne, *Iron Curtain: The Crushing of Eastern Europe*, Penguin, 2013

Barnes, John and David Nicholson (eds.), *The Leo Amery Diaries*, Hutchinson, 1988

Bechhofer Roberts, C. E., *The Trial of William Joyce: With Some Notes on Other Recent Trials for Treason, Etc.*, Jarrolds, 1946

Beckett, Francis, *The Rebel Who Lost His Cause: The Tragedy of John Beckett MP*, London House, 1999

Beevor, Antony, *Berlin: The Downfall 1945*, Viking, 2002

Beevor, Antony and Artemis Cooper, *Paris: After the Liberation 1944–1949*, Penguin, 2007

Bellamy, Richard, *We Marched with Mosley: The Authorised History of the British Union of Fascists*, Black House Publishing, 2013

Bew, John, *Citizen Clem: A Biography of Attlee*, riverrun, 2016

Boothby, Robert, *I Fight to Live*, Victor Gollancz, 1947

Boveri, Margaret, *Treason in the Twentieth Century*, Macdonald, 1956

Brome, Vincent, *The Way Back: The Story of Lieut. Commander Pat O'Leary*, Cassell, 1957

Brown, John, *In Durance Vile*, Robert Hale, 1981

Bulloch, John, *The Traitors*, New English Library, 1970

Burleigh, Michael, *Sacred Causes: The Clash of Religion and Politics, from the Great War to the War on Terror*, HarperPress, 2006

Burt, Leonard, *Commander Burt of Scotland Yard, By Himself*, Heinemann, 1959

Carrère, Emmanuel, *My Life as a Russian Novel*, Metropolitan Books, 2007

Chesterton, Arthur Kenneth, *Portrait of a Leader*, Action Press, 1937

——, *Creed of a Fascist Revolutionary and Why I Left Mosley*, Steven Books, 2003

Cole, J. A., *Lord Haw-Haw & William Joyce: The Full Story*, Farrar, Straus & Giroux, 1965

Davies, Norman, *Vanished Kingdoms: The History of Half-Forgotten Europe*, Penguin, 2012

de Slade, Marquis, *Yeomen of Valhalla*, private printing, 1970
——, *The Frustrated Axis*, private printing, 1978
Doherty, Martin A., *Nazi Wireless Propaganda: Lord Haw-Haw and British Public Opinion in the Second World War*, Edinburgh University Press, 2000
Dorril, Stephen, *Blackshirt: Sir Oswald Mosley and British Fascism*, Viking, 2006
Drake, David, *Paris at War, 1939–44*, Belknap Press, 2015
Edwards, John Carver, *Berlin Calling: American Broadcasters in Service to the Third Reich*, Praeger, 1991
Faber, David, *Speaking for England: Leo, Julian and John Amery, the Tragedy of a Political Family*, Free Press, 2005
Farndale, Nigel, *Haw-Haw: The Tragedy of William and Margaret Joyce*, Macmillan, 2005
Flannery, Harry W., *Assignment to Berlin*, Michael Joseph, 1942
Gardiner, Juliet, *The Thirties: An Intimate History*, HarperPress, 2011
Gilbert, Adrian, *POW: Allied Prisoners in Europe 1939–1945*, John Murray, 2007
Gilbert, Martin, *The Roots of Appeasement*, Weidenfeld & Nicolson, 1966
Griffiths, Richard, *Patriotism Perverted: Captain Ramsay, the Right Club and English Anti-Semitism, 1939–40*, Constable, 1998
Holmes, Colin, *Searching for Lord Haw-Haw: The Political Lives of William Joyce*, Routledge, 2016
Joyce, William, *Twilight Over England: The Path to Democracy is the Road to Oblivion*, private printing, 1940
Kenny, Mary, *Germany Calling: A Biography of William Joyce Lord Haw-Haw*, New Island, 2004
Levine, Joshua, *The Secret History of the Blitz: How We Behaved During Our Darkest Days and Created Modern Britain*, Simon & Schuster, 2015
Lowe, Keith, *Savage Continent: Europe in the Aftermath of World War II*, Penguin, 2013
Lownie, Andrew, *Stalin's Englishman: The Lives of Guy Burgess*, Hodder & Stoughton, 2015
Martland, Peter, *Lord Haw Haw: The English Voice of Nazi Germany*, National Archives, 2003
Mazower, Mark, *Hitler's Empire: Nazi Rule in Occupied Europe*, Allen Lane, 2008

Moorhouse, Roger, *Berlin at War: Life and Death in Hitler's Capital, 1939–45*, Vintage, 2011

Mosley, Nicholas, *Rules of the Game / Beyond the Pale: Memoirs of Sir Oswald Mosley and Family*, Pimlico, 1998

Mosley, Sir Oswald, *My Life*, Nelson, 1968

Murphy, Brendan, *Turncoat: The Strange Case of Traitor Sergeant Harold Cole*, Macdonald, 1988

Murphy, Sean, *Letting the Side Down: British Traitors of the Second World War*, Sutton, 2003

Neave, Airey, *Saturday at M.I.9: The Inside Story of the Underground Escape Lines in World War II*, Coronet, 1985

Nicolson, Nigel (ed.), *Harold Nicolson Diaries & Letters 1930–39*, Collins, 1969

Overton Fuller, Jean, *The Starr Affair*, Victor Gollancz, 1954

Pierrepoint, Albert, *Executioner Pierrepoint*, Coronet, 1980

Pleasants, Eric, *I Killed to Live: The Story of Eric Pleasants as Told to Eddie Chapman*, Cassell, 1957

—— (ed. Ian Sayer and Douglas Botting), *Hitler's Bastard: Through Hell and Back in Nazi Germany and Stalin's Russia*, Mainstream, 2003

Pryce-Jones, David, *Paris in the Third Reich: A History of the German Occupation, 1940–1944*, Collins, 1981

——, *Treason of the Heart: From Thomas Paine to Kim Philby*, Encounter, 2011

Pugh, Martin, *'Hurrah for the Blackshirts!': Fascists and Fascism in Britain Between the Wars*, Jonathan Cape, 2009

——, *We Danced All Night: A Social History of Britain Between the Wars*, Vintage, 2009

Raleigh, John McCutcheon, *Behind the Nazi Front*, George G. Harrap, 1941

Ranshofen-Wertheimer, Egon, *Portrait of the Labour Party*, G. P. Putnam's Sons, 1929

Rees, Lawrence, *Their Darkest Hour: People Tested to the Extreme in WWII*, Ebury Press, 2007

Richie, Alexandra, *Faust's Metropolis: A History of Berlin*, HarperCollins, 1999

Sante, Luc, *The Other Paris*, Farrar, Straus & Giroux, 2015

Selwyn, Francis, *Hitler's Englishman: The Crime of Lord Haw-Haw*, Penguin, 1993

Seth, Ronald, *Jackals of the Reich: The First Full Account of Hitler's British Korps*, New English Library, 1973

——, *A Spy Has No Friends*, Headline, 2008

Shirer, William L., *Berlin Diary: The Journal of a Foreign Correspondent 1934–1941*, Little, Brown, 1941

Skidelsky, Robert, *Politicians and the Slump: The Labour Government of 1929–1931*, Macmillan, 1967

——, *Oswald Mosley*, Macmillan, 1990

Speer, Albert, *Inside the Third Reich*, Phoenix, 1997

Spitzy, Reinhard, *How We Squandered the Reich*, Michael Russell, 1997

Stargardt, Nicholas, *The German War: A Nation Under Arms, 1939–45*, Bodley Head, 2015

Taylor, D. J., *Bright Young People: The Rise and Fall of a Generation, 1918–1940*, Vintage, 2008

Ullrich, Volker, *Hitler: A Biography, Volume I, Ascent*, Bodley Head, 2016

Weale, Adrian, *Patriot Traitors: Roger Casement, John Amery and the Real Meaning of Treason*, Viking, 2001

——, *Renegades: Hitler's Englishmen*, Pimlico, 2002

West, Nigel (ed.), *The Faber Book of Treachery*, Faber, 1995

West, Rebecca, *The Meaning of Treason*, Macmillan, 1952

Young, Gordon, *In Trust and Treason: The Strange Story of Suzanne Warren*, Edward Hulton, 1959

Index

Index

Abshagen, Major, 210n
Albert Hall, London: fascist
    meetings, 45
Alexander, William, 224
Ameln, Captain Konrad, 210n
Amery, Florence (*née* Greenwood;
    John's mother), 111
Amery, John: little known, 3;
    contributes to German war
    effort, 74; appearance and
    personality, 111, 116, 150, 214,
    253; idealism, 111; eccentric
    behaviour, 112–13; education,
    112–13; leaves for continent,
    112; sets up film company,
    113–15; dishonest practices,
    114–15; marriage, 115–16;
    bankruptcy, 116; mental in-
    stability, 116, 213; patronises
    prostitutes, 116; embraces
    fascism, 117–18; in Spanish
    Civil War, 118–19; relations
    with Jeanine Barde, 119, 123;
    improvidence, 123–4; in San
    Sebastian, Spain, 123; attitude
    towards Britain, 125–6; claims
    to have TB, 127; imprisoned
    in Vichy France, 127; moves
    to Berlin, 128; broadcasts for
    Germans, 129–32; friendship
    with Plack, 129; antipathy to
    Joyce, 131, 138; anti-Semitism,
    132, 143–4; family's reaction to

treachery, 132–3; drinking,
    137, 213–14; inadequacy as
    broadcaster, 137–8; leaves
    Berlin for Paris, 138; linguistic
    abilities, 138; and life in
    wartime Paris, 141; and
    Doriot's pessimism over
    Germany in war, 143; and
    Jeanine's death, 144–5; and
    Michelle Thomas, 145–6, 252;
    plans to raise British unit from
    POW camps (Legion of St
    George), 149–54, 157, 168; on
    Prince of Wales's possibly
    joining BFC, 170; prospective
    government post in Britain
    under Germans, 194; boastful-
    ness, 205–6; John 'Busty'
    Brown watches, 205–7; speaks
    at rallies across Europe,
    207–13; acts against SOE and
    French resistance, 210n;
    British prepare case against,
    210n; booed in Norway,
    211–12; declining reputation,
    211–13; motives as traitor, 212;
    letter from Berry, 220;
    Pleasants meets in Berlin, 222;
    claims to be Spanish, 223,
    267; prospective execution,
    223, 234; heroism in Berlin air
    raid, 234; political aims, 241;
    destructive behaviour, 251–2;

Cole, Harold (*cont'd*)
85–7, 94; union with Suzanne
Warenghem, 89, 175 & n, 176;
deceptions, 93–4; dissipated
life-style, 93–5; dishonesty
with money, 95, 99;
mistrusted by fellow resistance
members, 95–6; reckless
behaviour, 95; plot to kill,
97–8; judged and condemned
by resistance tribunal, 99–100,
176; interrogated by Germans
and betrays comrades, 100–2,
107; turns against Britain,
101–2; fever, 106; Carpentier
denounces, 107; tries to find
Suzanne Warenghem, 178–9;
works with Kieffer in France,
181–3; affair with Charlotte
Leblanc, 183–6; leaves Paris
on Allied advance, 187;
British gather information on,
207; political indifference, 241;
apprehended, 258–60; in
prison awaiting court martial,
270; evades capture, 273–4;
shot in Paris, 274; fate, 277;
effect of treachery, 278
communism: fascist hostility to,
28; Mosley condemns, 51
Conservative Party: pre-war
condition, 9–10
Cooper, Thomas, 194, 196,
198–9, 201, 205, 218, 219n
Cortés, Hernan, 117
Costantini, Pierre, 142
Courlander, Roy, 194–5, 201, 206n
Crépel family, 178–9
Cripps, Stafford, 11

Croisé, Georges, 179
Czechoslovakia, 52

D-Day landings (June 1944), 218
Dalton, Hugh, 11
Darling, Major Donald, 86
Dean, August, 103
Déat, Marcel, 141–3, 208, 211
Dechaumont, Maurice, 87, 103
Deloncle, Eugène, 119, 141–2
Deram, Madeleine, 100
Deuxième Bureau (Vichy
France), 104, 176n
Didry, Désiré, 103, 177
Dietrich, Marlene, 277n
Dietze, Eduard, 72, 131, 234n
Doriot, Jacques, 117, 141–3, 158,
206, 208, 211
Dowding, Bruce, 98–100, 103,
177
Dresden, 241–2
Dubois, Drotas, 103, 177
Duhayon, Marcel, 177
Duprez, François, 83–4, 95,
98–100, 102, 177, 181
Duprez, Henri, 85, 87, 95–7
Durand, Eugène, 88–9,
179–80
Dureng, Lieutenant, 258
Dyer, Geoff: *The Missing of the
Somme*, 225

Edward VIII, King (*earlier* Prince
of Wales; *later* Duke of
Windsor), 170, 192, 194
Einstein, Albert, 139
El Alamein, Battle of (1942), 132
Emergency Powers (Defence) Act
(1939), 55

Warenghem, Suzanne (*cont'd*)
178; evacuated from France by
SOE, 183; changes name to
Warren and marries, 276
Webb, Beatrice, 13
Wedgwood, Josiah, 19
Weiss, Madame (of Toulouse), 182
White, Margaret Cairns *see* Joyce,
Margaret Cairns

Wilson, Tug, 199, 220
Wodehouse, P.G., 129
Wolkoff, Anna, 268n
Wood (Australian in BFC),
201
Workers' Challenge (Nazi radio
station), 69n

Zweig, Stefan, 139